THE LENT PAPERS

Oberstleutnant *Helmut Lent wearing the* Ritterkreuz *(Knight's Cross) with* Eichenlaub *(Oak Leaves),* Schwerter *(Swords) and* Brillanten *(Diamonds).*

The Lent Papers
HELMUT LENT

PETER HINCHLIFFE

CERBERUS

First published in 2003.

PUBLISHED IN THE UNITED KINGDOM BY;
Cerberus Publishing Limited
22A Osprey Court
Hawkfield Business Park
Bristol
BS14 0BB
UK
e-mail: cerberusbooks@aol.com
www.cerberus-publishing.com

British Library Cataloguing in Publication Data.
A catalogue record for this book is available from the British Library.

ISBN 1 84145 105 3

PRINTED AND BOUND IN UK

I swear by God this holy oath,
that I will render to Adolf Hitler,
Leader of the German nation and people,
Supreme Commander of the Armed Forces,
unconditional obedience,
and I am ready as a brave soldier
to risk my life at any time for this oath.

The German Armed Forces oath of allegiance to Adolf Hitler

No man can serve two masters:
For either he will hate the one and love the other;
Or else he will hold to the one, and despise the other.

St. Matthew Chapter 6, Verse 24.

Lena Lent.

Meinen beiden Kindern,
Christina und Helena,
zur Erinnerung an ihren Vater.

Stade, 31. August 1945.

Contents

Acknowledgments

To all who helped me so willingly, each in his or her own individual way, with the writing of this book, my most sincere thanks. To pick anyone out for special mention would be invidious – except, if I may, for one lady, Christina Delavre, the elder daughter of Helmut Lent. Without her cooperation I would simply have been unable to undertake the writing of her father's biography. I list below those who also gave me indispensable help. I have listed them in alphabetical order, and I have not included ranks, decorations and so on. It is an interesting and gratifying fact that almost exactly half of those listed served in the *Luftwaffe* during the war. To those whom I have omitted, my apologies. It was not intentional.

Many of those named provided photographs for me, and a lot of them were duplicated. I decided, therefore, not to source individual illustrations. I hope I have disappointed no one.

In doing basic research for a book such as this, one reads very many books as background. It would be virtually impossible to list them all, but I would like to mention three that were essential as reliable reference soures: '*Wespennest Leeuwarden*', by Ab A. Jansen; 'RAF Bomber Command Losses of the Second World War' (six volumes), by W. R. Chorley; and '*Die Geschichte der deutschen Nachtjagd*' by Gebhard Aders.

My warmest thanks, therefore, go to my friends Heinrich Becker; Walter Briegleb; Bill Chorley; Helmut Conradi; Tina Delavre; Horst Diener; Otto Dombrowski; Martin Drewes; John Duffield; Wolfgang Falck; Georg Fengler; Kurt Frasch; John Gaye; Willi Göbel; Georg Greiner; Cato Guhnfeld; Walter Heidenreich; Jeremy Hinchliffe; Werner Hoffmann; Heinz Huhn; Hans-Joachim Jabs; Jochen Jahrow; Hans Ulrich Kettling; Claire Knott; Peggy Langdown; Mark Langdown; Eduard Lohse; Reg. Luce; Karl Pütz; Horst Römer; Alain Rosseels; Fritz Rumpelhardt; Harry Shinkfield; Peter Smit; Peter Spoden; Rudolf Tyrassek; John Vasco; Rob de Visser; Andreas Wachtel; Ton Weulink; David Williams; and Paul Zorner.

Foreword by Major a.D. Paul Zorner, Kommandeur II./NJG 100

O NCE again Peter Hinchliffe undertakes the tricky task of describing the life of a Second World War German Air Force officer – a 'German hero' – to an English-speaking readership. When he asked me to write a foreword to his book I was very happy to agree to do so. For one thing, I have been a friend of Peter Hinchliffe for a number of years. During the war he was a member of a British bomber crew, while I was a German night fighter. This is not the first book of this type that Peter has published, and by doing so he has contributed greatly to the very relaxed, and in many cases friendly, relationship that exists today between erstwhile enemies, the men who crewed German night fighters and those who crewed Allied bombers. Therefore I see his request as evidence of our friendship. On the other hand, however, I should like to rebut any impression that might be given that we feel it necessary to justify our actions during the war. In my view Peter Hinchliffe did not write this book with that in mind, nor do I myself believe that any self-justification is called for.

In July 1942, when I was posted as a lowly pilot to II./NJG 2 at Gilze Rijn in Holland after serving as an instructor at an advanced flying training school and flying operationally on transport aircraft, Helmut Lent was already a *Hauptmann* and the *Kommandeur* of II./NJG 2 at Leeuwarden, a short distance to the north: decorated with the Oak Leaves to the Knight's Cross, and with thirty-nine night victories in addition to his eight by day, he was the leading pilot of the *Nachtjagd*, the German night-fighter force. It was not until much later that I came to know him personally, but for every 'new boy' in the *Nachtjagd*, myself included, he was the example, the model for us to emulate.

Helmut Lent originated from a small village in East Pomerania, which now belongs to Poland. His father was the Protestant priest there. This background had a strong formative effect on the young Lent's personal outlook on life, his sense of duty, his relationships with his fellow men, in short in every respect. Had he been born twenty years earlier he would probably have become a priest, but in the early nineteen-thirties the whole world was fascinated by the rapid development of aviation and every young man, Lent included, longed to fly. And so, when it came to choosing a career, he decided to become an Air Force officer. In July 1942, of course, I was not aware of that. It was to be about eleven months before I would meet this 'ace of aces' face to face.

The first time that I saw Lent was one night in June 1943 when I was diverted to Leeuwarden. My stop-over there only lasted two-and-a-half hours. Two days later I was attached to Lent's *Gruppe* and spent a whole week there, but we were only together at mealtimes in the Officers' Mess and in the Operational Readiness Rooms during the evening standby periods. But during those periods at readiness particularly I was able again and again to observe this tall, slim man with the Oak Leaves to the Knight's Cross, and I was impressed by the quiet way in which he waited for things to happen with all the rest of us. Even though he was the one with the most experience, he was just another pilot among all those at readiness. He was of course responsible for us operationally, but otherwise he was simply my host. As *Kommandeur* Lent had the reputation of always concerning himself with the training of his crews, but unfortunately no enemy bombers entered our area that week and so there was no opportunity for me to see him in action as a teacher. All in all after this week Lent left me with the impression that he was by nature a rather serious man who could, however, sometimes show signs of boyish exuberance. But then, after all, he had only just passed his twenty-fifth birthday.

Only six weeks later, on 1 August 1943, Lent, who had in the meanwhile been promoted to *Major*, became *Kommodore* of NJG 3 at Stade. Following the heavy attacks on Hamburg a few days previously this meant that he was faced with a difficult task at the very doors of this devastated city. As a result of new radar-jamming methods by the RAF the *Nachtjagd* had been virtually crippled. Lent was now my commanding officer, but as I was only the *Kapitän* of one of his *Staffeln* and stationed some distance away at Lüneburg our personal connection remained remote. But a new commanding officer is inevitably talked about, and soon we were hearing of his belief that a senior officer should not demand respect from his subordinates on the grounds of his badge of rank alone but that he must earn it by personal example, by always being prepared to fly operationally, by his attention to the welfare of his troops, by always striving to improve their state of training and so on. And indeed Lent was an outstanding example to his officers. An incident at the very beginning of his night-fighter career is typical of his attitude. He had just become the leader of a new *Staffel* that had been transferred from the *Zerstörer* force to the night-fighter force. At first, however, and much to his chagrin, his pilots were gaining more operational successes than he was. This rapidly caused him to request a posting back to day fighters, because he considered that in the circumstances he was not an example to his men and therefore was unfit to be in command of them. His *Kommandeur*, Wolfgang Falck, refused his request and advised him to be a little more patient with himself.

I was never stationed on the same airfield as my *Kommodore*, Lent, and so had very scant opportunity to get to know him as a human being. The *Geschwader* Staff was at Stade, whereas my *Staffel* and I were at Lüneburg at that time. I can recall only one gathering of all unit commanders of the *Geschwader*, a short time after Lent had assumed command. He spoke to us with great seriousness about the catastrophic situation in which the night-fighter force found itself. From the words he used we could visualise the complete helplessness of the night-fighter leadership at that time. Yet he tried to encourage us, telling us that we would soon overcome these new difficulties.

Two personal meeting with him will always remain in my memory, two meetings that say a great deal about Lent the human being. Peter Hinchliffe tells of these encounters in this book.

In April 1944 I had to leave Lent's *Geschwader*. I was appointed *Kommandeur* of II./NJG 5 and thus ended my official contact with Lent. But when I was myself decorated with the Knight's Cross in June 1944 Lent send me a letter of congratulation. In it he wrote, 'My most sincere congratulations on your Knight's Cross . I share your pleasure at this distinction, which I am certain will save you a lot of trouble... I hope that you will not overlook those men who still do not hold this award, but are nevertheless doing their utmost for victory. Please remain my old, unassuming Zorner.'

I never saw this endearing man Lent again. After a period of operational flying in Northern France I was sent to the Vienna area in October. Just a few days before I took on my new responsibilities Lent's tragic fate overtook him. I was then given the great honour of standing guard over his coffin at the State ceremony in the *Reich* Chancellery in Berlin and accompanying him the following day on his last journey, to his grave in Stade.

It is symptomatic of the different attitudes prevailing in the Federal Republic of Germany and in English-speaking countries such as Great Britain, the Unites States, Canada, Australia and New Zealand that even positive biographical literature connected with the Second World War finds very little interest in Germany. In the nature of things such books are mostly written in the English language by English-speaking authors, and because of the low level of public interest they are seldom translated into German. I hope that this book by Peter Hinchliffe is more successful. Particularly today, when our young folk often experience difficulty in finding a direction in life, people should be made aware of men like Lent. With his high sense of duty, his readiness to subordinate his personal interest, his preference for working for the common good rather than for self-fulfilment, he would be an example to today's young men. One would, of course, have to make it clear that no matter how great one's idealism might be one must guard against becoming enmeshed in the schemes of evil men. But in the generation that Lent belonged to young Germans were not alone in the history of the human race.

Major a.D. Paul Zorner,
Kommandeur II./NJG 100

Nachtjagdgeschwader 3   O.U., den 4.7.1944.

Kommodore

Lieber Zorner !

Meine allerherzlichsten Glückwünsche zum Ritterkreuz.
Ich freue mich mit Ihnen zu dieser Auszeichnung, denn dadurch
bleibt Ihnen tatsächlich mancher Ärger erspart. Aber insbe-
sondere in Ihrer Stellung als Gruppenkommandeur werden Sie
feststellen, dass Sie mit dieser Auszeichnung fester im
Sattel sitzen. Ich hoffe, dass Sie nun nicht diejenigen
Menschen übersehen, die ohne diese Auszeichnung verblieben
sind, aber dennoch ihre ganze Kraft für den Sieg einsetzen.
Bleiben Sie bitte mein alter schlichter Zorner.

Hals- und Beinschuss,

Ihr

Lent's letter of congratulations to Paul Zorner on the latter's award of the Knight's Cross.

Introduction

WITHOUT question Helmut Lent was one of the most important members of the *Nachtjagd*, the force set up in 1940 to counter the British bomber offensive against Germany, which by the end of the war had shot down approximately 5,800 bombers, mostly four-engined 'heavies' operating by night and each carrying seven men. Lent's personal tally of confirmed night-time victories was 102, and he also shot down eight enemy machines by day, which brought his total score to 110. Yet even so he was not the highest-scoring German night fighter: that distinction went to *Major* Heinz Schnaufer, whose total score was 121. Lent's importance in the history of night fighting lies in the fact that he was not only a superlative fighter pilot but also an outstanding leader who, as a founder member in the *Nachtjagd*, rose rapidly to positions of command in which, by means of example and qualities of leadership, he had a considerable influence of the way in which the night-fighter force evolved. I wrote about Heinz Schnaufer because he was the highest-scoring night-fighter pilot ever, and after that it seemed a natural progression to write about his runner-up in terms of victories, Lent. When I began to look for sources I came up against a number of difficulties: above all I wanted reliable sources, which meant going back, as far as I could, to primary sources and not simply regurgitating other published material, a great deal of which is manifestly apocryphal and inaccurate. When writing about Schnaufer I had the advantage, for example, of being able to talk with his radio operator, Fritz Rumpelhardt, who had been in his aircraft with him for 100 of his kills. I was also helped by members of his family and a number of his wartime comrades who had known him closely. When Helmut Lent was killed in 1944, however, his crew perished with him.

Born four years before Heinz Schnaufer, Helmut Lent entered the *Luftwaffe* in 1936 and was already a front-line fighter pilot in Poland when Schnaufer enlisted in September 1939. This difference in age and service, short though it might seem, meant that when I came to gather material about Lent and his career very few of his close wartime colleagues and friends were still available for consultation.

My first lucky break was when I came into contact with Jochen Jahrow, a retired judge who during the war had been adjutant to *Oberst* Günter Radusch, who took over the command of Lent's night-fighter *Geschwader* when Lent died. In the months following Lent's death Herr Jahrow had come into possession of a sort of personal album about Lent, a hard-backed volume containing nearly two hundred typed and duplicated pages and a number of photographs, which he kindly made available to me. He was not aware who had compiled it but it was clear that the author, whoever that was, had had access to family papers, because the 'Lent Portfolio', as I called it to myself, contained extracts from personal letters written home by Lent.

My second stroke of good fortune occurred when I came into contact with *Frau* Christina Delavre, Helmut Lent's elder daughter, resident in Frankfurt am Main. When I first spoke with her on the telephone she welcomed my proposal to write about her father but told me that she did not remember him – after all she was only two years old when he died – and that the family possessed very little in the way of original material about him. Somewhere in her house, she said, there was a 'case' that contained some papers that might be of some slight interest to me – telegrams from Hitler and Göring and things like that. No, she assured me when I asked, Lent's flying logbook was not among the papers – that had disappeared a long time ago. She would be very happy to welcome me in Frankfurt and show me the papers and talk with me about her father as far as she could, but she doubted whether my visit would be really worth my while.

I accepted her invitation, of course. The case, an attaché case of moderate size, proved to be a metaphorical gold-mine, and among its contents were all four volumes of her father's flying logbook, containing details of all but a very few of his 2045 flights and 110 victories in combat. Not only that, there was another copy of the 'Lent Portfolio' which, *Frau* Delavre told me, had been compiled by her mother in the months following her husband's death and which she had dedicated to her two children, Christina and Helma (see page vi). In addition the 'case' contained a large number of original and copied documents and some photographs, including both personal and official letters of undoubted authenticity and great value to a biographer, and *Frau* Delavre willingly allowed me to copy them.

Yet another valuable document to which I gained access was a copy of what I call the 'Nonnenmacher list'. Emil Nonnenmacher was a pilot in the *Nachjagd* who after the war devoted himself in his spare time to building up an archive of material on the night-fighter force based almost entirely on official documents that had survived from wartime. I met Nonnenmacher in about 1989 when I was gathering material for an earlier book, and he showed me what he said was virtually a complete list of all German night-fighter claims during the war. Subsequently I had many occasions to consult him on specific kills, and he never failed to provide me with the information that I sought, nor did I ever detect any inaccuracy in his records. By the time I began to think of writing about Lent, however, Emil Nonnenmacher had sadly died, and it was said that all his archival papers had been sold to a collector abroad and were no longer available for consultation. Then, out of the blue, I was advised to contact Andreas Wachtel, who told me that he did indeed have a copy of the list and sent to me details from that list of all of Lent's kills. Andreas has also been of great help to me in the writing of my book in several other ways .

I now had a very good fund of reliable material on which to base my book, and after much deliberation I decided to call it 'The Lent Papers' because, unlike many other similar works, it is based more on authentic written and printed material than on individual memory, hearsay or myth. That is not to say, of course, that it does not contain anecdotal material from people who knew Lent during the war, but as I explained earlier such people are few.

Helmut was born into a Prussian family of profound religious faith. His father, his two brothers, and his two grandfathers were pastors in the Lutheran Church. From an early age, however, a military career had more attraction for Lent than an a clerical one did, but his religious faith remained unswerving throughout his life. He believed that he enjoyed the special favour of his God, who protected him in combat, and, as he once told his friend and fellow commander of a night-fighter *Geschwader*, Hans-Joachim Jabs, he said a prayer for his victims each time a bomber fell to his guns. Lent was trained as a *Zerstörer* pilot and had already scored victories in Poland, the German Bight and Norway when his unit was arbitrarily transferred to night-fighter duties when the Royal Air Force began its night-time bombing offensive against the Fatherland in 1940, a change of assignment that he accepted with marked reluctance. After a slow start, however, he proved himself to be not only a very competent night-fighter pilot, but also, as a member and then leader of the most successful *Gruppe* of the *Nachtjagd*, an influential factor in the development of night-fighter tactics and the training of the night-fighter crews. A modest, sensitive and devout man, he achieved high rank and distinction at an early age. His life ended in tragic circumstances only a short time before the family into which he was born and to whom he was deeply attached also became victims of the catastrophic war that had been launched by the Führer to whom, as a German officer, Helmut Lent had sworn and given his unquestioning allegiance.

As the war progressed and Lent was appointed progressively to positions of higher command he inevitably became more remote from the fighter crews whom he commanded, even though he continued to participate personally in the night battles right up to his death. At the same time the day-to-day pressures of the bitter fight against the bomber offensive and the steadily declining fortunes of the German armed forces meant that records were not kept as conscientiously as they had been in the earlier and more leisurely stages of the war, with the result that nor nearly as much reliable material, anecdotal, documentary and photographic, about Lent's career survives, so that in this book his earlier history, until the middle of the war, is covered in more detail that its later stages. Despite this inadequacy in the record Lent was a unique and outstanding example of the many thousands of young men who fought and who gave their life in the bitter aerial battle by night over Europe, and I think that his story merits telling and preserving.

Peter Hinchliffe
March 2003

CHAPTER ONE

June 1918 to March 1936
Family background, childhood and youth

'If you travel eastward by train from Berlin towards Landsberg an der Warthe a slim church steeple comes into sight to the right of the railway line just past Küstrin and before Döllensradung. It belongs to the village of Pyrehne.'

T HIS was written in either late 1944 or very early 1945. Today the church is no longer to be seen on the skyline; it was blown up and bulldozed by the Russians in February 1945 to make way for an airfield from which the Russian Air Force could operate in support of the Red Army's final apocalyptic advance on Berlin. Nor is there any longer a village called Pyrehne: today, as a consequence of the reshaping of Europe after the Second World War it now bears the name 'Pyrzany' and is no longer in Germany but in Poland. A boy was born there in 1918, and the church once visible from the railway, and the nearby vicarage,

The church at Pyrehne, where Helmut's father Johannes Lent was pastor

were the focus of his early life and a strong formative influence in the development of his character. His father Johannes was the Evangelical priest there, the *Pastor*. At the time of the boy's birth Germany had been engaged for nearly four years in bloody hostilities, the 'war to end all wars' which later, less emotively but more realistically, came to be called the First World War. Within five months of his birth that war had ended in Germany's collapse and there had begun for the Fatherland a period of troubled peace, internal ferment, strident nationalism and militant expansion, culminating soon after his twenty-first birthday in a return to – or, some would say, a renewal of – war. The interval of twenty-one years between the end of the First World War and the start of the Second World War meant that as a class the men of his generation were predestined to become soldiers, sailors and airmen and to be sacrificed in vast numbers, the victims of the second drastic culling of German youth in the Twentieth Century. The war in which he and so many other young men were fated to fight and to die was even more murderous than the one that had preceded it, although overall it was of a much different character. Air power, in its infancy between 1914 and 1918, had expanded and stamped its authority on the pattern of international conflict, bringing with it, among other things, forces of bomber aircraft that conveyed the terror of the front line into the

Helmut Lent's birth certificate. Old German handwriting was still the norm.

towns and the homes and the workplaces of the civilian populace, exacting an enormous toll in non-military lives, vast numbers of them those of women and children. The way in which the air war in Europe developed dictated that much of the bombing was done during the hours of darkness, and specialised forces of night fighters were brought into play to combat the bombers. It was in this new branch of military aviation that the boy was destined to excel and to achieve lasting fame. Born in the early hours of the morning of the thirteenth of June 1918, he was christened Helmut Johannes Siegfried Lent. The fifth child of his parents, Helmut Lent had two older brothers, Werner and Joachim, and

The vicarage at Pyrehne, Helmut's home from birth.

two older sisters, Käthe and Ursula[1].

Friedrich II, Frederick the Great, King of Prussia, is reputed to have founded the village of Pyrehne in the eighteenth century, although there are traces of settlements there from as early as the fourteen-hundreds. Pyrzany, as it now is, is situated in the low-lying, flat, sandy and marshy region adjacent to the River Warthe[2] that was known when Germans lived there as the *Warthebruch*, the Warthe Marshlands. It is said that at some stage the Lent family had enjoyed the patronage, or at least the favour, of Frederick the Great, as evidence of which there were a number of articles in the family home – a ring, a Meissen dinner service, a longcase clock and a portrait of Frederick, for example – which, family legend has it, were gifts from Prussian King himself.

The family, large and widespread, is thought to have originated in Holland, possibly near Nijmegen, where there is a village called Lent. One theory has it that the first Lents arrived in the *Warthebruch* when Friedrich Wilhelm, the 'Great Elector' of Brandenburg and the great-grandfather of Frederick the Great, who had lived in Holland and studied at the University of Leiden, imported Dutch labour and technology to carry out drainage and reclamation work in the area in the mid-seventeenth century. Another suggestion, not necessary exclusive, is that the Lents had first migrated from Holland to Westphalia and subsequently moved further east.

The Lents were of the Evangelical faith[3] and without exception devout

---

[1] It is possible that there had been a sixth child who had died in infancy, but details do not survive.
[2] The present, Polish, spelling is 'Warta'.
[3] At the time in question more than 95% of the population of the region belonged to the Evangelical church.

Christians. On his father's side, Helmut Lent's family can be positively traced back to one Christian Lent, whose son, Andreas Johann Lente (sic) was born in June 1738 and died in 1801 in Genthin, to the west of the town of Brandenburg[4] in which area there seem to have been Lents for several generations. The town itself lies to the west of Berlin and is therefore some long distance from Pyrehne. Christian's profession is recorded as 'carabineer' and that of his son Andreas, quaintly, as 'carabineer and master shoemaker'. Andreas' son, Christian Andreas (1766 to 1855), became an Evangelical pastor: *his* son Albert (1815 to 1879) followed the same profession, as, in turn, did *his* son, Johannes Karl Philipp, Helmut's father. There are also other members of the clergy recorded among Helmut Lent's forebears, as well as an *Oberstleutnant* (Lieutenant-Colonel) and an 'Officer and Landowner' with the splendid name of Wilhelm August Wobislaw von dem Borne (1768 to 1828). Helmut's mother was Marie Elisabeth, née Braune, and her father was also a pastor. Her side of the family tree – which is far from comprehensive – indicates that the family were mainly small farmers, but even so there are a number of clergymen to be seen among her ancestors, including another pastor, a preacher, a superintendent and a rector. Given a lineage such as this it is unsurprising to learn that there was a tradition in the Lent family that boys should make their career in either the Evangelical Church or the armed forces. Both of Helmut's elder brothers, Werner and Joachim, became Pastors.

The flat landscape of the *Wartebruch*, the marshland in which Pyrehne was set.

---

[4] Not to be confused with the former vast Province (now a *Land* in the Federal Republic of Germany) of the same name.

Helmut with his mother
in about 1920.

The family into which Helmut Lent was born was a very close, loyal
and loving one founded and brought up on strong Christian principles,
strict but fair, confident in its holy beliefs, its traditions and its respected
position in the community. In material and monetary terms the Lents
were by no means wealthy, but what the family lacked in worldly goods
it more than made up for in mutual love, security and solidarity.
Helmut's childhood was a happy one, and from a very early age it was
apparent that he was more likely to opt to follow a military career than
one in the Church. His favourite characters from history and literature
were soldiers and airmen, and his favourite games were war games, in
which he showed himself to be a natural and imaginative leader. He
founded and led, for example, the '*Schwarze Band*' ('Black Gang'), which,
together with his best friend Heini Hahn[5], he ran on strictly military lines
and with appropriate secrecy and discipline. From Easter 1924 until

---

[5] Heini Hahn was just one of the many school-friends of Helmut who did not survive the war.

Easter 1928, when he was approaching ten years of age, he attended the
local *Volksschule*[6], where he impressed as an intelligent and diligent
scholar. Then, having been successfully coached at home for the entrance
examination by his father and eldest brother, Werner, until Easter 1930,
he moved on to the *Staatliches Reformgymnasium*[7] (State Reform Grammar
School) in Landsberg, about fourteen miles distant from Pyrehne, where
he entered the top stream. An account of that period survives in the
family records; these are extracts from it:

The Lent family in
about 1921. Left to
right: Ursula ('Ulla');
Käthe; Helmut; Werner;
Marie Lent (Helmut's
mother); Joachim.

> Like every normal youngster he enjoyed model making, and he showed
> great interest in every new technical development, which found its practical
> expression in repairing wireless sets and other pieces of equipment. Walks in
> the woods, sometimes lasting hours, strengthened his powers of observation
> and his love of the *Heimat*, the homeland. He would often cycle from Pyrehne
> to Landsberg and back to save money, and he used to make a little pocket
> money by chopping firewood at home, so becoming accustomed to simplicity
> and thrift.
>
> History was one of his favourite subjects, which was probably why later in
> life he enjoyed reading books with a historical theme, but he also liked
> German. Physical training was not neglected, and when gymnastic displays
> were given he was called upon to demonstrate his skill on the horizontal and
> parallel bars, his favourite pieces of apparatus. He was always ready to react to
> provocation from the biggest and strongest members of the class, when his

---

[6] *Volksschule*: Literally 'people's school', providing basic primary and secondary education.
[7] After 1933 the school was renamed the '*Hermann Göring Hochschule*'.

Helmut with his sister
Ulla in about 1923/24.

agility and dexterity were a great advantage to him in playground scraps.

In the winter months Helmut used to lodge with his father's sister, *Tante* Lies, in Landsberg. Often the murmur of Latin or Greek vocabulary would interrupt the pleasures of a grown-up game of cards when *Tante* Lies opened the door to check that the afternoon visit of his friends was genuinely for the purpose of doing school work. Often, too, a pillow fight would take place in the evening, but the noise would change to snoring and deep breathing when *Tante* Lies came in to impose discipline.

Helmut passed his *Abitur*[8] at the age of seventeen. His quick understanding, his good memory and his ability to draw logical conclusions, as well as his powers of concentration, made him a good scholar, although he was anything but a swot.

In February 1933, it seems, Helmut Lent found another outlet for his liking for things military and his talent for leadership; he joined the *Jungvolk* ('*Young People*'), the junior branch of the *Hitler Jugend* (Hitler Youth). The Hitler Youth organisation had been in existence since about 1926 as an integral branch of the National Socialist Party, but had not enjoyed great popular support. In 1932 its membership was only just over 100,000, compared to the ten million or so members of the numerous other youth organisations, many of which connected to churches, that existed in Germany at that time. With Hitler's accession to the position of Reich Chancellor in January 1933, however, the Hitler Youth became a state-controlled organisation and membership began to grow rapidly, triggered by the upsurge of nationalism generated by Hitler's success. By 1935 it comprised almost sixty percent of the

[8] *Abne* examination which, when successfully passed, qualified a student for entry to University. It was, and still is, normally taken at the age of eighteen. The English equivalent in the nineteen-thirties was Higher School Certificate or Matriculation.

country's young men. Entry to the Hitler Youth was voluntary. Young boys (there was an equivalent organisation for girls, the *Jungmädel*, the junior branch of the *Bund Deutscher Mädel* or League of German Maidens) could join the *Jungvolk* at the age of ten, transferring to the *Hitler Jugend* proper when they became fourteen. One of the main incentives for boys to join was undoubtedly the smart, military-style uniform that went with being a member. Lent's father wrote proudly about his son in the following terms: 'When he was in the *Jungvolk* he had the most dashing troop in the whole district. The boys thought he was great. It wasn't long before he had formed a band, with himself playing the trumpet. When he marched through the village in the morning with his *Jungvolk* troop, with the band leading the way, it was as if the Potsdam Guards were marching past.'

When Helmut Lent joined the *Jungvolk* he was already well past the normal upper age limit for membership of the junior organisation.

Studienrat (teacher) Weber with his class at the *Volksschule* at Pyrehne in about 1926. Helmut's face can be seen just to the right of *Herr* Weber in the second row.

Helmut Lent aged
about twelve.

Young men specially selected for their leadership qualities, however, could work with the *Jungvolk* as leaders and trainers, and that is the function that Lent performed. From March 1933 he acted as a *Jungzugführer* (Platoon Leader, in charge of about twenty youngsters) and from April 1935 as a *Fähnleinführer* (Troop Leader, in charge of between sixty and seventy boys). He seems never to have joined the Hitler Youth proper. Another former night-fighter pilot[9] comments: 'The *Fähnleinführer*, usually sixteen or seventeen years of age, was the senior

---

[9] *Hauptmann* Peter Spoden, *Kommandeur* I. /NJG 6.

member of the Group. There was, of course, also the introduction of National Socialist ideas. We received the printed material from the Hitler Youth, but mostly it was fun for young boys who, like me, wanted to get away from their parents, playing games in the countryside in the open air. I became a *Jungzugführer* myself like Lent at the age of fourteen or fifteen and I enjoyed it for some time, but I never officially joined the *Hitler Jugend* – clearly Lent didn't either.'

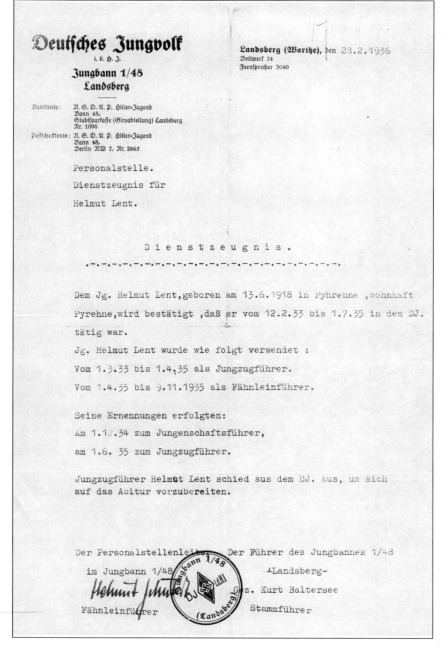

Helmut Lent's Record of Service in the *Deutsches Jungvolk*. It shows him having served from 1933 to 1935, when he left the organization in order to prepare for his *Abitur* (matriculation examination).

We can but conjecture as to what motivated Lent belatedly to join the *Jungvolk*, particularly when he did. It might, of course, have been nothing more than the attraction that quasi-military organisations held for him, but in that case one might well wonder why he had not already joined the *Jungvolk*, or a similar group such as the *Pfadfinder* (the equivalent of the Boy Scouts) earlier than in his fifteenth year. As noted above, he entered the *Jungvolk* immediately after Hitler's nomination as Chancellor - could that have had anything to do with his decision? It seems, however, unlikely that genuine enthusiasm for Hitler and his policies played a part: the Lent family had little sympathy for National Socialism and would, one might think, have been opposed in principle to their son associating himself with the Party, whether it was in or out of power, unless, perhaps, there were some possible benefit to be perceived. One attractive possibility is that Lent, having already decided that he wanted to make a career as an officer in the armed forces, and possibly advised by his father, foresaw that membership of the *Hitler Jugend*, even in its junior branch – or possibly *particularly* in its junior branch, because there were real opportunities there for leadership experience – would count strongly in his favour when his application for officer training came to be considered.

Helmut Lent left the *Jungvolk* in either July or November 1935 (the record is ambiguous) in order to concentrate on preparation for his *Abitur* examination, a prerequisite for officer training. In the normal course of events he should not have taken the examination until March 1936 at the earliest, when he would still be three months short of his eighteenth birthday. In December 1935, however, having gained his *Abitur* on the 12th of the month but still six months short of his eighteenth birthday, he left school, and on 2 February 1936 he began an eight-weeks period of compulsory labour service[10] at Mohrin, no great distance to the west-northwest of his native village. It seems likely that his *Abitur* examination had been brought forward, possibly at the request of the military authorities, to allow him to take up a cadetship in the *Luftwaffe*. That he was able to do so is a strong indication that he was a pupil of above-average abilities.

It is unsurprising that Lent should have opted to make his career in the Air Force rather than in one of the other two branches of the *Wehrmacht*, the Army or Navy. The *Luftwaffe*, prohibited under the terms of the Versailles Treaty of 1918, officially emerged from clandestinity in March 1935, although its existence had in fact been an open secret for some time: it did so amid considerable publicity and a wave of patriotic triumph and pride. Since the Wright Brothers had made their first powered flights in December 1904, aviation, both military and civil, had developed to an extent and at a rate that could scarcely have been foreseen in those first days, the process being accelerated by the

---

[10] *Reichsarbeitsdienst* - State Labour Service, introduced in June 1935. Young Germans had to serve a period of *Arbeitsdienst* before entering the armed forces.

demands of the First World War leaders for better, faster and more
potent flying machines for both attack and defence. The first decades of
the twentieth century might well be called the age of the aeroplane, with
flying attracting to itself a great aura of novelty, romance and adventure.
Speed records, long-distance records, altitude records were being made
and broken, new, exciting machines were being introduced – and the
constraints of the Versailles Treaty were such that Germany was able to
share in these triumphs to only a very limited degree. Almost everywhere
else in the developed world men – particularly young men – dreamed of
being able to share the unique experience of flight, and in Germany the
Versailles restrictions made the forbidden fruit of flying even more
attractive. Now, in March 1935, the official announcement by the hero of
the First World War, Hermann Göring, that Germany now had a
Luftwaffe, followed by an intensive recruitment campaign for that service,
suddenly opened the way for fulfilment of the dream. Exactly when Lent
himself applied to join the air force as a trainee pilot and officer-cadet is
not known, but presumably it was after the announcement; or possibly
he had already applied for a cadetship in the *Wehrmacht* but changed his
application to one specifically for the *Luftwaffe* when the opportunity to
do so arose.

Be that as it might, in Spring 1936 Helmut Lent, the youngest son of
the Evangelical priest of a small village in rural eastern Germany, began
his career in the renascent *Luftwaffe* of the Third Reich. Just a month
before he did so Germany had begun her programme of territorial
expansion by marching into the demilitarised Rhineland.

CHAPTER TWO

April 1936 to September 1939 Enlistment, training, posting to an operational unit. To war.

THE official date of Helmut Lent's enlistment in the *Luftwaffe* was 1 April 1936, when he was still more than two months short of his eighteenth birthday. He entered as a *Fahnenjunker*, or officer-cadet, and he began his training on the sixth of the same month at the *Luftkriegsschule* (Air Warfare School) at Gatow, on the south-western outskirts of Berlin. On 21 April he swore the National Socialist oath of allegiance: 'I swear by God this sacred oath, that I shall render unconditional obedience to Adolf Hitler, the Leader of the German Reich, supreme commander of the armed forces, and that I shall at all times be prepared, as a brave soldier, to give my life for this oath.'

Immediately following the official confirmation in March 1935 that a German military air force now existed, a number of Air Warfare Schools had been established to meet the demand for suitable young men of high quality to train as permanent long-service aircrew officers of the *Luftwaffe*. In effect that meant, almost without exception, as pilots. The only other crew member who was likely to be a commissioned officer was the observer (*Beobachter*), and as often as not he himself was also qualified as a pilot and he would, if he were senior in rank to a pilot with whom he flew, act as captain of aircraft. The young men selected for aircrew-officer training were the elite of the flying service, the cadre from which, in due course, its senior commanders would be drawn. Other flying men, such as radio operators, gunners and flight mechanics, were usually co-opted from the ranks and trained separately. Unlike their RAF counterparts they were not exclusively volunteers.

A contemporary of Helmut Lent, Werner Baumbach, who was destined to achieve great distinction as a bomber pilot during the war, was a member of the same course:

> My call-up orders as a *Fahnenjunker* to the Air Warfare School at Berlin-Gatow came into operation with effect from the 6th April 1936. There, according to the syllabus, we were to receive a careful training in all branches of military and air-force service. We were one of the first officer-cadet intakes for the new Luftwaffe. Out of tens of thousands only a few hundred had the

Werner Baumbach, seen here as a *Hauptmann* and wearing the Knight's Cross with Oak Leaves and Swords, was one of the most influential bomber pilots of the Second World War. He survived the hostilities with the rank of *Oberst*. In 1948 he emigrated to South America, and he died there when the aircraft he was flying, ironically an Avro Lancaster, crashed.

good fortune to be selected.

From the moment that we entered the establishment we formed the impression that neither trouble nor expense had been spared. Our accommodation, the sports ground, the gymnasium and the swimming pool, our flying field, the hangars, the lecture rooms and the aircraft were all the most modern of their kind. The whole atmosphere of the place breathed the spirit that motivated Hermann Göring, Commander-in-Chief of the Luftwaffe, in building up the new branch of the Wehrmacht. We swore our oath to the Führer and we worshipped Göring as the greatest hero of the First World War.[11]

---

[11] This extract is quoted in translation from Werner Baumbach's book *'Zu spät?'* (Too Late?), first published in 1949.

Lent during training at the *Luftkriegsschule*, Gatow, Berlin.

The basic training that a cadet had to complete at Air Warfare School before obtaining his commission and winning his pilot's 'ticket', together with the coveted flying badge that went with it, lasted in the region of twenty-two months. It was divided into three courses or '*Lehrgänge*': *Lehrgang* 1 lasted four months, *Lehrgang* 2 ten months and *Lehrgang* 3 eight months. The first of the three courses was devoted entirely to basic military recruit training – parade-ground drills, weapons drills, field exercises, games, physical fitness, classroom instruction and so on. High standards were demanded, and the training was intensive yet, to the highly motivated and healthy young students, greatly enjoyable. The second and third courses comprised primarily flying instruction, with, of course, officer training and theoretical and practical work proceeding in parallel. Cadet pilots trained and qualified on single-engined aircraft alone, aiming for the 'A' and 'B' pilot's licences. Broadly speaking, *Lehrgang* 2 covered the syllabus for the 'A' licence and *Lehrgang* 3 that for the 'B' licence, the students being awarded their Military Pilot's Licence and their flying badge[12] after a period of training lasting about eighteen months. Multi-engined training, for those fledgling pilots who were selected to fly bigger aircraft, for which they needed the 'C' Licence, and continuation training for those selected to fly single-engined aircraft, were carried out afterwards on attachment to operational or specialised units. Subject, of course, to his making satisfactory progress and successfully negotiating the necessary examinations and assessments

---

[12] The German equivalent of the RAF wings was the *Flugzeugführerabzeichen* (Pilot's badge) and the Pilot's Licence was the *Militärischer Flugzeugführerschein*.

Cadet Lent on field exercises during his initial training.

throughout the training programme, a cadet could expect a number of intermediate promotions on his way to becoming an officer, but their timing was not, seemingly, tied directly to the three courses outlined above. One entered the *Luftwaffe* as a *Fahnenjunker* (Officer-Cadet) and then after six months came promotion to *Fahnenjunker-Gefreiter* (Lance-Corporal Cadet): then two months later the cadet would be promoted to *Fahnenjunker-Unteroffizier* (Corporal Cadet) and then, after a year's service, to *Fähnrich*[13]. The latter step was a big one, because appointment to this rank was virtual confirmation that one had now, after the most

---

[13] *Fähnrich* was a rank somewhere between that of Senior NCO and the first commissioned rank (*Leutnant*). It was normally peculiar to men scheduled to become commissioned officers, and has been translated as, for example, Warrant Officer, although it did not equate to a man of that rank in the British armed forces.

Heinkel He 72 '*Kadett*'.

careful scrutiny, been finally and positively adjudged to be a fit and proper person to become a professional officer of the *Wehrmacht* – one might almost say that a *Fähnrich* was an officer on probation. Finally, shortly before commissioning, one could expect to go up one more rank and be promoted to '*Oberfähnrich*' (Senior *Fähnrich*).

Flying training, as already noted, began with the second of the three courses. In Helmut Lent's case the long-anticipated event occurred on Monday, 7 August 1936. At 1125 hours that morning a Heinkel 72 '*Kadett*' single-engined biplane, registration letters D-EYZA[14], took off from Gatow with one Becker at the controls and Lent in the pupil's seat: the purpose of the flight was logged as 'familiarisation'. The *Kadett* was a machine similar in size and design to its British counterpart, the de Havilland Tiger Moth, although it had a radial engine of about 160 horsepower as opposed to the Moth's slightly less powerful in-line power plant. The flight lasted a scant five minutes, but it marked the beginning of a flying career of great distinction. By the 15th September, *Fahnenjunker* Lent had entered sixty-three flights in his logbook, although the total flying time to his credit, only six hours and twenty minutes, an average of little more than six minutes per trip, was still modest. After the first few days the He 72 had yielded way to another biplane basic trainer, similarly powered, the Focke-Wulf Fw 44 '*Stieglitz*' ('Goldfinch'). Lent's regular instructor was called Lehnecke, but another pilot, presumably senior, by the name of Schumann, occasionally checked him out. Following a check flight by Schumann on the 14th September Lent flew three short dual trips with Lehnecke on the early morning of the 15th. After his next trip, his sixty-fourth in all – it began

[14] Some of the aircraft used for training still carried civil registration letters. Soon changed to four-letter identifications with the German '*Balkenkreuz*' in the centre - e.g. EM+RE.

Focke-Wulf Fw 44
'Stieglitz'.

at 0948 and lasted for five minutes – he was able to enter in his logbook, doubtless with no little pride, *'Alleinflug'* – Solo! Possibly, because it was a tradition in the *Luftwaffe*, he was met by his fellow-pupils and his instructors when he landed and subjected to a ceremonial 'bottom-smacking' – good pilots flew 'by the seat of their pants'. Or possibly the ceremony was delayed until later in that morning's flying programme, because very shortly after landing Lent flew a further four short solos in quite rapid succession. The important thing was, however, that he had now experienced the indescribable joy, freedom and self-fulfilment of flying an aircraft with no one else on board to monitor his performance.

Other 'firsts' followed in rapid sequence – his first aerobatic experience for example, with Lehnecke at the controls, on 29 September on his 106th flight. The trip lasted thirty-two minutes, and presumably Lent suffered no adverse effects, because two minutes after landing he took off solo for a couple of sessions of local flying. Then came the first practice forced landings, the first tentative cross-country flights, the first landings away from base, the first overnight stops. The average length of exercises

Helmut Lent's logbook shows his 64th flight, in Focke-Wulf Fw 44 registration EMRE on 15 November 1936, to be his first *Alleinflug* – solo.

Lfd. Nr. des Fluges	Führer	Begleiter	Muster	Zulassungs-Nr.	Zweck des Fluges	Flug							
						Abflug Ort	Tag	Tageszeit	Landung Ort	Tag	Tageszeit	Flug- dauer	Kilo- meter
									Übertrag			365 Min	
59.	Lehnecke	Lent	FW 44	EMRE	Schulflug	Flu.-Gatow	14.9.36	8⁴⁵	Flu.-Gatow	14.9.36	8⁴⁹	4 "	
60.	Schümann	"	"	"	Übungsflug	"	"	8⁵⁴	"	"	8⁵⁸	4 "	
61.	Lehnecke	"	"	"	Schulflug	"	15.9.36	9⁴⁵	"	15.9.36	9⁴⁸	3 "	
62.	"	"	"	"	"	"	"	9³⁰	"	"	9³⁵	5 "	
63.	"	"	"	"	"	"	"	9³⁷	"	"	9⁴²	5 "	
64.	Lent	/	"	"	Alleinflug	"	"	9⁴⁸	"	"	9⁵³	5 "	
65.	"	/	"	"	"	"	"	9⁵⁶	"	"	10⁰¹	5 "	
66.	"	/	"	"	"	"	"	10⁰⁵	"	"	10¹⁰	5 "	
67.	"	/	"	"	"	"	"	10¹³	"	"	10¹⁸	5 "	
68.	"	/	"	"	Platzflug	"	16.9.36	7⁵⁸	"	16.9.36	8⁰³	5 "	
69.	"	"	"	"	"	"	"	8⁰⁶	"	"	8¹²	6 "	

Bücker Bü131

Arado Ar 66

increased, and Lent was sometimes flying an hour or more at a time, and on one occasion he was airborne for two hours and a quarter. Then came the first night-time take-offs and landings, marking the beginning of the transition to the 'B' licence syllabus. There were new aircraft to be mastered too, the Bücker Bü 131, another basic training biplane, on 22 October; and the Arado Ar 66, a more powerful biplane with a 240

horsepower engine, the following week. The Gotha Go 145, of similar   Gotha Go 145
design and similarly powered, was first flown by Lent on 5 November
1936, when his total flying time amounted to 27 hours. A break in flying
occurred from the 18th December 1936 to the 7th January 1937,
presumably for Christmas leave.

    Until now all the aircraft that Lent had flown had been single-engined,
open-cockpit trainer biplanes, but on the 12th of January 1937 he
graduated on to a bigger aircraft, a passenger-carrying and light
transport monoplane, the Junkers Ju (W) 34. This machine, reminiscent
in general appearance of its bigger and much better-known cousin the   Cockpit of a
three-engined Ju 52, had the same corrugated-metal bodywork as the   Junkers Ju (W) 34

Lent as a *Fähnrich* under training at Gatow.

Ju 52, but only one engine. That engine, however, was a BMW 131 A of 660 horsepower, an engine very much more powerful than anything that Lent had handled so far. By the fourth of February 1937 his total flying time amounted to a fraction over 63 hours.

Aircraft were not the only machines that the cadets had to learn to handle; they also had driving lessons on motorcycles and cars, and at about this time Lent was involved in an road accident in the course of such instruction, breaking his right upper leg badly enough to prevent him flying for five months. The passage of time has obscured the details of the occurrence: presumably he was able, in one way or other, to carry

on with the classroom aspects of his training, and indeed the record
shows that his promotion pattern was not adversely affected by his
enforced absence from 'hands-on' flying training. On 1 April 1937, after
taking his commissioning examination, he was made a *Fähnrich*, the
penultimate step before promotion to *Leutnant*, and for the month of
May he was attached to a bomber unit, the Third *Gruppe* of KG 152
(Hindenburg) in Schwerin, presumably to occupy his time profitably and
to gain broad general experience. Whatever the reason, he did not fly
during the attachment.

Focke-Wulf Fw 56
'Stösser'

Back at Gatow Lent resumed his flying course in the 15th of July,
making two take-offs and landings totalling ten minutes in a Go 145, with
an instructor at the dual controls. Apparently the instructor was satisfied
that the pupil's flying ability had not suffered by his enforced absence,
because he then handed the machine over to Lent, who made a number
of local solo flights. Between the 17th and the 25th of the month Helmut
Lent carried out a total of fifteen cross-country trips in the Go 145,
presumably making up for lost training time. Then he flew another new
type, the Focke-Wulf Fw 56 'Stösser' high-wing monoplane, a number of
times before beginning a comparatively long period flying the Ju (W) 34.
During September 1937 he made a number of trips, with and without
instructors, in such disciplines as cross-country flying, target landings by
day and night, blind flying, aerobatics and so on, marking them in his
logbook '*für B2*', indicating that they were practical tests for Part 2 of his
'B' Licence.

It was at about this time that Helmut Lent, one might reasonably
assume, was faced with something of a moral dilemma. By all accounts
and all evidence he was a deeply convinced Christian, and as a member
of the Evangelical Church he had accepted and acknowledged a personal
commitment to Christ. As a German officer candidate, however, he had

also sworn allegiance to the Führer, Adolf Hitler. Now Church and State came into conflict in a way that directly affected him and his family. Among papers in the possession of the Lent family there survives an extract from a letter that Helmut wrote to his parents from Gatow on the 10th of October 1937, and it is marked, 'On the occasion of Werner's arrest'.

Like their father, both of Helmut's elder brothers, Joachim and Werner, were Evangelical pastors. One branch of the Evangelical Church, the so-called Confessional Church (*Bekenntniskirche*), led by Pastor Martin Niemöller, was in outspoken opposition to the Nazi Party's intention to merge all religions in Germany into one organisation under State control and sympathetic to national-socialist policies. Niemöller declared that the Nazi doctrines of race and leadership were incompatible with Christianity. Both Joachim and Werner were members of the Confessional Church, and possibly – the record is not clear on the point – their father was too. Pastor Niemöller was arrested on 1 July 1937 after preaching an anti-Nazi sermon, and Lent's brother Werner was arrested soon afterwards. One must wonder how Lent reacted to this action by the National Socialist authorities, and because the extract that we have from his letter home is only very brief, what words of sympathy he had for his mother and father and the rest of the family. One must wonder, too, what his innermost feelings were. All that survives of the

March 1937. Lent as a newly commissioned *Leutnant*, with his mother.

letter is:

I hope that the journey to see him did you good both physically and spiritually. Perhaps it also gave you some small degree of courage. It is a strange fact that those people for whom, when looked at from the general point of view, things are going badly, are often the happiest.

On 19 October 1937 Lent was awarded his A/B Licence, making his final flight from Gatow six days later. His wings followed on 15 November. On 1 February 1938 he was promoted to *Oberfähnrich*, and on 1 March to

Hartmann Grasser, a co-student of Lent at Gatow. He became a *Major* and was awarded the Oak Leaves to the Knight's Cross.

Another fellow-student at Gatow. Alfred Druschel is seen here as a *Major* and is wearing the *Eichenlaub mit Schwertern*.

Leutnant. He had made 434 flights, the overwhelming majority by day, in eight different types of single-engined training aircraft, and he had accumulated 112 hours and 48 minutes flying time. His only experience of multi-engined aircraft had been as observer on three short local trips in a Ju 52 logged as, 'photographic and reconnaissance instruction'.

So ended Helmut Lent's basic training as a career officer of the

Wehrmacht and a pilot of the *Luftwaffe*. There were, of course, other aspects of training over and above the purely professional: not only young Germans but also young men of all nationalities found the experience of learning to fly and to command exciting, stimulating and self-fulfilling. But the social and 'fun' sides of being a young man learning to make his way among like-minded fellow-pupils in a privileged and heady environment were certainly not neglected. One

Hans Philipp, seen here as an *Oberleutnant* with the Oak Leaves to the Knight's Cross. He subsequently reached the rank of *Oberstleutnant* and was awarded the Swords.

reflection of this survives, written after his death by an unknown pen:

He liked to look back on his period of training, when maximum effort and duty were interspersed with crazy horseplay. Years afterwards, when he was already a *Kommodore*, he would smile when he described how, at a party during that time, the cadets shaved a somewhat unpopular instructor's dog in the shape of a tonsure; they then gave the dog some beer and cognac to drink and took him to a quiet spot in the ablutions and left him there, where eventually his master, who had gone looking for him, found him fast asleep. The outcome of this episode, which was soon on the social grapevine, was that the cadets of that entry, among whom where a number of other fliers – Baumbach, Nordmann[15], Grasser[16], Druschel[17] and so on, all of whom were subsequently highly decorated – became the heroes of the Berlin dance circuit.

In his book '*Zu spät*' Werner Baumbach[18], quoted earlier and mentioned immediately above, also commented on the cadets' course at Gatow. By the end of the war Baumbach was probably the outstanding bomber pilot of Göring's *Luftwaffe*. Decorated with the Oak Leaves with Swords to the Knight's Cross of the Iron Cross, the highest award to be given to a bomber pilot, he attained the rank of *Oberstleutnant* and the function of *General der Kampfflieger* – General of the Bombers – just as Adolf Galland became *General der Jagdflieger*. His comments on the course, on a more serious note than those already quoted, were critical:

The first shock to our young enthusiasm came during the preliminary infantry training. Our drill instructors were not fliers, and we were dealt with on strictly military lines. We learned to see Mother Earth as if through the eyes of a frog, and we were given to understand that thinking for ourselves could have unfortunate consequences.

At this flying school there was precious little feeling of a flying spirit. The teaching syllabus was in effect more a list of drill regulations going back to the days when the horizon of a young *Leutnant* was no further away than the depth of his platoon. It was in no way suited to make us into open-minded and self-reliant individuals. These institutions did not turn out aircrew officers capable of mastering the complicated mechanisms of a modern air force. Little wonder that 'rebels' soon gravitated to each other, among them some of the most successful fliers of the Second World War. They included Lent, Philipp[19] and Claus. We were among the last to pass the officer's examination, and I can still

---

[15] *Major* Theodor Nordmann became one of the leading Stuka and ground-attack pilots of the war and was awarded the Oak Leaves to the Knight's Cross. As *Kommodore* SG 3, and with approximately 1,200 operational flights to his credit, mostly on the Ju 87 and the Fw 190, he was killed in a mid-air collision on the Eastern Front in January 1945.

[16] *Major* Hartmann Grasser, also awarded the *Eichenlaub*, ended the war as *Kommodore* JG 210 with 103 'kills' to his credit.

[17] *Oberst* Alfred Druschel, decorated with the *Schwerter*, was an outstanding fighter-bomber pilot and was killed in action on 1 January 1945 when *Kommodore* SG 4.

[18] Baumbach also served as *Kommodore* of the elite KG 200

[19] *Oberstleutnant* Hans Philipp, a leading fighter pilot, was killed in October 1943 in combat with American Thunderbolts when, as *Kommodore* JG 1, his tally of victories stood at 206. He was a holder of the *Schwerter*.

remember the parting words of the *Kommandeur* of the Air Warfare School: 'I   Dornier Do 11
am letting you go not only with great concern for your own careers, but also
with great concern for the entire *Luftwaffe*.'

It seems possible that at this stage in Lent's career it was envisaged by the
Luftwaffe personnel department that his future utilisation would be on
multi-engined aircraft, because when he left Gatow with the rank of
Leutnant he was posted to the *Grosse Kampffliegerschule* (Main Bomber
Crews' School) at Tutow, in the north-east of Germany between
Greifswald and Neubrandenburg. He spent three months there training
as an observer, beginning his attachment on 1 March 1938 and
completing it on 30 May, totalling about 50 hours flying time, much of it
as trainee observer rather than in the pilot's seat. Bombing practice,
often using cement bombs, alternated with training in reconnaissance
and navigation, sometimes using radio beams, and cross-country flying
featured prominently. Much of the training was done on familiar single-
engined biplanes and on the Ju (W) 34, but two fresh types were
sometimes used, the Dornier 11 and the Dornier 23, obsolescent twin-
engined bomber aircraft with high wings and fixed undercarriage.

Just before Lent's course at Tutow was due to end there occurred an
incident which, when viewed in connection with his traffic accident the   Dornier Do 23

previous year at Gatow, might have suggested that he was accident-prone. He described it in a letter home on the 26th June:

> I'm afraid that this Sunday greeting comes to you from a hospital once more. On Wednesday it happened to me again. A car drove into me at a road junction on the airfield. The result: a broken lower jaw, concussion and internal bleeding, bruises and other nice things. Now they have made my jaw more or less straight again with a splint that a professor or a dentist fixed in my mouth with a great deal of skill and fuss. Because of this stupid concussion I'm afraid I've got to stay in bed for three weeks. But when they are over I'll soon be up and about again. Let's hope, with God's help, that everything will soon be back in good order.

Arado Ar 68

On 1 July 1938 Lent was posted – presumably on paper only until such time as he recovered from his injuries – to the Third *Gruppe* of *Jagdgeschwader* 132 (Richthofen) (III./JG 132). The estimate of three weeks in bed seems to have been accurate, because by the 19th of July he was flying again, carrying out fighter training with II./JG 132 at Jüterbog-Damm, south of Berlin, albeit with the *Drahtverhau* (wire entanglement), as he called it, still in his mouth. After a couple of days of local flying in his old friends the Fw 44 and the Fw 56 he graduated to the Arado 68, a single-seater biplane fighter with a 640 horsepower Jumo engine, which since 1935 had been one of the front-line fighter aircraft of the new *Luftwaffe*, but was soon to be replaced by the Messerschmitt Bf 109. By early August he was intensively practising formation flying and air-to air firing, occasionally varying such disciplines with cross-country flights at the controls of a Ju (W) 34 or an Fw 56.

September 1938 was a month of great tension in Europe. To observers outside Germany Hitler's increasing self-confidence and bellicose territorial expansionism seemed to be leading to certain war; inside Germany he was overwhelmingly perceived as the charismatic leader who would restore the greatness of the Fatherland and deliver it from the repressions and injustices of the Treaty of Versailles – the *Versailler Diktat*, as it was generally referred to – which he had unilaterally renounced just a year previously. The irresolution of the western powers in face of Hitler's territorial demands served to affirm to the German public the correctness of his political decisions and the justice of his claims. In March 1938 German troops had marched into Austria without opposition - indeed, to great welcoming acclaim from the German-speaking population. Now Hitler's eyes had turned to Czechlosakia and the German-speaking Sudetenland, part of Bohemia adjacent to Germany that had formerly belonged to Austria but had been awarded to the newly formed state of Czechoslovakia in the settlement following the First World War. The rapidly increasing tension arising from Hitler's avowed determination to absorb the Sudetenland into the Third Reich and the strong threat of imminent war led to the three visits to Munich in September by the British Prime Minister, Neville Chamberlain, from the last of which, on 30 September, he returned by air to England announcing his belief that he had achieved 'peace in our time'. In truth he had given in to Hitler's demands: the Sudetenland became part of the Third Reich and Europe was one more step closer to war.

At the beginning of September Lent's *Staffel*, probably 7./JG 132[20], moved south from Jüterbog to Grossenhain near Dresden, about 45 miles from the border with Czechoslovakia. On the 11th of the month he could write home to his parents, 'The comic wire entanglement has been removed and now my jaw can do its duty unsupported,' and on the 29th, in another letter home, he gives a glimpse of the nature of his Christian belief. A young boy, possibly the son of Helmut's sister Käthe, had died. In his letter to his parents Helmut said, 'I wrote to Käthe at once. Who can say what the reason for it is? But what it is quite certain is that the dear child is better off then we humans are.'

On the 21st of September 1938 the *Staffel* returned to Jüterbog, and on the 29th redeployed to nearby Rangsdorf. The following day, the same one that saw Neville Chamberlain flying back to London from his meeting with Hitler in Munich, Lent flew the first of a short series of armed patrols in the Ar 68, part of the *Luftwaffe*'s show of strength to mark Germany's acquisition of the Sudetenland and to deter any counteraction by the Czechs. For the very first time he could enter in his logbook *'Jagdflug'*, the equivalent of 'Operational Patrol' in an RAF flier's log.

The tension over the occupation of the Sudeten territories having eased, Lent's unit returned to Rangsdorf, where he immediately began a course of conversion on to the Messerschmitt Bf 108 *'Taifun'*, a single-engined, low-winged touring aircraft of all-metal construction and with a retractable undercarriage. The aircraft bore a distinct family resemblance to the Bf 109 fighter, which, having proved itself in the Spanish Civil War with the *Legion Kondor*, was rapidly being adopted by the *Luftwaffe* as its standard single-engine interceptor. The fighter arm of

---

[20] The 3rd *Gruppe* of a *Geschwader* comprised the 7th, 8th and 9th *Staffeln*. In the *Luftwaffe* the *Staffel* was the smallest operational unit to operate independently.

the German Air Force was undergoing extensive – and confusing – reorganisation and re-equipment at this period, and it is possible that Lent's conversion on to the Bf 108 was because it was foreseen at that time that his *Gruppe* would exchange their Ar 68s for Bf 109s. On 1 November III./JG 132 moved to Fürstenwalde, between Berlin and the German-Polish border at Frankfurt/Oder, and was renamed II./JG 141, and Lent was posted to the 6th *Staffel*.

In the reshaping of the fighter arm of the *Luftwaffe* that was under way two distinct types of fighter unit were to be formed, *Leichte* (Light) and *Schwere* (Heavy) *Jagdgeschwader*, the former to be equipped with the

Messerschmitt Bf 108

Bf 109, largely for territorial defence, and the latter with its twin-engined stablemate the Bf 110, which was originally conceived as a 'strategic fighter', intended as a high-performance, heavily-armed and long-range escort for deep-penetration bomber formations. By naval analogy, the class of fighter – but not only, be it noted, the Bf 110 itself – came to be known as '*Zerstörer*', or 'Destroyers'. Possibly as a result of a late change of plan, II./JG 141 was now designated a Heavy Fighter *Gruppe*, to be re-equipped in due course with the Bf 110.

In January 1939 Lent, in addition to routine 'keeping-in-practice' flying on the Bf 108 and the Ar 68, began to learn to fly the three-engined Ju 52, presumably in preparation for more advanced qualifications as a pilot – the 'C' Certificate, confirming proficiency on multi-engined aircraft, the Blind-Flying Certificate, and the ELF, the *Erweiterter Luftwaffen-Flugzeugführerschein* or '*Luftwaffe* Advanced Pilot's Certificate', a standard qualification for active pilots. On the eighteenth of the month he soloed on the Bf 109, and in February he added the Do. 23 to the list of aircraft that he was qualified to pilot. From the flying point of view, this was a very busy period for Helmut Lent, during which he was broadening his flying experience and polishing his flying skills. It was also a period in which the Germans took the world another step towards war: on the 14th of March, in blatant contravention of their undertakings at Munich six months earlier, they annexed the

Czechoslovak provinces of Bohemia and Moravia, and the following day Adolf Hitler made his triumphal entry to Prague. By the end of the month Lent was flying the Bf 109 from Pardubitz[21], and could write home, 'Flying is great fun. You can really let off steam without having to worry about being reported by a gamekeeper. Our Messerschmitt makes a great impression on the Czechs. And it really is a splendid machine. Like a real racehorse, I would say.'

On 1 May 1939 II./JG 141 changed its designation to I./ZG 76, ZG being the abbreviation for '*Zerstörergeschwader*', at the same time moving to another airfield in Czechoslovakia, Olmütz[22]. Re-equipping of the *Gruppe* with the Bf 110 began, but it was not until the 7th of June that Lent made his first flight in one of the new machines, going solo after

Junkers Ju 52

one very short local flight monitored by another pilot. In the meanwhile, however, on the 12th of May, he had passed the necessary tests and obtained the ELF. During June, July and August Lent flew a broad selection of aircraft – the Bf 109; the Bf 110; the Ju (W) 34 (for blind-flying practice); the He 70 (a fast two-seater multi-purpose low-wing monoplane with glazed cockpit and retractable undercarriage); and the Ju 52 (also for blind flying practice). In the Bf 109 and the *Gruppe*'s new operational aircraft, the Bf 110, he flew patrols and practised air-to-air gunnery, and in the 110 he also flew '*FT-Flüge*', radio-homing practices.

The specific version of the 110 with which I./ZG 76 was now equipped was the Bf 110C-1, powered by two Daimler-Benz DB 601A engines and boasting formidable armament – two 20-mm MG FF cannon and four 7.9-mm MG 17 machine-guns in the nose and a single flexible, rearward-firing, MG 15 machine-gun in the rear of the glazed crew compartment. The aircraft normally carried a crew of two, pilot and radio-operator (*Funker*), who sat back-to-back in tandem, and it was the *Funker*'s task, in addition to operating the aircraft's radio equipment, to man the rear machine-gun as necessary. The machine had an economical cruising

---

[21] Pardubice, Czechoslovakia, about sixty miles to the east of Prague.
[22] Olomouc, a comparatively short distance to the south-east of Pardubice.

Heinkel He 70

speed of 217 m.p.h. at 13,500 feet and a maximum range at that speed of 680 miles, but supplementary fuel tanks could be fitted in the wings to increase the distance that it could fly. Depending on altitude, the aircraft had a maximum speed of between 295 m.p.h. at sea level and 336 m.p.h. at 20,000 feet. Flying at maximum speed, of course, would greatly reduce its range.

While converting on to the Bf 110 *Leutnant* Helmut Lent did not have a regular *Funker* in the rear seat, but on the 14th of August he was accompanied in M8+AH for a sixteen-minute air-to-air firing detail by *Gefreiter* (the equivalent of Leading Aircraftman) Walter Kubisch. Born on 7 September 1918 in Helbigsdorf in Saxony, the son of a machine fitter, Kubisch had served his apprenticeship as a blacksmith before volunteering to join the *Luftwaffe*. First, however, in common with all volunteers at that time – including Lent – he had to serve his period of compulsory labour-service. Following his call-up he was trained as a radio operator and then as an air gunner. In about July 1939 he was posted to I./ZG 76, where he was allocated as *Funker* to Helmut Lent. From the very first the two found each other compatible both personally

Messerschmitt Bf 110C

and professionally.

Following the annexation of Czechoslovakia in March, the Germans had made no secret of the fact that the next object of their territorial ambitions was Poland, mounting an unbridled campaign of virulent propaganda and threats against that country. The world looked on, unable or unwilling to intervene. War was now inevitable. On 25 August 1939 I./ZG 76 deployed to a forward airfield, Ohlau, just to the southeast of Breslau, poised to play its part in the Germans' long-planned assault on Poland. Ohlau lay about thirty miles, only eight minutes flying time, from the border with south-western Poland. The following day Helmut Lent wrote a letter to his family in Pyrehne, conforming to censorship requirements by heading it simply, 'Greater Germany'. He assured his parents that they need not worry, but at the same time he expressed strong belief in the rightness of the German cause:

> I'm writing sitting on the edge of a camp bed with a leisurely pipe in my mouth to send you a Sunday greeting so that you don't need to worry. We have left Olmütz, heading east. But all the same, things are sure to get a bit worse. After all, I didn't become a soldier so that I could stroll about in my dress suit! We have a fine task to do, and we're all looking forward enormously to carrying it out – to take back the eastern territories that were stolen from us and to revenge the Poles' atrocities.

The Second World War began when German troops and armour crossed the Polish border at 0445 hours on the morning of Friday the 1st of September 1939. Just one minute before that precise time Bf 110 M8+DH lifted off from the grass field at Ohlau with *Leutnant* Helmut Lent at the controls, one of the *Zerstörer* briefed to escort a force of He 111 bombers heading eastward for Krakow.

CHAPTER THREE

September to December 1939
The Polish Campaign and the
Battle of the German Bight

To THOSE in the German hierarchy privy to such matters, the top-secret plan to invade Poland was known as *'Fall Weiss'*, which may be translated as 'Contingency White'. There were also similar colour-coded contingency plans for other possible military scenarios: *'Fall Rot'* (Red) and *'Fall Grün'* (Green) had for instance been plans for war with Czechoslovakia, while *'Fall Blau'* (Blue) referred war with England. The invasion of Poland was to be the first practical implementation of the German strategists' theory of *Blitzkrieg*, a swift and concentrated attack on enemy strongpoints with the maximum use of air support aimed at overwhelming and incapacitating the defences while achieving optimum surprise, an attack as unexpected, as precise and as potent as the flash of lightning from which its name derived. At a strategic level, admittedly, the action against Poland could not be described as unexpected, but when the German armies moved the tactical surprise was almost complete. The Germans, with a vastly superior aerial armada comprising about 1,250 aircraft – bombers, dive-bombers, fighters and *Zerstörer* – made it their priority task to gain air superiority by destroying the Polish air force on the ground and in the air. The Poles' front-line air strength was in the region of 360 machines, most of which were obsolescent and of which only 160 were fighters. Once having achieved air superiority, the *Luftwaffe* would be able to concentrate on providing close support for the German armour and ground troops that had had thrust simultaneously into Polish territory.

Weiss envisaged simultaneous attacks on Poland from three directions, the north, the west and the south, beginning at 0445 hours on the morning of the 1st of September. 1./ZG 76, positioned on the south-western flank of Poland, was allocated to operate in support of the XIVth Army, one of the three German armies that made up Army Group South.

On the morning of the invasion Helmut Lent, with Walter Kubisch as his wireless operator and rear gunner, was flying 'his' aircraft, M8+DH, escorting a formation of Heinkel 111 bombers of I. and III./KG 4[23]

---

[23] KG = Kampfgeschwader (Bomber *Geschwader*).

attacking the airfield at Krakow. His own words, written after the campaign, describe his first taste of action:

> For several days now the *Staffel*[24] has been positioned on one of the many airfields in Silesia from which we will meet with the foe. Tonight the ultimatum the *Führer* made to Poland runs out. The old adage '*Alia iacta est*'[25] is as good as in operation.
>
> In the spirit of a Richthofen, a Boelke, an Immelmann and so on every man in the *Staffel*, from the pilots to the youngest mechanic, is ready and in his place to further the fame of German arms. Our *Staffel*, which until recently carried the '*Richthofen Geschwader*' ribbon, will do its utmost to prove itself worthy of the name.
>
> At last, on the late evening of the 31st August, the *Staffelkapitän*[26] comes back from a commanders' briefing. We officers of the *Staffel* are already lying down on our beds and listening to the latest news. The boss comes in and whispers, 'It's on for tomorrow.'
>
> Then he is gone, leaving us to our own thoughts, which on this particular night churn around in our minds. We are woken up at 0230 hours. Before take-off the *Gruppenkommandeur*[27] makes a short speech to remind us once more of our duty. It is scarcely necessary. Each one of us knows that today there begins a fateful chapter in the history of the world, and it will not be written in words on paper, but in blood.
>
> Every one of us is aware of his responsibility, aware that he has to play his part in ensuring that the German people can stand up proud in the eyes of history, that the spirit of German aviation can shine forth, that the great hopes that the *Führer* places in his *Luftwaffe* shall not be disappointed.
>
> Take-off is scheduled for 0430 hours. In brief, our job is to provide escort for our bomber formations attacking the airfield at Krakow at 0530 hours. Well ahead of time the pilots and their wireless-operators are seated in their aircraft, checking their machines yet again. Because there is still time to spare each one of us is plagued with a mass of questions. What will the coming hours bring? How will the enemy react? Will he accept our challenge? Will our long-held wish to defeat the enemy in chivalrous man-to-man duel be fulfilled? Or will there be a clash in massed squadrons?
>
> All at once the boss, in whose *Schwarm*[28] I am flying as wingman, gives us the sign to start up our engines. All our wayward thoughts disappear. We have only one aim in mind, to destroy the enemy whenever we meet him. My twin engines start up perfectly. A rapid look at my instruments, a quick question to my faithful wireless operator – 'Everything OK?' Then the engines of the boss's aircraft roar out. A few seconds later my *Rotte*[29] follows after him.
>
> The weather is not particularly good. At about 600 to 800 metres there is a sheet of stratus. Visibility is bad. At first we fly below the layer of cloud. As we

---

[24] 1./ZG 76.
[25] 'The die is cast.'
[26] *Oberleutnant* Werner Hansen.
[27] *Hauptmann* Günther Reinecke.
[28] *Schwarm* – tactically, a section. Three or four aircraft.
[29] *Rotte* – tactically, a pair of aircraft.

fly east, however, the cloud lifts. When we have crossed the border a bright sun is shining in our face. It is as if it wanted to wish us '*Hals- und Beinbruch*'[30]. We are already over enemy territory. Many pairs of eyes scan the horizon for the enemy, but there is nothing to be seen.

Far below us the formations of our bombers move on, the ones who will be the first to present our compliments in Poland. In the distance I can already see a narrow, silver ribbon – the River Weichsel. So Krakow must soon come into view. Right – there it is ahead of us in the distance. Tension grows. Surely the Poles must have been alerted by now. We search eagerly, but there is nothing to see.

By now the airfield is below us. Suddenly mushrooms of fire shoot up from the landing ground, from the hangars, from the barracks. Our bombers have unloaded their all-destroying cargo. Below us there are bright fires burning.

Gradually the Polish flak begins to fire. It is as if they have been aroused from a deep sleep. Their aim is so bad that all we can do is to laugh at it. Only slowly do they seem to wake up. The accuracy of their aim seems to improve a little, but it is still too bad to cause any of us any harm. In the meanwhile attack follows attack beneath us. Formation after formation, *Staffel* after *Staffel*, roars over the airfield and we *Zerstörer* hover above the whole arena like eagles, ready to dive on our prey if the Poles dare to harm a hair of one of our bomber pilots. But nothing happens. The attack finishes. We fly back home, a little disappointed. Where were our enemies hiding? All our dreams and expectations have come to naught. Nothing turned out as we had imagined it would. All we can answer to the excited questions of our mechanics asking how things were is, 'Not one single bastard to be seen!'

At midday the *Staffel* takes off on another operation with the brief to fly escort for the bombers again. Let's hope something will happen this time. But it doesn't look as if it will. Our bombers' target this time is the fortifications on the River Warthe near Wielun. As far as can humanly be predicted Polish fighters are not to be expected there. We take off on time and fly our escort duty. The attack goes ahead, but as expected there is no contact with the enemy. Really disappointed, we return to base. Where is the famous spirit of the Polish fighter pilots, then? Now, when they have a chance to prove their heroism, they are not there. As we often say in flier's jargon – 'Something stinks!'

It is in such a frame of mind that we wait for the 2nd of September. We are not scrambled during the morning because it's the turn of the 2nd and then the 3rd *Staffel*, who had to stay behind yesterday afternoon. Towards mid-day rumours that there is heavy fighter opposition in the area of Lódz gather strength. We hope we will have a chance to measure ourselves against these opponents. We begin to suspect that the enemy has withdrawn his flying units to the rear, as he has done with his ground troops. Will we be in time to have a go at him?

Then the boss comes back from a conference. 'Lads, we're taking off in an hour. Freelance sweep over Lódz.' We jump into the air with joy. For us, who were formerly interceptor pilots, freelancing is as if someone has taken the

---

[30] *Hals- und Beinbruch* - a flier's good-luck wish. Literally, 'Break your neck, break a leg!'

PZL 24

harness from a two-year-old and he can run around just as he wishes.

Until now our escort duty had always tied us firmly to the bombers. Now, however, we can go out and look for the enemy, attack him where we find him. Now our fighter pilot's dream can come true. We can hardly believe it.

The *Staffel* takes off in the direction of Lódz at 1630 hours. We climb up to height so that we can attack the enemy from above. The sun is behind us – excellent tactical conditions. At 4,000 metres we are flying in beautiful weather, with fabulous visibility to the east. We can see the town of Lódz in the distance. A few hundred metres below a *Staffel* of German fighters sweeps past on the opposite heading. We waggle our wings to them, but they have already disappeared.

Lódz lies at our feet. Tense, we search the horizon. There – what is that? I don't have time to think this question through, but instinctively I put my aircraft into a steep dive. Three hundred metres below us, almost on a reciprocal heading – a PZL 24. Unfortunately the Pole recognises my attack much too quickly and dives away into the depths. Shit! It's a pity he got away. But I don't need to fret for long. Slightly above me there is a small black blob coming towards me from ahead, and it reveals itself as a PZL. Apparently he thinks I am a bomber because I have two engines and it is well known that our bombers are twin-engined. He opens fire when he is still at long range. The four ribbons of his machine-gun fire, made visible by phosphorous smoke, pass about five metres over my head. Calmly I let him approach to 400 metres. Then in my turn I press on the firing button. I can tell from the erratic way he steers that my burst of fire has worried him. But both of us remain steadfast and head stubbornly for each other. At the last moment I pull my machine up to starboard. He dives down to port. All that my *Funker* sees is a smoke-trail and then he has disappeared in the depths. What a pity he didn't catch fire. I don't have any time to think things over. At a range of one thousand metres ahead of us a Pole is trying to sneak up to height to one side of the confusion of battle, hoping to pick out one of my comrades from above and out of the sun.

But just you wait, young man! Hidden by his wing I pull up on him from astern and below. I am almost sweating with fear that he might get away from me again. But no, he doesn't see me. I open fire at 100 metres. There – he's on fire! He hurtles to the earth in a number of separate, burning pieces. From sheer joy both my *Funker* and I throw our hands up in the air. That is the only way in which we can announce our victory at the moment. We can't jump up in the air, because we're strapped in. In his machine my old wingman, *Feldwebel* Jänicke, who has stayed with me throughout, beams all over his face and waves to me. When all is said and done, it was to some extent his success as well, because by sticking close behind me so splendidly whatever my position he has guarded my tail the whole time.

Because we had drifted out of the operational area of the *Staffel* during the dogfight we turn back to look for our comrades. But we haven't time to do so. Just as we had done before we see another Pole sliding towards us.

In the same way as previously I attempt to creep up on him from astern. But this fellow is more careful than his comrade, the one who has just been shot down. He realises what I am trying to do and attempts to escape in a dive. This time, in my eagerness for combat, I follow him. At high speed we roar down – my wingman is still there – almost to the ground. The fellow hopes he can escape at low altitude. But we are on his heels. In his great danger he throttles back suddenly and begins to wallow and to swing from side to side. With my faster machine, I fear, I can't do the same.

Unfortunately I have to pass him, and I head away. I can't worry about him any longer, because in my present position flak from below and fighters approaching from above spell danger to me. Once I am out of the combat area I climb up again with my *Rotte*. In doing so I find my *Staffel* and join up with them to return to base. After we have landed I can report proudly to my *Staffelkapitän*, 'Second *Rotte* landed OK. Crews and aircraft undamaged. One

A copy of the certificate from the *Reich* Ministry of Aviation and Commander in Chief of the *Luftwaffe* confirming Lent's first kill, which took place in Poland on 2 September 1939. The Polish aircraft in question was a PZL 24. It was also the first kill made by Lent's *Staffel*.

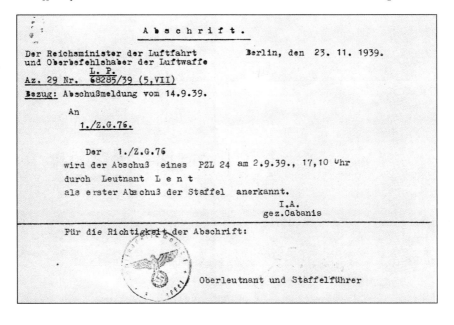

PZL destroyed – one PZL destroyed'. I think that was the proudest report I ever made.

Lent also told of his first victory in the air in a letter home on the 3rd September, the day on which Britain and France declared war on Germany,:

> 'Now the war has begun. On Friday morning we were over Krakow by twenty-five past five protecting our bombers. The Poles shot at us with their flak, but they didn't hit us. It wasn't until yesterday that we were in combat over Lódz, our baptism of fire. I shot down a single-seater Polish fighter. My first victory. God in His mercy protected me. It was a hard fight. They were very manoeuvrable. But we have the advantage in fire-power and speed.'

He was partly correct: the PZL 24, a single-seat high-wing monoplane, was more manoeuvrable than the Bf 110, but the 110 was faster. In terms of firepower, however, the 110's advantage was not overwhelming. Both machines had two forward-firing 20 mm. cannon, but the Messerschmitt also had four machine-guns in its nose as against the two carried by the PZL 24. Lent's kill, made at 1750 hours on the 2nd September, was the first one ever achieved by his *Gruppe*, I./ZG 76.

Lent made one further operational flight on the 3rd of the month, and another one on the 4th, taking off from Ohlau for his second mission and landing at Breslau. By now the Polish air force had been so badly mauled that the Bf 110s could switch from the task of escorting bombers to that of ground-attack. On the 5th September M8+DH, with Lent at the controls and Kubisch in the rear cockpit, took off from Breslau, and at 0530 hours they destroyed a twin-engined low-wing monoplane on the   PZL 37 *'Elk'*

Poland, 14 September 1939. The *Führer* visits front-line *Luftwaffe* units, including that of Helmut Lent. Here he is seen shaking hands with Lent, who has a patch above his left eye covering a slight injury he incurred in a forced landing following an encounter with a Polish aircraft. The fourth officer from the right is Gordon Gollob, destined to become one of the leading fighter pilots of the *Luftwaffe*.

ground, possibly a PZL 'Wilk'[31], and landed an hour later. Airborne again at 0934 hours, Lent disposed of another Polish aircraft on the ground at 1035, this time an unidentified biplane with a radial engine. The *Staffel* was plying its tactical trade from a number of airfields in the Breslau area at this period – Breslau, Ohlau, Gleiwitz, Gross-Stein, Tschenstochau – and Lent landed back at Gross-Stein, flying a third operational flight later that day. There were more sorties on the 6th and the 7th of the month and then, on the 9th, came the destruction of his third aircraft on the ground, a PZL 24, the eighth by the *Staffel* overall. In a letter home he spoke of these achievements - and of an unexpected encounter on the 12th September with another Polish aircraft:

> Since I last wrote to you I have set fire to another three Polish machines on the ground. As I was having a go at a fourth a Pole took me by surprise and attacked me, shooting my starboard engine out. I had to make a forced landing behind our lines[32]. On Sunday the *Führer* was with us, and he congratulated me on my successful emergency landing. (There was a picture of me in the newspaper as well). Göring visited us on Wednesday and spoke of our *Gruppe*'s great successes. Greetings from your son, who enjoys merciful protection.

On the 17th of September the Soviet Army, attacking from the east, crossed the border into Poland, virtually unopposed. By the end of the

---

[31] Probably a PZL 37 *'Elk'*, a twin-engine, low-wing monoplane.
[32] Lent force-landed near the small village of Pogorzela.

Hauptmann Reinecke, *Kommandeur* of I./ZG 76, decorates officers of his *Gruppe* with the Iron Cross Second Class during the Polish campaign. Left to right: *Oberleutnant* Böhmel; *Leutnant* Kettling; *Leutnant* Ewers; *Leutnant* Graef.

month the Poles had surrendered and the Germans and the Russians occupied their country. Following his forced landing Lent had flown just five more sorties during the Polish campaign. Describing one, he wrote home proudly on the 24th, 'I picked out a flak battery that was having a bit of a go at us and silenced it. On Friday I was awarded the EKII (Iron Cross Second Class). I had the good fortune to be one of the first ten to get it.' The Iron Cross, first established in 1813, was awarded in wartime for bravery in action, and could not be won in peacetime. Re-introduced by Adolf Hitler on the 1st September 1939, the first day of World War Two, it was awarded progressively in three grades, Second Class, First Class and Knight's Cross. As the war went on, higher classes of the order were created. Helmut Lent was justifiably proud of being one of the first ten men of the *Wehrmacht* to wear an Iron Cross and, although he was destined eventually to progress to a much higher class of the order, he would often say that the decoration of which he was most proud was the EKII.

On 29 September I./ZG76, its part in the seizure of Poland completed, moved westward to the Stuttgart area to take part in the defence of the *Reich* against the threat presented by France and Britain, who had been at war with Germany since the 3rd of the month.

From early October to the middle of December I./ZG 76 operated from a series of airfields in the Stuttgart and Ruhr areas, set back some distance from the border with France. This was the beginning of the seven-month lull, characterised by a lack of major offensive initiative by either side, that came to be known as the 'phoney war', a period of watching and waiting, of planning and of consolidation, of the building up and reinforcing of opposing armed forces for the inevitable clash that lay ahead. Shifting from airfield to airfield the *Zerstörer* flew armed defensive patrols in the border area by daylight without coming into contact with the enemy, and in between their operational flights they flew training exercises in preparation for more serious tasks to come.

Of the two main enemies that the Germans faced, the British and the French, the British posed the greater threat. Bomber Command – the French did not have an equivalent strategic force – formed in 1936, went to war with a number of contingency plans, the so-called 'Western Air Plans', broadly based on the assumption that Germany would make her first aggressive moves, on the ground or in the air, against the United Kingdom and/or France and Belgium. In response to any such move, and dependent upon its nature, the Air Plans foresaw that the RAF bombers would respond by hitting at targets such as German airfields and supply depots, communications and lines of supply to the battlefields, and German war industry, particularly oil production facilities. There was no contingency for the possibility that Germany's first move would be against Poland.

On 1 September, immediately after the start of the German attack, the President of the United States of America, Franklin D. Roosevelt, appealed to the governments of all belligerent countries not to mount bombing attacks on undefended cities or other targets that might result in civilian casualties, and an Anglo-French statement approving his initiative was made on the following day. A German statement also welcoming the appeal was issued on the 18th of the month, but nevertheless the *Luftwaffe* mounted a series of devastating bombing attacks on Warsaw, maintaining that the Polish capital was a defended city and hence a legitimate military target within the context of the ground war between the two countries.

Vickers-Armstrong
Wellington 1A

Partly in response to Roosevelt's appeal, but doubtless also for other expedient reasons – there was great uncertainty about the likely

December 1939, Jever.
A Bf110C of I./ZG 76.

effectiveness and possible consequences of initiating unrestricted bombing – Bomber Command received orders to the effect that no targets on German soil were to be attacked. The ban extended, even, to the bombing of German naval vessels if they were moored alongside dockside wharfs. For the first months of the war, therefore, the operational activities of the bombers of the RAF - apart from the single-engined Fairey Battles of No. 1 Group operating in France as part of the Advanced Air Striking Force – were restricted to the dropping of propaganda leaflets over Germany by night and to looking for, and occasionally finding and attacking, German naval vessels at sea by day.

The RAF anti-shipping operations focused on the German Bight (*Deutsche Bucht*)[33] sea area to the north of the great naval base of Wilhelmshaven and bounded to the east by the coast of Schleswig Holstein. A number of low-strength reconnaissance flights carried out by the RAF between September and early December were virtually unopposed, but a comparatively heavy attack on the 4th of September against capital ships in Wilhelmshaven harbour and Brunsbüttel at the mouth of the Elbe resulted in heavy RAF casualties, seven of the thirty aircraft sent out failing to return. From another major attack by Hampdens, Wellingtons and Whitleys on ships north of Wilhelmshaven on the 14th of December, five of the 12 Wellingtons despatched were lost. At first German claims that they had been shot down by fighters were not believed by the High Command of the RAF, who were at this stage confident that heavy bombers flying by day in a defensive formation could hold their own against fighter attack.

A further heavy attack against shipping off Wilhelmshaven was mounted four days later, on the 18th of December. This time the force was an all-Wellington one, made up of 24 of the twin-engined machines

---

[33] Also known as the Heligoland Bight (*Helgolander Bucht*).

Oberstleutnant Carl Schuhmacher, *Kommodore* JG1, Jever, December 1939.

from Nos. 9, 37 and 149 Squadrons. The bombers formed up over Norfolk into four 'self-defending' formations and headed east. Two aircraft aborted the mission due to mechanical defects, but the remaining 22 continued on their way, heading for the island of Heligoland, 45 miles to the north of Wilhelmshaven, where they turned south towards their search area. Unknown to the RAF the *Luftwaffe*, possibly in response to the repeated British activity in the German Bight, had installed experimental *Freya* radars on the East Friesian islands. One of them, on

Oberstleutnant Carl Schuhmacher in his Bf 109E3, December 1939.

the island of Borkum, picked up the approaching bombers and alerted the fighter units in the area, including 1./ZG 76, which had redeployed two days previously from Dortmund to Jever[34], just to the west of Wilhelmshaven, in anticipation of further RAF raids. Here they had joined the so-called '*Jagdgeschwader* Schumacher', an *ad hoc* miscellany of fighter units flying Bf 109s and Bf 110s from Jever and Wangerooge and commanded by *Oberstleutnant* Carl Schumacher, which had been formed to provide flexible and rapid-reaction defence in the area of the German Bight. Schuhmacher, officially *Kommodore* JG 1, exercised the function of *Jagdführer*[35] *Deutsche Bucht* ('Fighter Leader German Bight).

Aircrew of I./ZG 76 in 1939, prior to the move to Jever to join *Kommando Schuhmacher*. Helmut Lent is on the extreme right.

---

[34] The airfield was in a part of the town of Jever called 'Upjever' and was originally known by that name. With the passage if time the name 'Jever' became more usual.

[35] '*Jagdführer*', a title used quite frequently, was very often abbreviated '*Jafü*'.

Wolfgang Falck, *Staffelkapitän* of 2./ZG 76, at Jever in December 1939.

In the early afternoon of the 18th Helmut Lent flew an armed patrol, landing back at Jever at 1415. local time. Fifteen minutes later, refuelled, M8-DH was airborne again in time to join in later stages of the battle raging to the north. Bf 109s from II./JG 77 and 10./JG 26 and the Bf 110s of 1./ZG 76 took a heavy toll of the attackers. The first interception had taken place just to the east of Heligoland at about 1410 hours, but

Hauptmann Wolfgang Falck with the pilots of his *Staffel* at Jever. The aircraft is Bf 110 G9+GA, Falck's personal machine.

the Wellington formations, despite repeated attacks, had maintained their course for the target area, where they had photographed enemy shipping in the port of Wilhelmshaven. In keeping with the crews' orders, no bombs were dropped. The aerial battle resumed when the heavy bombers turned off and headed for home: over Wilhelmshaven the fighters had stood off to allow the intense German *Flak* an unrestricted field of fire. Of the 22 Wellingtons in the attack ten were shot down in flames and two, badly damaged, ditched in the North Sea on their way back home. Three others crash-landed in England.

The *Staffelkapitän* of 2./ZG 76, the *Marienkäfer-Staffel* ('Ladybird *Staffel*) was *Hauptmann* Wolfgang Falck, later to play an important part in Helmut Lent's *Luftwaffe* career. He too flew in the Battle of the German Bight, as it came to be known, having arrived at Jever the previous day. In the very early afternoon of the 18th he took off on what was intended to be a flight to acclimatise him to operational flying over the sea, something that he had not previously experienced. He takes up the story:

> I was in the vicinity of Juist when I had an R/T message from the Ops. Room at Jever to the effect that a force of British bombers was attacking Wilhelmshaven and that I should attempt to engage it, even if it was already on its way home. I set course for Heligoland to intercept the Englishmen's track. We soon saw flak bursts in the sky, and then we saw the outward-bound bombers, which were under attack by Me 109s. We could also see burning bombers going down. As we got near I saw that they were Wellingtons. The formation was scattered, and the aircraft were heading to the northwest, flying homeward singly and in small groups. When we caught up with the bombers I gave the order to attack. I myself approached a Wellington from slightly above and obliquely astern, coming under fire from the rear turret as I did so. His starboard engine began to burn immediately, and the aircraft went downwards in a flat glide. As we were almost out of fuel I didn't wait to see it crash in the sea, but I looked round for another target. Again I attacked from astern, but this time I went in nearer and fired with all my guns. The first attack had no visible effect, so I made a second one, going in even closer. Now the Wellington started to burn, and it went straight down into the sea. But during my second attack the rear gunner had done his job excellently. My starboard engine stopped and from in front of me, where the ammunition boxes for the four machine-guns were located, thick smoke was coming into the cabin. What was left of my ammunition was apparently on fire. I had scarcely got over the shock when the port engine, in its turn, stopped. It was the first time I had ever flown a glider!
>
> My first reaction was to bale out, but we were to the west of Heligoland and the North Sea beneath us was covered in ice-floes. In the meanwhile, however, the fire had apparently gone out, although petrol was pouring out from holes in the wing tanks. I decided to get as close to the coast as possible, and of course I sent out a distress message in the hope that if we had to ditch they would fish us out of the cold sea as soon as possible. My *Funker* and I had a whole *Geschwader* of guardian angels on our side that day! Thanks to the fact that we were almost at the end of our endurance, the remaining petrol was leaking out and the majority of our ammunition had been expended, that the

wind was from a favourable quarter and we still had height to spare, we were able to reach the airfield on the island of Wangerooge.

Helmut Lent himself claimed three Wellingtons destroyed in the action, of which two, achieved at 1440 and 1445 hours respectively, were subsequently confirmed. He wrote home to his parents that same day:

> Today was eventful. I hope that I did my duty for my Fatherland. I shot three English bombers down; God's help was with me. It happened like this. I had just got back with my *Staffel* from an operational patrol without anything untoward happening, and I was having my aircraft refuelled. Then a number of English bombers – between 40 and 50, it is estimated – appeared in the region of Wilhelmshaven. No sooner had I tanked up that I turned round and took off directly from the refuelling point. I was lucky enough to catch up with them and shoot down three one after the other.
>
> Today, with God's help, I achieved my greatest success. To Him be honour and gratitude that He grants his favour to us poor sinners. I would dearly have loved to drop my rubber dinghy for the Englishmen, but some of them were burned to death and the majority of them drowned. War is nonsensical: first you shoot them down, and then you want to help them.

Later, in February, he wrote another letter home:

> I've just received photographs of the aircraft I shot down on Borkum from a naval NCO, who took some of them only half an hour after the crash. I am very pleased with one of the photos that shows that the British fliers were put into the ground with full military honours. On the ribbon on the wreath it said, 'To a brave enemy.'

Lent photographed immediately after the Battle of the German Bight. Four kills are marked on the fin of his BF110, representing one in Poland and three over the German Bight. One of the latter three claims, however, was not confirmed.

The two aircraft that Lent shot down and were later confirmed were
both from No. 37 Squadron, stationed at Feltwell in Norfolk. Captained
by Flying Officer P. A. Wimberley and Flying Officer O. J. T. Lewis
respectively, both these machines came down in the shallow sea off
Borkum. Only two crew members survived, and one of those succumbed
to his injuries soon afterwards. It is likely that the third bomber that Lent
claimed, but which was not confirmed, was also from No. 37 Squadron,
Wellington 1A N2396, LF-J, captained by Sergeant H. Ruse, which crash-
landed on the sand dunes of Borkum. Three of the five-man crew
survived to become prisoners of war, the other two having been killed in
the air during the fighter attacks.

*Hauptmann
Günther Reinecke.
Kommandeur* I./ZG 76.

Following this action the *Kommandeur* of I./ZG 76, *Hauptmann* Günther Reinecke, wrote an operational report, commenting as follows: 'The Bf 110 is capable of catching and destroying this English type quite easily, even at low speeds, when attacks can be carried out in quick succession from both sides as well as from the front quarters. Such frontal quarter attacks can be particularly effective when the enemy machine flies into the cone of fire. The Wellington burns easily and is very prone to catching fire.' Reinecke was right about the inflammability of the Vickers Wellington: as a result of a well-nigh incredible oversight by the aircraft's designers its fuel tanks were not self-sealing.

This operation by Bomber Command, and the earlier one on the 14th of December, were of great significance in the history of the development of the RAF bomber offensive, in that they gave the emphatic lie to the belief that heavy bombers, by flying in formation and bringing their combined defensive fire to bear on attacking fighters, could operate by daylight over enemy territory without incurring prohibitive losses. As a direct consequence of the inescapable realisation that such was not the case, Bomber Command, when the time came to attack targets in

Wreckage of Wellington bombers shot down in the Battle of the German Bight, 18 December 1939.

Germany, went over to a policy of night bombing, only very rarely penetrating German air space by daylight, and then only against specially selected targets.

For Helmut Lent, too, the Battle of the German Bight was a very significant event, because, as will be described, the RAF decision to operate in the hours of darkness gave rise in its turn to the Germans introducing and building up a night fighter force, the *Nachtjagd*, in which Lent achieved eminence unequalled in his lifetime.

In another way – lesser or greater, whichever way one chooses to consider it – the battle had an effect on Lent's life. In the letter quoted above, in which he spoke of the photographs sent to him, Lent also wrote: 'In recent weeks I have had quite a lot of letters to answer from girls who have made me the object of their desires. Sometimes I have laughed, but sometimes the women are quite mad. In any event, you would enjoy reading them.'

One of the girls who wrote to Helmut Lent signed herself 'Elisabeth Petersen'.

Successful Bf 109 and Bf 110 crews after the Battle of the German Bight. Helmut Lent is the third from the left of the photo. Other pilots who achieved great distinction during the war were Gordon Gollob (first left) and Johannes Steinhoff (two to Lent's left).

CHAPTER FOUR

January to August 1940
The Norwegian Campaign and
a short visit to England

AFTER the excitement of their decisive confrontation with Bomber Command's Wellingtons over the North Sea in December 1939, 1./ZG 76, together with the other *Luftwaffe* units defending Germany, settled down to a further period of routine flying with very little operational excitement. Lent's logbook shows that during this period, still flying from Jever, he made about forty flights, roughly half of them uneventful operational patrols and the remainder routine flying and training exercises. Bomber Command continued its anti-shipping patrols in the North Sea, but in general the crews were under orders not to approach the enemy coast unless there was cloud cover. From January 1940 the majority of shipping searches and reconnaissance flights were made by Blenheim light bombers, while by night the heavies went to Germany to drop vast quantities of propaganda leaflets. By April the number that had been dropped would exceed seventy million, but Bomber Command's navigational equipment and capabilities were such that there was no means of knowing whether even these innocuous cargoes had fallen in the target area, let alone what effect, if any, they were having on the German populace. The first Bomber Command raid on a German land target took place during the night of 19/20 March 1940, when fifty aircraft, Whitleys and Hampdens, were sent to attack the German seaplane base at Hörnum on the island of Sylt. Only one aircraft, a Whitley, was lost. The Hörnum raid was, it was said, in reprisal for a *Luftwaffe* bombing attack two nights previously on the British naval base at Scapa Flow, in the course of which one civilian, James Isbister by name, had been killed and a number injured. Forty-one of the RAF crews returning from Hörnum reported that they had bombed accurately, but it subsequently transpired that these claims were, to put it mildly, over-optimistic: virtually no damage had been caused to German installations. The reports of the crews, however, were very well received by the RAF senior commanders, strengthening as they did their firmly held, but unsoundly based, belief that night-time bombing could be carried out with accuracy and was therefore a viable alternative to bombing by day.

Die Ruhr-Arbeiter

Amtliches Blatt der Royal Air Force, England

| Luftpostausgabe | Herausgeber: R.A.F. Verlagsort: London. | Jahrgang 1 |

Man erzählt Euch, daß Ihr für deutschen Sozialismus und gegen die Plutokratien kämpft

Warum?

Warum
stehen die Arbeiterparteien und freien Gewerkschaften aller Länder geschlossen gegen das Hitlersystem?

Warum
wurden alle Eure Arbeiterorganisationen aufgelöst?

Warum
sind, mit Ausnahme von einem, alle Nazi „Treuhänder der Arbeit" ehemalige Angestellte der Unternehmerverbände?

Warum
können sich alle Naziführer Schlösser, Landhäuser und Paläste leisten?

Warum
stehen seit Kriegsausbruch alle Bergarbeiter an Rhein und Ruhr unter Kriegsrecht?

Zahlen sprechen!

Nach offiziellen Angaben in der „Frankfurter Zeitung" vom 28. Januar 1939 stieg die Zahl der deutschen Lohn- und Gehaltsempfänger seit 1932 um 9,5 %.

Aber das Gesamteinkommen aller Beschäftigten in Industrie, Handel, Gewerbe und Verkehr sank in derselben Zeit um fast 11 %, während die Lebenshaltungskosten um mindestens 10 % stiegen.

———

Für Hitlers Kriegsvorbereitungen zahlten die deutschen Werktätigen mit erhöhter Ausbeutung und sinkenden Löhnen!

Für Hitlers Krieg soll das deutsche Volk mit seinem Blut zahlen!

Warum reden alle Naziführer erst seit Ausbruch ihres Annektionskrieges so viel vom deutschen Sozialismus?

327

Typical of the primitive propaganda leaflets that the RAF were dropping in their millions over industrial areas in Germany in the early part of the war, this example, headed 'The Ruhr Worker', carries the headline, 'They tell you that you are fighting against the plutocrats and for German Socialism.' It then poses a number of leading questions headed, 'Why?' and provides answers under the heading, 'Figures speak for themselves.' Not surprisingly these leaflets failed completely to have any positive impact on the German population.

While Helmut Lent's professional life at this period might perhaps be described as rather uneventful, the same could not, it seems, be said about his personal life. After his success over the North Sea in December he had become a minor national hero: a successful fighter pilot, Aryan-blond, film-star handsome in his *Luftwaffe* uniform, he had been the subject of considerable coverage, written and photographic, generated by the Ministry of Propaganda and published in the media. Among other things a glossy postcard of him was published. As he had said in his December letter home, this publicity attracted a great deal of fan mail, mainly from young – and not-so-young – girls, among them Elisabeth Petersen. Helmut replied to Elisabeth's letter, and the contact developed.

Leutnant Lent, probably in the winter of 1939/1940. He was promoted to the rank of *Oberleutnant* on 1 July 1940.

Surviving details are scant, and it is not known whether Lent also replied to letters from other girls. What is known, however, is that he and Elisabeth agreed to meet 'blind' for dinner at the select *Reichshof* hotel in Hamburg, where Elisabeth lived and which was not a great distance from Jever. Elisabeth, by nature dark-haired, dyed her hair blond to present as positive an Aryan image as she could. The couple were attracted to each other, and they had mutual interests, one of which was skiing. In February 1940 they went together to Hirschegg for a skiing holiday.

The colour of her hair was not the only thing about herself that Elisabeth had changed so that she would make a favourable impression on Helmut Lent – or, more correctly, in order not make an unfavourable impression. She had also given herself a false name. She came from a very prosperous family in Hamburg, but was reluctant to take her new boyfriend home and introduce him to her parents, because to do that

would mean that she would have to admit to her act of deception. At what point in their courtship she revealed her secret to Helmut is not recorded, but as things turned out it clearly did not have the adverse effect on their relationship that she had feared.

'Elisabeth Petersen' was in fact Helene (Lena) Senokosnikova, and she was of Russian birth. She had been afraid that Lent would not reply to her first letter if she had used her real name – Russians were not popular in the Third Reich – and once having met him she then feared that if she were to do so he would want nothing more to do with her. Lena was born in Moscow in April 1914, which made her four years older than Helmut. She was the daughter of a very prosperous merchant, Trifon Senokosnikov, who had had to flee his country in 1918 after the Communist Revolution, moving first to London and then to Germany: his wife and two daughters were able to escape from the Soviet Union and join their father in the West about three years later, by which time he had set up a trading company in Hamburg, the *Britisch-Kontinental Handelsgesellschaft*[36], with offices there and in London. When she met Helmut, Lena was employed in her father's firm.

During the first months of the year 1940 the attention of both sides in the war, German and British, turned to the strategically important Scandinavian area. For the Germans, occupation of Norway and Denmark would not only protect their northern flank during and after the invasion of the Low Countries and France, which they were already planning, but it was also necessary to safeguard the passage of iron ore from neutral Sweden via the port of Narvik in the far north of Norway,

Lent relaxes at Hirschegg in the Tyrol, where he spent a period of leave in February 1940. Lena Senokosnikova, alias Elisabeth Petersen, accompanied him.

---

[36] The British-Continental Trading Company.

ore that was indispensable to the Germans' production of arms and for which they had an annual requirement of over sixty million tons. Of parallel importance was their wish to seize and to develop naval bases from which their submarines and surface vessels could dominate the North Sea and extend their activities into the North Atlantic. For the Allies, occupation of Norway would provide them with bases from which to disrupt German coastal shipping, including the transport of the Swedish iron ore, while affording them a strategic naval advantage in the northern waters. In addition it would have provided an avenue for the transport of military aid to Finland, engaged in a bitter struggle with Hitler's then allies, Russia. Both sides planned to occupy Norway, but Germany also aimed to move into Denmark. While the Allied action, 'Plan R-4', was to be limited in the first place to the occupation of the coastal areas around Narvik, Trondheim, Bergen and Stavanger, the Germans envisaged a much more comprehensive invasion. British and French troops were already aboard transport ships in the Clyde and the Firth of Forth, awaiting their passage to Scandinavia, and units of the Home Fleet were heading for Norwegian waters, when the Germans made their move. On the 8th of April eight aircraft of 1./ZG 76 led by their *Staffelkapitän*, *Oberleutnant* Werner Hansen, deployed northward from Jever to Westerland on the island of Sylt.

Weserübung, as the German operation was code-named, was scheduled to begin in the early hours of the 9th of April 1940. It was to be the first offensive action by the Germans involving all three components of the

Leutnant Helmut Lent in the cockpit of a Messerschmitt Bf 110 *Zerstörer* of I./ZG 76, early 1940.

The rear fuselage
of Lent's Bf 110,
M8+DH, on the
gun-
synchronisation
stand at Jever,
April 1940.

Wehrmacht - Marine, Luftwaffe and *Heer*[37] – in unison. An hour before dawn
on the chosen morning the Germans presented both countries with an
ultimatum stating that their troops would not come as enemies but
exclusively to protect the Danes and Norwegians against occupation by
Anglo-French military forces. The Danes accepted the ultimatum, and the
occupation of their country was bloodless. Norway, however, rejected the
German demands. Unlike Denmark, Norway had no land border with
Germany. She did however have a west-facing coastline well over a
thousand miles long, a coastline of mountains, islands, precipitous cliffs and
fjords, sparsely populated and hence vulnerable to assault from the sea.

The German plan for the attack on Norway envisaged simultaneous
amphibious attacks on the Norwegian capital, Oslo, and six other major
ports from Kristiansand in the south to Narvik in the north. Strategic
airfields were to be captured by parachute troops so that transport
aircraft could land at once and disembark ground troops and
equipment. Oslo, the primary target, was to be taken by troops landed
from a convoy of ships led by the pocket battleship *Lützow*[38] and the
cruiser *Blücher*, while simultaneously Junkers 52 transport aircraft would

---

[37] The Navy, the Air Force and the Army. The *Wehrmacht* comprised all three arms and can
perhaps best be translated as 'The German Armed Forces'.
[38] The pocket battleship *Lützow* had originally been named *Deutschland*, but Hitler had
insisted that her name be changed because of the loss of face which, he believed, would be
caused if a vessel bearing the name 'Germany' were to be lost.

Lent's *Zerstörer* on the synchronisation stand at Jever, April 1940.

drop parachute troops, the vaunted *Fallschirmjäger*, to secure the airfield of Oslo/Fornebu. Timing was tight: the wave of Ju 52s carrying troops and equipment was scheduled to arrive at Fornebu just twenty minutes after the parachute drop, by which time the airfield had to be in German hands. 1./ZG 76 was detailed to provide cover and ground-attack support for both waves, the one dropping the parachute troops and the one ferrying in the infantry and support troops and equipment. 2./ZG 76 and 3./ZG 76 would play a similar role at Aalborg in Denmark and at Stavanger/Sola respectively. Hansen's pilots, especially, had to be prepared to meet fighter opposition, because Norway's sole force of fighter aircraft, comprising ten Gloster Gladiators, was stationed at Fornebu for the protection of the capital city.

Led by Hansen, the eight *Zerstörer* of 1./ZG 76 took off at seven o'clock in the morning, aiming to synchronise their arrival at Fornebu to coincide with the first parachute drops at 0845 hours. Lent was flying M8+DH, and as usual his *Funker* was *Gefreiter* Walter Kubisch. The distance from Westerland to Fornebu meant that this would have to be a one-way operation; the Bf 110s would have to land at Fornebu when the airfield had been seized. The timing was critical: it was calculated that the *Zerstörer* would have only twenty minutes' fuel left when they arrived overhead at Fornebu.

Both the main attack on the city of Oslo itself and the secondary one on the airfield of Fornebu went agley. In the narrows of Oslo Fjord *Blücher* was hit at 0723 hours by shells and torpedoes fired from the shore and sank with the loss of 1,600 men. *Lützow*, too, was damaged, and the German fleet was forced to withdraw. The *Luftwaffe* also met with a further setback. Low cloud, drizzle and fog compelled the first wave of twenty-nine Ju 52s, those carrying parachute troops, to turn round and head for the Danish airfield at Aalborg, which, it was hoped, was already in German hands. Flying north some distance behind, the

eight *Zerstörer* of 1./ZG 76 also met the bad weather, but they continued towards Fornebu. Following them was the second wave of fifty-three Ju 52s, the troop carriers. Orders were broadcast from Command Headquarters for the attack to be abandoned, but *Hauptmann* Wagner, the commander of the troop-carrying aircraft, decided not to obey the recall order, claiming later that he thought that the radio message was probably an enemy attempt at deception. The Messerschmitts of 1./ZG 76, one of which of which, of course, was piloted by Helmut Lent, were already beyond their point of no return and so were compelled to press on, hoping against hope that somehow or other Fornebu would be in German hands and they would be able to land there. But even if Fornebu were still in the hands of the Norwegians, they reasoned, a forced descent on dry land would be preferable to one in the sea. The situation was confused. Helmut Lent himself later described that eventful day:

Lent at the controls of his *Zerstörer*. Walter Kubisch, his *Funker*, can just be made out in the rear cockpit.

> It isn't my job to write a *Staffel* history of our campaign in Norway, but I should like to put together a few significant experiences that will serve as a modest memorial to the deeds of German *Zerstörer* of this young arm of the German Air Force. I hope they will also be a proud memory for our own *Staffel* and for those who come after us.
>
> After a time of quiet in the months of January to March in the *Geschwader* Schuhmacher it was about time for something to happen again. On 7 April 1940 our *Staffel* had the task of escorting a formation of naval ships heading out to the north. The sight of this fleet, which included among others the two biggest German battleships, an imposing appearance manifesting the combined might of a nation, will forever remain with me. I can still see to this day our proud young *Marine* heading north in the morning sun of a splendid April day. Everyone was asking me, 'What does the German Fleet want in the

A Gloster Gladiator of the Norwegian Air Force piloted by Sergeant Per Schye and shot down by Helmut Lent on 9 April 1940.

North?' One could speculate, by one couldn't come up with any answers. It was to be the most daring operation ever in German history.

We moved to the north on 8 April. At a pilots' briefing we were told the reason for the move and why the German Fleet had sailed out on the 7th. Our *Staffel's* job in the overall war plan was to protect our paratroops landing on Oslo/Fornebu against attacks from the air and then to land there ourselves.

There is 'clag' up to an altitude of 3,000 metres in the Skagerrak. We climb up above it. After flying an hour and a half at economical revs we are at the entrance to Oslo Fjord. The blanket of cloud opens up. For the first time we see the land of Norway beneath us – as wonderful sight! We race on to Oslo at high speed. Suddenly I notice that the *Staffel* is becoming become restless and is veering to starboard, into the sun. At the same moment I see a Gloster to the left of me sitting on a comrade's tail. I pull to port automatically and fire in front of the Norwegian's nose to frighten him away. He gets the message and peels off.

But by now I'm involved in a vast dogfight. I fire and I am fired at, get on a Gloster's tail, find a Gloster on my own tail, I dive, pull up, turn. My attack fails. We *Zerstörer* are faster, but the Glosters are more manoeuvrable. So let's get out of it. We do so. But suddenly the enemy have disappeared as well. The *Staffel* regroups. I join it, and I find my old *Rottenkamerad*[39] *Feldwebel* Jänicke again. At the same time I see two Glosters coming down out of the clouds.

My *Rotte* attacks them immediately, and after a lot of twisting and turning one of the two has been accounted for[40]. Unfortunately the other one disappears somewhere in the rocky hills. We don't see him again. Perhaps after all he was

---

[39] *Rottenkamerad* – wingman.
[40] Lent is being modest. It was he who shot down the Norwegian Gladiator, which was flown by Sergeant Per Schye of the Norwegian Army Air Service. Per Schye was wounded in one arm but survived the ensuing crash.

damaged in the attack – we will never know.

But now we have to do our real job. We look for the transport aircraft carrying our paratroops. But there is nothing to see apart from a Ju 52 attempting to land at Fornebu, but it is coming under heavy fire. But that might be a good thing. We only have fuel for about another fifteen minutes. We can't go back. Under the leadership of the *Staffelkapitän* some of our friends have begun to put the defences on the ground out of action. So with my *Rotte* I too attack – machine-gun nests, flak positions, aircraft on the ground come under successful fire. But suddenly a machine-gun nest I haven't seen brings me under fire too. I dive down once more into the turmoil, holding on resolutely.

As I am pulling out my *Funker* suddenly cries out: 'Starboard engine on fire!' I shout back, 'Calm down, Kubisch! We'll land!'

I switch off the smoking engine. In a split second I have thought things through. I must get down whatever happens. The best place, in fact, is the runway. None of the *Staffel* has landed yet. But why shouldn't I be the first? Automatically I lower the undercarriage, then the flaps, and I turn in. I am rather too high, and the field is small – will I get away with it? I am being fired on again from the right. Cheers! I have put the aircraft down in the centre of the runway. I brake as well as I can. I nearly stand up on my nose.

(Left) A troop-carrying Ju 52 overflies Lent's belly-landed Bf 110 on the approach to Fornebu airfield, 9 April 1940.

(Right) Another view of a similar incident to that depicted in the previous photograph.

Suddenly I am at the end of the runway. I've no more time for thought. We are heading at breakneck speed for bushes ten to fifteen metres thick. But the aircraft is still going fast enough for it to fly. Finally we come to earth in a field. The undercarriage has gone – thank God we didn't turn over. I complete the remainder of my landing on my belly. My landing – anything but an everyday one – is completed just short of the fence of a Norwegian country house. There is no time for thinking. The first thing is to open the cabin roof and get out. A quick look at Kubisch reassures me. He is OK. From the house come a number of Norwegians showing varying degrees of interest.

Among them is an airman who is wearing a sweater and scarf: he is rather excited. That's not surprising – after all, only a few minutes he had been fired on by us and now we have force-landed on his airfield. From a safe distance he greets us with 'Heil Hitler!' That's all right, then, I think. He asks me hesitantly if I am going to open fire. I have my pistol in my right hand and Kubisch is standing in the back of the aircraft at the moveable machine-gun. I reply, 'If you don't fire, I won't.'

The armistice is agreed. We give our names to each other and introduce ourselves. We talk about the war in general and other things, and while this is going on I squint over to the airfield and am pleased to see that my *Feldwebel* Jänicke and the others have landed. We report by radio to the *Kommandeur* in Aalborg that the airfield is in our hands. Two hours later one transport machine after the other is taxiing across the field. What then happened is no doubt known to everyone from transport personnel and the *Wehrmacht* report. And by the way, my machine pistol wasn't loaded – it was a *ruse de guerre*.

Fornebu was taken, and the Junkers transporters could land and discharge their cargo of airborne troops. It was a comparatively small

Confirmation of the shooting-down of a Sunderland flying-boat by *Oberleutnant* Hansen and *Leutnant* Lent on the evening of 9 April 1940. Only Hansen was credited with the kill.

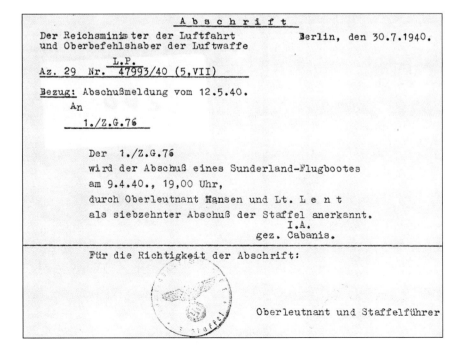

force, about five companies in all. That afternoon, led by a military band, they marched into Oslo unopposed. When at last the main German contingent, which was to have taken Oslo from the sea but had been forced to withdraw, arrived there the following afternoon, the city was already in German hands.

With perhaps rather more than a modicum of exaggeration – but it made very good propaganda – Lent subsequently received further official publicity as the *Luftwaffe* pilot, a mere *Leutnant*, who had accepted the surrender of the Norwegian airfield of Fornebu, thus making possible the successful capture of the Norwegian capital. In truth the attack on Fornebu, the German victory and the occupation of the airfield

Short Sunderland

represented an episode of no little confusion and uncertainty, but the fact remains that the small force of *Zerstörer* from 1./ZG 76, with slight loss to themselves, had secured the strategically important base, into which further air and ground reinforcements could now be poured, and with it came access to the capital city of Norway, despite the unpromising way in which the whole operation had begun.

In the company of *Staffelkapitän* Werner Hansen, whose Bf 110 had also been damaged in the morning's fighting, Helmut Lent took off on patrol from Fornebu at 1850 hours that evening, both of them flying undamaged machines. Lent was in M8+IH. The pair were only airborne for forty minutes, but in that time they came across a vast RAF Sunderland flying boat over Oslo Fjord, and they shot it down. Presumably the kill was credited to Hansen alone, because there is no mention of it in Lent's flying logbook. After landing Lent wrote home:

Photographed after their destruction of an RAF 'Sunderland' flying-boat on 9 April 1940. From left to right: *Unteroffizier* Gross, Hansen's *Funker*; Hansen; Lent; Kubisch. Lent's wrecked Bf 110 M8+DH can be seen on the edge of the copse in the background.

At the moment I am in Oslo. I landed here at 4 o'clock in the morning[41], but unfortunately I crashed. Before that I shot down a Norwegian. Then I got a direct hit from the ground in one of my engines and had to land. I got down safely under anti-aircraft fire. With paratroops we then cleared the airfield of Norwegians. In the late afternoon together with Hansen I shot down a British flying boat. In haste.

The Sunderland that Hansen and Lent destroyed was L2176, one of three aircraft from No. 210 Squadron, Coastal Command, that had been despatched that morning from their base, Pembroke Dock, to Invergordon, north of Inverness. From Invergordon L2176 had left at 1300 hours to carry out reconnaissance in the Oslo area, and Hansen and Lent took off at 1850 hours to intercept it. The huge flying boat, piloted by Flight Lieutenant P. W. H. Kite, exploded with the loss of all the crew except the wireless operator, who apparently fell into the sea from a height of 1,500 feet without a parachute yet survived.

Helmut Lent remained at Fornebu for about two weeks, during which time the German occupation was being consolidated in the face of localised resistance on the part of the Norwegians. The Allies, taken by surprise by the German *coup de main*, reacted by carrying out daring and telling naval attacks on German warships and merchant vessels in Norwegian harbours, and they landed contingents of troops from the sea

---

[41] This is an error. Lent's logbook shows that he landed at 0850 hours.

at several points in north and central Norway. The main focus of activity was Narvik, where two attacks by the Royal Navy completely destroyed enemy war vessels concentrated there and where a large force of Allied troops were landed. All three *Staffeln* of I./ZG 76 were tactically redeployed to Stavanger/Sola during this period, Lent himself flying there on the 22nd April. Walter Kubisch, in the meanwhile promoted to *Unteroffizier*, went with him. Lent resumes:

After we had left Oslo for Stavanger on 14 April there followed a period during which our *Staffel* was not overly blessed with good fortune. Although British aircraft often attacked Stavanger, the luck of the fight was more often than not with the 2nd and 3rd *Staffeln*. Disgruntled and disappointed, perhaps also a little envious, we saw the successes of our other comrades. But there was a new job coming for us. A small band of brave German *Gebirgsjäger*[42] were still fighting in Narvik against odds of ten to one under the leadership of *General* Dietl. Even though we were not fortunate enough to take part in the unique victory procession of our *Wehrmacht* on the western front on 10 May[43], we are nonetheless proud to belong to those who, far away from the homeland, had the opportunity to support that brave fighter *General* Dietl. This experience is perhaps the finest that my comrades and I were privileged to experience during the campaign.

During the course of the air operations in support of the *Gruppe Narvik* it

Stavanger 1940. Fitting a Bf 110 with the *'Dackelbauch'* supplementary fuel tank. The man wearing the life jacket is *Oberfeldwebel* Herzog, a pilot of 1./ZG 76.

---

[42] *Gebirgsjäger*: − Mountain Troops.
[43] Lent is, of course, referring here to the opening of the German *Blitzkrieg* offensive against Holland, Belgium and France.

was necessary for a long-range *Zerstörer Staffel* to take over the protection of the bombers and transport aircraft against attacks from the air. From our old *1. Staffel* I was selected for it with my *Rotte*. Our Narvik *Staffel* was formed and posted to Trondheim.

The special *Staffel* (*Sonderstaffel*) for which Lent was selected was under the command of *Oberleutnant* Hannes Jäger. It comprised three tactical pairs (*Rotten*) and was equipped with a long-range version of the Bf 110, the Bf 110 D-1/R1, which was fitted with a huge extra fuel tank beneath the forward fuselage, which gave rise to the unofficial nickname '*Dackelbauch*' – 'Dachshund Belly'. The crews, chosen from the whole *Gruppe*, were selected on the basis of their experience and their blind-flying capabilities. While he was with the *Sonderstaffel* Lent mostly flew M8+OL. He flew in to Trondheim on 18 May, and was destined to remain there until July. On the 13 May, however, just before he transferred to Trondheim, he was awarded the EK I (Iron Cross First Class). His description of his part in the Norwegian campaign continues:

> The 150-kilometre-long stretch of coastline from Trondheim to Narvik is in itself one of the most fantastic experiences that a flier can have. No Narvik-flier can ever forget the huge mountain ranges, the deeply incised fjords, the snow-covered glaciers, the huge vastness of this, possibly the most beautiful country in Europe. Whoever has the additional good fortune to do this flight in the midnight sun will be fulfilled forever by the experience.
>
> But now to the events themselves. After a number of operations flying escort for the bomber formations attacking units of the British Fleet in Ofot Fjord, we were briefed to fly escort for the transport units dropping paratroops, food and ammunition near Narvik for the hard-pressed *General* Dietl.
>
> We thought, because so far we had not had any contact with the enemy, that there wouldn't be any more aerial victories. But one day *Leutnant* Loobes came back from a Narvik flight waggling his wings. It turned out that Tommies, flying from the airfield at Bardufoss, 20 kilometres to the north of Narvik, had attempted to attack and shoot down our brave Junkers. On 27 May I was lucky enough to shoot down a Gloster near Bodö during a *Stuka* attack... Now the question was whether I too would ever succeed in shooting down a Tommy at Narvik under the eyes of our brave *Gebirgsjäger*.

The Gladiator that Lent shot down on the 27th of May was from No. 263 Squadron, Royal Air Force, and the pilot was a Rhodesian, Caesar Hull. Flight Lieutenant Hull was an experienced pilot. He had shot down one Heinkel 111 and shared two others over Britain before his posting to Norway and had already destroyed two He 111s, two Ju 52s and a Ju 87 in Norway, the Ju 87 only moments before he came up against Helmut Lent. In the engagement he was wounded in the head and one knee and was evacuated to England for treatment. Promoted to Squadron Leader and awarded the DFC (Distinguished Flying Cross), Caesar Hull flew from Biggin Hill during the Battle of Britain, scoring further victories before losing his life on September 7th, a short week after having been appointed Commanding Officer of No. 43 Squadron.

No. 263 Squadron's participation in the Norwegian campaign was dogged by ill fortune throughout. Its Gladiators had first arrived in Norway on 24 April after taking off from the aircraft carrier HMS *Glorious* in atrocious winter-weather conditions – despite the fact that none of the pilots had ever taken off from a carrier's deck before – and landing on the frozen Lake Lesjaskog, near Andalsnes, where, it was intended, they would make their operational base. Within a few days 263 Squadron's biplane aircraft and the makeshift landing strip of ice had suffered so badly at the hands of *Luftwaffe* bombers that the pilots had to be evacuated and taken to Scapa Flow by cargo ship, leaving behind only one serviceable machine. Then, re-equipped with replacement Gladiators, the squadron had returned to Norway on 22 May on board HMS *Furious*, landing this time at Bardufoss, to the north of Narvik.

Helmut Lent, with five confirmed kills to his name, was now officially classified as an *Experte* – an ace. His wish to shoot down an enemy aircraft over Narvik was soon to be realised:

> My chance came on 2 June. A *Schwarm* led by *Oberleutnant* Uellenbeck was briefed to cover a Stuka attack on Bardufoss. My *Schwarm* and I myself were under orders to take over the protection of our indefatigable transport aircraft near Narvik. It seemed to be beyond doubt that this time *Oberleutnant* Uellenbeck would have the greater chances of scoring. Events, however, proved the opposite.
>
> Over Bardufoss the weather was not good enough for the *Stuka* attack, but the weather over Narvik was good enough for us to carry out our orders.
>
> This was *the Zerstörer* operation of my life. Shortly before take-off from Trondheim the *Schwarm* had to split up because the clouds were so low that we could only get to Narvik flying blind. While *Stabsingenieur* (Staff Engineer) Thönes[44] with his *Rotte* flew through to Narvik independently, I, with my wingman *Feldwebel* Mütschele, flying in the place of Jänicke who was sick, climbed up through the clouds and found ourselves in an intermediate layer at 3,500 metres. After about 400 kilometres we caught sight of the ground again in the vicinity of Bodö. Near to Narvik, where there was about six-tenths cloud, I broke cloud and so reached our transport aircraft's dropping zone, which I knew very well. For a good ten minutes I had been orbiting above this place when I saw two aircraft appear suddenly from behind a mountain, which turned out to be *Stabsingenieur* Thönes and his wingman. We were very pleased that he too had got through despite the difficult conditions. We flew above our transport aircraft in a wide defensive circle while they were making their drop, like eagles protecting their charges with their wings.
>
> Then suddenly – I could scarcely believe my eyes – two Glosters come down out of a cloud 500 metres in front of me. In a split second I turn in and bring the outside one under fire. He tries to turn in towards me in combat. But I stick stubbornly on his tail. I fire my second burst ahead of him. I can already see that his prop is turning slowly and that he is going to try to crash-land in

---

[44] *Thönes* was in fact the wireless operator/gunner of the aircraft. His pilot was *Feldwebel* Neureiter..

this rock-fissured countryside. He waggles his wings to show that he cannot fight. I watch calmly to see where he will put down. He touches down on a small, rocky hill, turns over and explodes. Together with *Feldwebel* Mütschele, who has covered me impeccably throughout the entire engagement, I fly back to the dropping zone.

Where is *Stabsingenieur* Thönes' wingman? Uneasy minutes pass. After a time he appears again, and soon afterwards the second Gloster. He too is shot down after a short combat by *Stabsingenieur* Thönes and his wingman. I am immensely pleased that we have been able to shoot down two enemy fighters without loss to ourselves. But while I am thinking I see two more spots in the distance coming towards me. I fly towards them and identify them as two Hurricanes[45]. I can match them for speed, but they are better when it comes to manoeuvrability. I have only one thought – don't let yourself be drawn into a dogfight, which is what they're trying to get you to do. I am able to attack them from astern twice by clever use of the cloud cover. But unfortunately they see what I am trying to do too soon and I am unable to shoot one down. By this time seventy minutes have already passed while I have been over Narvik. I must be thinking of breaking off from the enemy, because I have a long journey ahead of me, most of it blind flying.

And the Tommies, too, don't show much inclination to fight. It's OK by them if I disappear. Far in the north I see them heading for home on a reciprocal heading. But we aren't back home yet. A hundred kilometres south of Bodö we pass through a cold front. This time I was hoping to get back to base below the clouds. But all at once there was no chance of that. I had to pull up. At 2,500 metres I was out of the layer of cloud again with my wingman, *Feldwebel* Mütschele, in close attendance. At the entrance of the Trondheim Fjord I find the 'duty hole in the clouds'. Now for the coast and landing permission!

But suddenly I am surprised to notice that the temperature of the port engine has risen from 80 to 100 degrees – the port radiator is out of action. That's all I need! I have to fly the final leg of the journey on one engine.

In spite of the excitement I find the approach lane. Back home soon! Anxiously I look for Mütschele – but where is he? It is as if he had been suddenly swallowed up by the ocean. I thought that perhaps he had gone on ahead with his two good engines to see that everything was ready on the airfield for my single-engined landing. I make my approach to the Värmes airfield rather shakily on one engine, touch down, taxi in and am welcomed enthusiastically.

Stabsingenieur Thönes, who had left Narvik ten minutes before me because of petrol shortage, was already there and had reported our success.

But where is *Feldwebel* Mütschele? Kubisch and I had seen him when we were at the entrance to the Fjord. It was a drop of vermouth in our joy. Somewhat depressed we go to our billets. By themselves two kills alone would not make it a complete success – it would only be that if all the crewmen came home safe.

---

[45] The Hurricanes were from No. 46 Squadron, which had flown into Norway from HMS *Glorious* on 26 May, landing at Skaanland and later joining No. 263 Squadron at Bardufoss.

Only a few minutes later Mütschele rings in from a naval post at the entrance to the Fjord to say that he had had to force-land there because of fuel shortage.

Now our joy is complete. His aircraft had incurred slight damage, but that is nothing. Machines – aircraft – can be replaced, but not men.

At 5 hours and 46 minutes, his was the longest operational flight that Helmut Lent had flown until then, a testimony to the long-range capability of the Bf 110 D-1/R1. Both the Gladiators, the one shot down by Lent and the one claimed by Thönes, were again from No. 263 Squadron, N5893 (Pilot Officer J. L. Wilkie) and N5681 (Pilot Officer L. R. Jacobsen). Wilkie lost his life, but Jacobsen, despite considerable damage to his aircraft, managed to fly back at low level to base and to land there.

On the 7th of June, in the context of the evacuation of British forces, the squadron commanders of No. 263 and No. 46 were ordered to destroy their remaining aircraft, ten Gladiators and seven Hurricanes respectively, before boarding ship. Reluctant to do so they asked, and were granted, permission to fly them on to HMS *Glorious*, which was about to set sail for Britain. The machines were not fitted with deck-landing arrester gear and none of the pilots had ever landed on a carrier before, yet they accomplished the hazardous feat safely in the early hours of the following day. A total of ten pilots from 46 Squadron and ten from 263 Squadron embarked. It was a remarkable feat of combined airmanship.

Then tragedy struck. That afternoon *Glorious* was intercepted on her homeward crossing by a German task force that included the *Scharnhorst* and the *Gneisenau* and was sunk with the loss of nearly all her crew, all the RAF fighters on board, their ground personnel and all but two of their pilots[46], a total of 1,519 souls in all. Among the dead was Flying Officer Jacobsen, DFC, who had survived the encounter with 1./ZG 76 just five days previously.

On the 9th of June the Norwegians formally laid down their arms, and the Scandinavian confrontation ended in a comprehensive victory for the Germans. The *Sonderstaffel* remained at Trondheim for a short time to act in a local defence role, and on the 15th of June Lent added a Bristol Blenheim to his tally of kills, writing home later: 'I can report to you the shooting down of a Blenheim – I got it the day before yesterday near Trondheim. I was very sorry that no one got out. But the young fellows shouldn't be so cheeky!' Lent's victim on this occasion, his seventh overall, was L9408 of No. 254 Squadron of Fighter Command, flying a reconnaissance mission in the Trondheim area from Sumburgh in the Shetlands. The pilot, Pilot Officer P. C. Gaylord, and his crew perished.

On 1 July 1940 Lent was promoted to *Oberleutnant*, and a few days later wrote home, 'If you looked at my last letter carefully you will already know that I am now an *Oberleutnant*. I had already stuck the

---

[46] The pilots who survived were Squadron Leader Kenneth Cross (Commanding No.46 Squadron) and Flight Lieutenant P. G. Jameson. Jameson later commanded No. 266 Squadron. He retired in 1959 as Air Commodore, CB, DSO, DFC (with Bar).

envelope down, and I didn't want to have to open it again. Just now my shoulders seem very heavy and can scarcely bear the weight of the pips!' On 13 July, once more flying M8+DH – it is not clear whether this was his old aircraft repaired or a new replacement – Lent rejoined 1./ZG 76, now at Stavanger/Forus.

On the world stage, events in Scandinavia had been overshadowed by those in Western Europe where, on 10 May 1940, the German armies had swept forward into France and neutral Holland, Belgium and Luxembourg in a text-book manifestation of *Blitzkrieg* that had enforced the surrender of the Dutch within five days and that of the Belgians

Hauptmann Restemeyer, *Kommandeur* I./ZG 76, shot down and killed over England on 15 August 1940.

within less than three weeks. On the 20th of May the evacuation of the British Expeditionary Force, pushed back to the Channel coast, had begun, and by the 4th of June the well-nigh miraculous withdrawal had been completed and 'Dunkirk' had become a household word. On the 14th of June the triumphant German troops had entered Paris and by the 22nd of the month, only six eventful weeks after the beginning of the German offensive, France had capitulated. In London there was a new Prime Minister, Winston Spencer Churchill, who on the 17th of June had said in a memorable speech to the House of Commons, 'What General Weygand called the Battle of France is over. I expect that the Battle of Britain is about to begin. The whole fury and might of the enemy must very soon be turned on us.'

He was right. Beginning at the end of June the Germans directed the might of the *Luftwaffe* against the British Isles, confidently expecting to achieve the air superiority without which invasion could not succeed, and the Battle of Britain had begun. The outcome is history. For the

Hans Ulrich Kettling, seen here as a *Leutnant,* was a close friend of Helmut Lent.

crews of 1.ZG/76, detailed to remain in Norway to defend against British attacks from across the North Sea, this was a frustrating period. They were kept reasonably busy, it is true. From the beginning of June to the end of August, when he finally left Norway, Lent made twenty operational flights, many of them entered in his logbook as '*Alarmstart*' (emergency scramble), without any success apart from the Gladiator on the 2nd June and the Blenheim on the 15th. But other *Zerstörer* units stationed in France, including II./ZG 76 – and later III./ZG 76, formed in June – were in the thick of the battle over the British Isles, where there was high adventure to experience and glory to be won. But there were also daunting losses to be suffered as the inferiority of the Bf 110 under battle conditions and in direct combat with the single-engined Spitfires and Hurricanes of the Royal Air Force became apparent, and some might say that the crewmen of I./ZG 76 had been fortunate when Fate decided that they would remain in Norway rather than move to France.

Helmut Lent did, however, experience one taste of action in the Battle of Britain. On 15 August the Germans, in addition to raids against Southern England, mounted a heavy attack against targets in the north-east of England as part of an all-out assault on the island. Lent was flying 'his' M8+DH, one of twenty-one Bf 110s of I./ZG76 escorting He 111 bombers of KG 26 that were briefed to attack targets in Yorkshire and the Newcastle/Sunderland area. He later described this operation in these terms in a letter to his parents:

Lent and Kettling share a few quiet minutes at Trondheim-Vernaes in the summer of 1940, before Kettling was shot down over England.

Recently we were in England. Unfortunately I didn't shoot anything down this time either. I had a technical fault in my aircraft, so that I was at a serious disadvantage. In addition I had a scrap with six Spitfires by myself – a bit much all at one time! Otherwise I got back home OK. But once again God the Father mercifully spared me. I landed safely with only a couple of bullet holes. In passing I had a go at two balloons over Hull.

This was the most costly day of the battle for the *Luftwaffe*, which mounted approximately 2,000 sorties against the British Isles and lost about ninety aircraft. I./ZG 76 despatched twenty-one aircraft and lost seven, among them that of *Hauptmann* Restemeyer, the *Gruppenkommandeur*, who was killed when RAF Spitfires of No. 72 Squadron shot him down in the sea off the Durham coast. A Spitfire flown by Pilot Officer Ted Shipman of No. 41 Squadron shot down *Oberleutnant* Hans Ulrich Kettling from Lent's *Staffel*, but he survived to become a prisoner of war. Lent was diverted to Jever when he got back to Germany, and the round-trip took him four hours and twenty-nine minutes. It had been his 98th operational flight as a *Zerstörer* pilot, and, although he did not know it at the time, his final one. Kettling had been a close comrade and friend of Lent since pre-war days.

In July Lent had had a letter from home telling him of the death in action of a number of friends and acquaintances. His reply showed that neither his allegiance to the Fatherland nor his belief in the omnipotence of the Almighty had weakened:

> Jo and Ulla had already written to me about the hero's death of acquaintances from Pyrehne and thereabouts. No matter how sad any individual death might be, we must be proud that by their heroic death they not only made our Fatherland great and strong but also added immortal laurels to the banners of German military tradition. Our *Gruppe*, too, has experienced several losses in the course of this war. But their sacrifice only shows its true glory when seen alongside their success in the form of enemy aircraft destroyed. It is God who decides who just who precisely has to make the sacrifice.

CHAPTER FIVE

August 1940 to May 1941
Becoming a Night Fighter

W ITH the Germans' invasion of Scandinavia the phoney war in Europe – the Germans called it the *Sitzkrieg* – had come to its end, and the speed with which the war situation had changed in the following weeks was as bewildering as it was unpredictable. When Helmut Lent had flown north to Westerland as a member of 1./ZG 76 on the 8th April 1940 the front line between Germany and the Allies lay along the Franco/German border, while Belgium, Luxembourg and Holland still enjoyed their neutrality. By the time Lent left Norway just under five months later, France had been comprehensively defeated and the Germans were firmly ensconced in the Low Countries as well as in Norway and Denmark. Their front line with the one unconquered enemy, Britain, had been shoved back, almost effortlessly it seemed, to the Channel coast, and Britain was under intense siege from the *Luftwaffe*, with the pilots of the Hurricanes and Spitfires of Fighter Command struggling desperately to prevent the Germans gaining the air supremacy they needed before they might consider launching an invasion. The pastor's son from Pyrehne was by then a recognised ace, but, in common with other fighter pilots whom arbitrary decisions by higher authority had kept away from the Western Front, he felt frustrated at being stationed in Scandinavia, very much a sideshow to the principal theatre of action, and he feared that the war might be over before he had his chance to prove himself fully in decisive battle against the main enemy. He need not have worried: his chance was to come, although not in the way that he had hoped it might.

At the outbreak of war in 1939 the two main front-line operational Commands of the Royal Air Force were Fighter Command and Bomber Command. The German advances to the north and the west in Spring 1940 had created a war situation in which both of these forces were to be put to the test. Fighter Command passed that test, as the outcome of the Battle of Britain was to show, although it was a close-run thing. The way in which Bomber Command, still a comparatively small force, was to be used was uncertain, a matter of debate, indecision and pragmatism. A large proportion of the aircraft with which the Command was equipped were obsolescent medium- and long-range 'heavies', so-called 'strategic' bombers, designed to carry a large bomb-load to distant targets at high altitude, although there were even bigger and better strategic bombers on the drawing board. But navigation training in peacetime had been a very casual business, totally unsuited to the task of finding such distant targets. In particular, navigation by night had been grossly neglected. Until late 1939 the general assumption had been that accurate attacks on enemy targets could be carried out in formation in daylight, when sight of the ground would, it was optimistically assumed, ensure accurate target finding and bomb aiming. It had also been assumed that the bombers were sufficiently well armed to fight off fighter interception by day, but this assumption had been proved wrong in the most unambiguous way by German fighter pilots, among them Helmut Lent, over the German Bay in December 1939.

During the Scandinavian Campaign the RAF, forced to operate largely in the hours of darkness, had mounted raids against airfields such as Stavanger, Trondheim, Oslo, Kristiansund and Aalborg that were occupied by the *Luftwaffe*. At about three percent of the bombers despatched, losses were tolerable, but, as was later established, very little damage was caused to the targets – although that contention would have been strongly denied at the time by both the senior officers who had planned the raids and the crews who had carried them out, an interesting example of the power of either wishful thinking or self-deception. With the escalation of the war in Spring 1940 the ban on striking at land objectives in Germany was lifted and leaflet raids were discontinued. Directives from the Director of Plans to the Air-Officer Commanding-in-Chief, Bomber Command, specified the targets for Bomber Command as 'identifiable oil-plants, electricity plants, coking plants, gas works, "self-illuminating objectives", troop concentrations, moving trains, marshalling yards' and so on, completely overlooking the fact that the Whitleys, Wellingtons and Hampdens of Bomber Command were neither equipped nor had crews trained to hit such targets, even if they were able to find them, which itself was highly unlikely.

The first attack by Bomber Command in the vicinity of an inland German town took place on the night of 11/12 May 1940, when thirty-seven Hampdens and eighteen Whitleys were sent to bomb road and rail communications near to Mönchengladbach, a town west of the Ruhr industrial area and near to the German border with Holland, in an attempt to hinder military traffic heading towards the invasion front. In return for three bombers lost, five aircrew men and four civilians killed and one airman taken prisoner, only very slight damage to property was caused. It was an unimpressive beginning to a bomber campaign that was destined by the end of the war to have resulted in incalculable damage to property, including the total destruction of an estimated 3,370,000 dwellings in Germany, and to have cost the lives of more than 50,000 Bomber Command aircrew and an unrecorded number of German night-fighter crewmen[47], not to mention an estimated 600,000

---

[47] The number of German night-fighter crew members killed in action has been estimated at approaching 4,000.

German civilians, the great majority of them women and children.

British bombers were in action in small numbers over the Rhineland and the North German coast on the following three nights, but then, during the night of 15/16 May, there came the first major attack directed against strategic objectives in Germany. Ninety-nine bombers were sent out to hit sixteen separate targets in the Ruhr area. From then on raids on Germany in varying strength by Whitleys, Wellingtons, Hampdens and Blenheims were an almost nightly occurrence, oil and tactical communications targets predominating. On average about 75 bombers were over Germany each night, and the pattern was as it had been on the 15/16th of May, with small numbers of bombers being sent individually to each of a number of separate targets without any attempt to concentrate the attacks in either space or time. In June, with the evacuation of the British Expeditionary Force from France completed, Bomber Command began to increase the number of heavies it was sending out by night and to seek targets deeper in Germany. On 3/4 June the number of bombers despatched was 142, and targets ranged from Hamburg in the north to Frankfurt in Central Germany. Italy declared war on France and Britain on 10 June, and the following night a force of 36 Whitleys was sent to attack Turin. Bad weather prevented the majority of the heavies from crossing the Alps, but eleven did succeed in getting through, nine of which reached the city and bombed it, missing their allocated targets – despite the lack of any black-out – but killing 17 people and injuring a further 40. Two Whitleys were lost. In terms of hard profit and loss, this was certainly not an auspiciously successful operation, but its psychological impact was considerable. Bomber Command was letting it be known that no part of enemy Europe was safe from aerial attack.

On the 15th of June the armistice between Germany and France came into effect. Britain finally stood alone against the Reich and the defence of the British Isles lay firmly in the hands of Fighter Command, while Bomber Command represented, for the time being, the only means of carrying the war to the enemy. As Winston Churchill would later, at the height of the Battle of Britain, tell his Cabinet, 'The Navy can lose us the war, but only the Air Force can win it. The fighters are our salvation, but the bombers alone can provide the means of victory.' Stirring words – but looking back it is clear that Bomber Command, as then equipped and led, was far from equal to such a responsibility. If that is surprising, however, it is even more so that the *Luftwaffe*, thus far so outstandingly successful in its attacking role, had also been guilty of a significant miscalculation in devoting only scant attention to the necessity for a night-fighter force. It was not that the threat of attack from the air had not taken seriously, despite Hermann Göring's boast in a widely distributed and quoted newspaper interview shortly before the German invasion of Poland that not a single enemy bomb would ever fall on German soil.

When the *Luftwaffe* had emerged from clandestinity in 1935 it had brought with it the strong nucleus of an anti-aircraft artillery force, the

Flakartillerie[48], or '*Flak*' in common usage. The *Flak* had two primary functions, the defence of metropolitan Germany against air attack and the protection of the armies in the field.[49] The seriousness with which the threat from the air was regarded by the Germans – despite Göring's flippancy – is indicated by the fact that when the war began the anti-aircraft arm had a strength of nearly one million men, approaching two-thirds of the total establishment of the *Luftwaffe*. It is a matter of no little puzzlement, therefore, that only relatively scant and casual attention seems to have been given to the provision of a fighter force that could intercept and destroy enemy bombers during the dark hours.

There had, of course, been experiments with night-time interception in the closing stages of the First World War, and there were further experiments in the nineteen-thirties after the rebirth of the *Luftwaffe*, and these involved single-seat day fighters, frequently with the cockpit canopy removed, working in co-operation with searchlights. Results were promising enough for a small force of fighter *Staffeln* be detailed in June 1939 for night-fighting duties, but this was a short-lived initiative and the *Staffeln* concerned, with the exception of two, returned the following month to the day-fighter force. After the outbreak of war, in late 1939 and early 1940, when the *Kommando Schuhmacher*[50] was installed at Jever, two of its Bf 109 *Staffeln* were theoretically there for night-fighting contingencies, and it is believed that *Oberfeldwebel* Hermann Förster of IV./(N)JG 2, flying a Bf 109, shot down a Hampden[51] from No.

Handley Page
Hampden

---

[48] May also be written '*Flak-Artillerie*'. '*Flak*' is an abbreviated form of '*Flieger-Abwehr-Kanonen*' – 'Guns for defence against aircraft'.

[49] Later in the war the *Flak* was also used to considerable effect in a ground-artillery role.

[50] Also known as '*Jagdgeschwader Schuhmacher*'. See Page 47.

[51] The Hampden was P1319, and it was piloted by Pilot Officer A. H. Benson. The crew of four perished.

Hauptmann Wolfgang Falck. He became *Kommodore* of NJG 1, the very first night-fighter *Geschwader*, in June 1940.

49 Squadron laying mines off Sylt on the night of the 25/26th April, probably the first RAF bomber to be destroyed by a German night fighter during World War Two.

In June 1940, with Bomber Command penetrations of German airspace on the increase, so that some nights well over one hundred RAF aircraft were dropping their bombs apparently indiscriminately on the Third Reich and with comparative immunity, Göring decreed that a night-fighter force should be formed at once. The officer whom he charged with the task was the *Zerstörer* ace Wolfgang Falck, since February 1940 *Kommandeur* of I./ZG 1.

During the Norwegian Campaign *Hauptmann* Falck's unit had been based at Aalborg in Denmark, located near to the northern tip of the

Jutland peninsula and the recipient of frequent visits by Bomber
Command aircraft. Mindful of the Battle of the German Bight, in which
he (and Helmut Lent) had successfully taken part and in which early
warning of the approach of the British force had been provided by a
Freya radar on the island of Borkum, Falck contacted *Leutnant* Werner
Bode, the officer in charge of a *Freya* station on the coast, and asked him
to inform the Operations Room at Aalborg when his radar picked up
bombers approaching from the west: the *Freya*, with a range of about 100
kilometres against a target at 10,000 feet, might be expected to provide
about fifteen minutes' warning of the arrival of enemy aircraft, long
enough for Falck to get his *Zerstörer* into the air. Aircraft from Falck's
Gruppe took off in this way on a number of occasions, but without success.
Then, on the night of 30 April/1 May 1940, fifty RAF Whitleys,

Generalfeldmarschall
Erhardt Milch,
State Secretary
for Aviation.

Wellingtons and Hampdens attacked Scandinavian airfields, including Aalborg. Forewarned of the bombers' approach by the *Freya* station, Falck, together with three of his best pilots, *Oberleutnant* Werner Streib, *Oberleutnant* Günter Radusch and *Feldwebel* Thier, took off. They were successfully directed into visual contact with a bombers and opened fire, themselves coming under return fire, but could make no claims. Nevertheless the feasibility of Falck's concept, interception with the aid of ground radar, had been established.

Immediately after this encounter with Bomber Command Wolfgang Falck wrote a report and sent it 'through channels' to the Aviation Ministry, where it came to the attention of *Generalleutnant* Erhard Milch, Director General of Equipment (Air), who was so interested that he paid a visit to Aalborg to discuss Falck's thoughts about night-time interception with him in considerable depth. Soon after this visit I./ZG 1 moved south to play its part in the *Blitzkrieg* against France and the Low Countries, and by the 22nd of June it was positioned on an airfield in the vicinity of le Havre, poised to join in the assault on Britain. Then, on the 23rd or 24th of June, there came a telephone call from *General* Albert Kesselring, Commanding *Luftflotte* 2, that not only changed the way in which Falck's own *Luftwaffe* career developed but also marked the beginning of a unique aerial battle between bombers and night fighters that was destined to continue until the very last night of the war. Kesselring told Falck that he and his *Gruppe*, with the exception of one

Generaloberst Ernst Udet, Director General of Equipment, in conversation with Wolfgang Falck, probably about August 1940.

Staffel[52], were to leave France that very day and move to Düsseldorf to fly night-time operations against RAF bombers in defence of the Ruhr area. Falck was most reluctant to give up his successful career as a *Zerstörer* pilot and commander and enter the uncharted and unpromising world of night fighting, but his protests were to no avail. On 26 June, a scant few days after Falck's arrival with his *Gruppe* in Düsseldorf, he was summoned to attend a conference in Wassenaar in Holland. A mere *Hauptmann*, he found himself in the daunting presence of some of the most eminent and influential personalities of the *Luftwaffe*, senior among them the Commander-in-Chief, *Feldmarschall*[53] Hermann Göring himself. There were Generals there, too, including Ernst Udet and Albert Kesselring, as well as a number of other less highly ranking officers. Göring summarised the war situation, coming round to the war in the air: he described the RAF bombing attacks on targets in Germany as '*ärgerlich*' – annoying. He had, he said, decided to form a night-fighter force, and he was appointing Falck as *Kommodore* of the first night-fighter *Geschwader*, NJG 1. For the moment the *Geschwader* would comprise just two *Gruppen*: two *Staffeln* of Falck's *Gruppe*, I./ZG 1, would become I./NJG 1, and IV(N)/JG 2 would form the nucleus of II./NJG 1.

Falck himself received promotion to the rank of *Major* on the first day of July. The task that faced him was a formidable one. When the Bf 109D-1s of IV(N)/JG 2 had practised night fighting they had attempted to work in cooperation with the searchlights, but without any ground control. The fighters simply took off and headed in the general direction of the area in which bombers were expected, hoping to see one illuminated by searchlights and to be in a position to carry out an attack on it. Several claims were made, but only one 'kill' seems reasonably certain, that of the No. 49 Squadron Hampden mentioned earlier in this chapter, which had come down in the sea off Sylt during the night of 25/26 April, and that interception had been made without the aid of searchlights. The Bf 109 was, indeed, totally unsuited to night fighting, and was soon to disappear from the operational scene. The Bf 110 D-1, however, as flown by the *Zerstörer* units, was a better prospect: indeed it might have been tailor-made for night fighting. It could stay in the air considerably longer than its single-engined cousin; it was twice as heavily armed (two 20 mm. MG FF cannon and four 7.9 mm. MG 17 machine-guns as against one 20 mm. MG FF cannon and two 7.9 mm. MG 17s); it carried a wireless operator/navigator ('*Funker*') and was fully equipped for blind flying; and, very importantly, most of the pilots flying the Bf 110 in the *Zerstörer* rôle had, as part of their training, undergone a blind-flying course.

---

[52] A *Gruppe* usually comprised three *Staffeln*, each of nine aircraft, although there were exceptions to this rule. There was also a Staff Flight of three aircraft. There were usually three *Gruppen* to a *Geschwader*.

[53] Göring was appointed by Adolf Hitler to the unique rank of *Reichsmarschall* (the equivalent of a six-star General) about three weeks later, on the 19 July 1940.

Even although there was an aircraft suitable for night fighting immediately available, however, there remained the difficulty of finding the RAF bombers in the darkness, preferably before they reached their allotted targets. Ground radar, such as the *Freya* that Falck had used at Aalborg, could give warning of the approach of enemy machines, but in the closing stages of the interception the pilot of the night fighter had to rely on his eyesight to pick up a bomber and to carry out an attack. Falck, therefore, still had to look to the searchlights for help. A method of bringing fighter and bomber together was rapidly developed: called '*Helle Nachtjagd*' (bright, or illuminated, night fighting), it required the fighters to scramble when approaching bombers were picked up by radar and to patrol behind a belt of searchlights, ready to head into the belt as soon as the lights were switched on and focused on a target. Some successes were achieved, but it was becoming increasingly clear that some form of control of the fighters from the ground was needed.

Josef Kammhuber

On 17 July 1940 Göring announced the formation of a Night Fighter Division (*Nachtjagd-Division*) and appointed *Oberst* Josef Kammhuber (later *Generalmajor*) to command it, so relieving Falck of a great deal of the staff work that went with the command of NJG 1. During August Kammhuber set up a Divisional HQ in Brussels and an operational HQ in a country house at Zeist near Utrecht in Holland. Once in being, the night-fighter force began to expand rapidly, with existing units being divided to form the nucleus of new units, and fresh personnel, together with their aircraft, being brought in from other, mostly *Zerstörer*, *Gruppen*. Expansion was rapid, so that by October 1940 NJG 1 comprised three *Gruppen*, while a second and a third *Geschwader*, NJG 2 and NJG 3, were

Slot Zeist above, was Kammhuber's wartime headquarters. The lower photo shows it as it is today.

in being. It was during this period of rapid expansion that Helmut Lent reluctantly became a member of the fledgling German night-fighter force, the *Nachtjagd*[45].

When Lent had made his only operational flight against England on the 15th of August 1940 his *Gruppe*, I./ZG 76, stationed at Stavanger/Forus, had already been earmarked to join Falck's *Nachtjagd-Geschwader*, NJG 1[55], as II./NJG 1. It did so officially on 7 September. Typical of the confusing and seemingly haphazard way in which the *Nachtjagd* was mushrooming was that the existing II./NJG 1, which, as described above, had been formed from IV(N)/JG 2, became the nucleus of the First *Gruppe* of the Second *Nachtjagdgeschwader* (I./NJG 2) with the task of converting to twin-engined aircraft such as the Ju 88, the Do 17 and the Do 215 to fly long-range intruder missions against the British Isles from Gilze-Rijen in the Netherlands. They were known as *Fernnachtjäger* – long-range night fighters.

At the end of August Lent wrote home, 'We are currently converting to night fighting. We are not very enthusiastic. We would sooner head directly for England.' Instead he headed south: his logbook shows that he left Stavanger in 'his' M8+DH on the 29th of the month for Lager Lechfeld, a bomber training school in Bavaria, west of Munich and south of Augsburg, making an overnight stop on the way. Walter Kubisch was in the rear seat of the Bf 110. Their stay at Lechfeld was very short. On the 4th September, after two local flights practising beacon approaches, they flew seven night-time 'circuits and bumps' and then, the following day, moved the short distance to the airfield at Ingolstadt, where, that very evening, they flew more take-offs and landings. Then, according to his logbook, Lent had a week's respite from flying. When he resumed on the 12th of September the aircraft he was piloting bore the identification markings G9+EM, 'G9' being the indicator for NJG 1 and the final 'M' indicating the 6th *Staffel*. For the remainder of his time at Ingolstadt Lent used a variety of 'G9' machines: what became of M8+DH is unknown. Possibly she was repainted black[56] and became a 'G9' aircraft or possibly she went to another unit. On 1 October 1940, after completing about twelve hours night flying at Ingolstadt, Lent moved to Holland to begin operational night fighting.

It will be recalled that Lent's friend Hans Ulrich Kettling had been shot down over England on 15 August 1940. Clearly, news that he was a prisoner of war had reached his former *Staffel*, because during their time at Ingolstadt a number of them, during what was obviously a convivial party at a *Gasthof* in the nearby village of Geisenfeld, wrote a letter to him reading, 'Dear Kettling, the *Staffel* remembers you in comradeship and

---

[54] Literally 'night hunting'. In German a fighter aircraft is a *Jäger*, a hunter, and air fighting in general is *'die Jagd'*, 'the hunt'.

[55] There is a degree of oversimplification here. Only two *Staffeln* of I./ZG 76 were used to form the new II./NJG 1.

[56] At this early period all night-fighter aircraft were painted matt black. Later more imaginative camouflage patterns were adopted.

wishes you an early return.' The letter was signed by *Staffelkapitän* Hansen and all the '*Waffenjodler*', as they styled themselves[57]. Lent's contribution was, '*Holzauge sei wach!*' (A colloquialism for, 'Look after yourself!').

The airfield in Holland to which Lent was posted was Deelen, just

GASTHOF FUCHSBÜCHLER · GEISENFELD
TELEFON NUMMER 7
Erstes Haus am Platze. Fließendes Warm- u. Kaltwasser in allen Zimmern
Eigene vorzügliche Biere
Eigene Hausmetzgerei
"SCHUTZMARKE"
BRAUHAUS MÜNCH. BRAUEREI TELEFON NUMMER 53

Ihre Zeichen
Ihre Nachricht vom
Unser Zeichen
Tag
Betreff
GEISENFELD (Hallertau), den

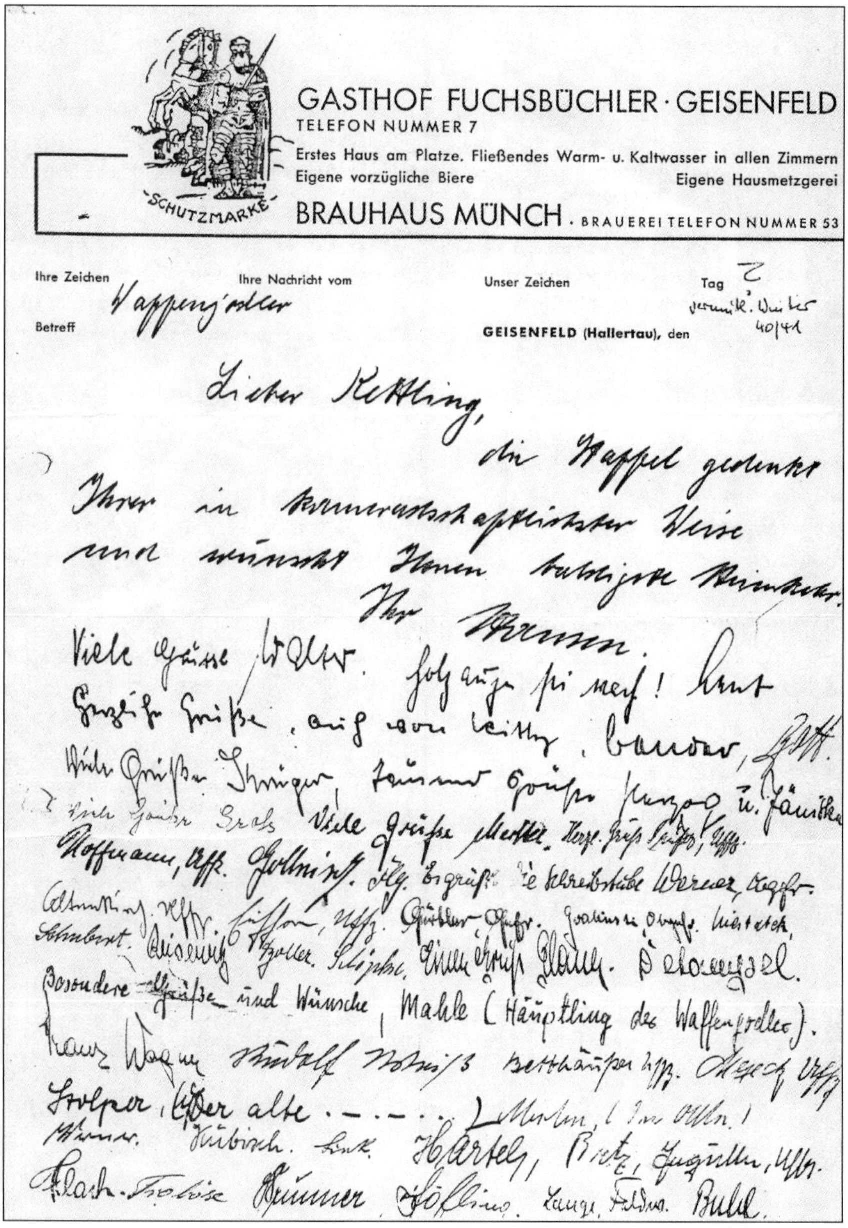

This letter, written to Kettling by comrades from 1./ZG 76, was forwarded 'through channels' and reached him in his PoW camp. Old German handwriting makes it difficult to read. Lent's contribution may be seen below the signature of *Staffelkapitän* Hansen (fourth line of letter), while Kubisch's signature can easily be made out near the bottom left-hand corner of the page. An interesting signature is that of Mahle, five lines from the bottom, who has added in brackets, 'Boss of the *Waffenjodler*'. In 1943 Paul Mahle worked closely with Rudolf Schoenert on the design and fitting of the *Schräge Musik* weapons system.

[57] '*Waffenjodler*' translates as 'Weapon yodellers', and was a nickname for the armourers. Kettling had been Armaments Officer of 1./ZG 76.

north of Arnhem, and he was *Staffelkapitän* of 6./NJG 1. A glance at the map of Europe makes it clear that any fighter force defending German airspace against attacks coming from England would have to be very largely concentrated in Holland and, to a lesser extent, in Belgium and France. It was virtually impossible for Bomber Command aircraft to avoid crossing, or passing very near to, at least one of those countries, especially Holland, when heading for any of the Command's main targets, the majority of which lay in North Germany – the ports and naval bases of Kiel, Hamburg, Bremen, Emden, Wilhelmshaven and so on; the sprawling concentration of coal- and steel-producing towns, oil refineries and armament factories that made up the Ruhr industrial area, with major cities such as Düsseldorf and Cologne just to the south; and, of course, Berlin further east. Fighters stationed in Belgium and France would additionally defend against bombers attempting to approach along a more southerly route, either making a tactical approach from an unexpected direction or heading for targets in, for example, Southern Germany, Austria or Italy. Quite certainly, however, it was in Holland that the maximum defensive effort would have to be deployed.

Immediately the necessity for an organised night-fighter force was acknowledged, therefore, the Germans had selected suitably located airfields in Holland, the majority of them little more than grass aerodromes used for private and commercial flying, and intensive work had been begun to expand and to equip them to meet the needs of the rapidly developing *Nachtjagd*. Leeuwarden and Venlo were destined to become the two most important night-fighter bases in Holland. The former, situated in Friesland, to the east of the Ijsselmeer, covered the RAF's most frequently used approach route. Venlo lay in the east of Holland. Between these two geographical extremes such airfields as Schipol[58], the main airport of Amsterdam, Deelen, Bergen, Gilze-Rijen, Eindhoven and Twente and other bases eventually accommodated night-fighter units.

Oberleutnant Helmut Lent arrived at Deelen, flying in from Ingolstadt in G9+GP, on 1 October 1940. After a one-hour local familiarisation flight the following day he flew his first night-fighter operation in the very early hours of the 4th of October. Overall this was his 100th operational sortie. Bomber Command did not mount a major attack that night, although it seems possible that a small number of Blenheims and Wellingtons flew individual raids on targets on the coasts of France and Holland. Lent spoke of this flight in a letter home:

> We are night fighting in earnest now. Yesterday I too was airborne. Unfortunately the Tommy didn't show himself. Even though it was a clear night no incoming flights were detected. But the chances of shooting the brothers down by night have risen considerably. Very recently someone shot three down in a night! An outstanding performance.

---

[58] Night fighters were based at Schipol for only a comparatively short period.

The pilot who had shot down three British bombers in a night was *Oberleutnant* Werner Streib, and he had performed the feat during the night of the 30th of September, the eve of Lent's arrival at Deelen. The bombers that he destroyed were either two Wellingtons and a Hampden or three Wellingtons[59]. Streib was *Staffelkapitän* of 2.NJG 1 and was flying from Vechta, roughly halfway between Osnabrück and Bremen. Two of the Wellingtons that he claimed were in all probability both from No. 115 Squadron, R3292, KO-F (Captain Sergeant. C. Wessels) and T2549, KO-K (Captain Pilot Officer A. J. J. Steel). Their target was the railway

Hauptmann Werner Streib, later *Kommandeur* I./NJG 1, wearing the Knight's Cross awarded to him on 6 October 1940.

---

[59] Two contemporary lists of kills that night give conflicting information on the type of aircraft shot down.

marshalling yards at Osnabrück, and Streib shot them down within two minutes of each other at the villages of Badbergen and Menslage, about fifty kilometres north of the target, respectively. The 'Hampden' that he claimed is more difficult to identify, as no Hampdens are recorded as having been lost that night. Possibly it was a Whitley, or even another Wellington – misidentifications were not infrequent.

Armstrong Whitworth Whitley V

Werner Streib was one of the outstanding German night-fighter pilots, surviving the war with the impressive total of 65 night-time victories to add to the one that he had gained as a *Zerstörer* pilot. He is credited with having achieved the second confirmed kill[60] of the newly-formed *Nachtjagd* when he shot down a Whitley Mark V, P5007 of No. 51 Squadron, captained by Flight Lieutenant S. E. F. Curry, at Ibbenbüren in the early hours of 20 July 1940. Curry and five of the six-man crew died. The three kills that Streib scored on 30 September were his fifth, sixth and seventh respectively.

When Kammhuber had been appointed to command the Night Fighter *Division*, and with *helle Nachtjagd* being the only obvious way forward for the time being, one of the his first actions was to set up a long belt of searchlights and acoustic listening-posts, a so-called '*helle Gürtel*' or 'illuminated belt' centred to the north-west of the city of Münster, to guard the Ruhr area against bombers approaching from the north. It was in this belt that the pilots of I./NJG 1 were operating at this period.

---

[60] The first confirmed *Nachtjagd* kill was made by *Feldwebel* Förster of 8./NJG1, who destroyed a Whitley during the night of 8/9 July1940. His victim was almost certainly Whitley N1496 of No. 10 Squadron, Dishforth (Captain Flight Lieutenant D. A. ffrench-Mullen).

When a British raid was expected the fighters would take off and position themselves to the east of the lights and, if at all possible, at a greater altitude than that of the incoming bombers: the *Flak* was under orders – not always observed – not to fire. When a searchlight beam illuminated a bomber, the pilot would head for it and attempt to shoot it down. It was not unusual for the searchlights, having 'coned' a bomber, to keep it coned for up to six minutes or more before the fighter successfully attacked it or it escaped from the beams. Many mistakes were made, of course, but progress was being made.

As *Staffelkapitän* of 6./NJG 1, and with a rank equivalent to that of a Flying Officer in the RAF, Lent had nine aircraft and their crews under his direct command and was responsible to his *Gruppe*, II./NJG 1, not only for the operational readiness and efficiency of his *Staffel* but also for overseeing its administration. It was, of course, accepted that a *Kapitän* would lead his unit in battle, if not literally at least by example, which meant that he would fly operationally whenever possible and, ideally, score victories. It was not long before his impatience with his own performance was reflected in his letters home. On 10 October, when he had been at Deelen no more than ten days, he wrote:

> The reason that I can't take leave has nothing to do with either me myself or my poor performance, but because I can't leave my *Staffel*, which is still, of course, very much in its infancy. If I can, I should like to get a few kills first. It is extremely difficult. By now, however, if the stupid searchlights had been more on the ball, I should have at least one or perhaps, with a bit of luck, two. I'm flying nearly every night. Things have got to take a turn for the better sooner or later!

We do not know whether Lent mentioned in this letter – only an extract survives – that his friend the *Kommandeur* of II./NJG 1, and formerly of I./ZG 76, *Hauptmann Graf* von Stillfried, had been killed in a flying accident just four days previously. *Oberleutnant* – soon to be *Hauptmann* – Walter Ehle was appointed to take over command.

As Lent's letter indicates, the night fighters were still completely dependent on the efficiency of the searchlights, and the searchlights themselves could only operate if there was no, or only broken, cloud cover. Nevertheless, the units of NJG 1 that had gone into action progressively since the formation of the *Nachtjagd* had performed quite well, considering that they were exploring territory hitherto unknown. So far they had claimed twenty-two kills, among them four over England in the course of long-range intruder operations. But, as Lent himself had said in his letter, his *Staffel* was very new to the world of night fighting, and he was perhaps being too self-critical in expecting quick results. It would not be until January 1941 that his unit would score its first success. In November, his appointment as *Staffelkapitän* having been confirmed – seemingly it had until then only been officially on an acting or temporary basis – he wrote home that 'night fighting at the moment is suffering to some extent from bad weather and the stupid Flak.' Bad weather in autumn was not unexpected, and misunderstandings between night fighters and anti-aircraft gunners would persist to the very end of hostilities, despite many attempts to achieve co-ordination. In principle it did not seem too difficult to arrange that the guns should stop firing when a bomber was under attack by a night fighter – or even to persuade the gunners not to engage friendly aircraft when there were no bombers in the immediate vicinity – but 'itchy trigger fingers' remained a problem.

Lent had not taken leave since February 1940, when he and Lena Senokosnikova had spent a skiing holiday together in Hirschegg. Between April and September and until his arrival in Deelen on 1 October he had been in Bavaria training to be a night fighter. There had, it seems, been very little opportunity for the couple to meet unless, possibly, Lena had made a fleeting visit to see him in Jever in March, or in Bavaria or Deelen from September onwards. Nevertheless, the relationship had prospered to the extent that Helmut now looked upon her as his future wife. We can only speculate as to Helmut's family's attitude to their son's involvement with Lena: he was only twenty-two years old – young for marriage, particularly in wartime – and Lena was four years his senior; furthermore, she was of Russian birth and, as she herself had known when she had thought it necessary to use a false name when first writing to him, the Russians did not enjoy great popularity in Germany. Apparently intending to let his family meet Lena and to obtain their approval of her, Helmut wrote home on the 1st of December:

> Today is the first day in Advent. This year, particularly, I can celebrate it especially happily. Beneath a magnificent Advent wreath that my dear Lena has sent me I am thinking not only of you, but also of her. Looking ahead to my leave, which I hope she and I can spend with you over the New Year, my heart is filled with a special joy and thankfulness.

In January 1941 another letter home announced the first victory of Lent's 6./NJG 1, scored by *Oberleutnant* Reinhold Eckardt on the 9th of the month. Armstrong-Whitworth Whitley Mark V of No. 78 Squadron, serial number T4203, had taken off at 1757 hours from Dishforth in Yorkshire for a raid aimed at synthetic oil plants in Gelsenkirchen in the Ruhr Valley. She came down on the way home at 2318 hours between Millingen aan de Rijn and Kekerdom, on the Dutch/German border southeast of Arnhem. The five-man crew, all sergeants[61], died. The profit and loss figures of this raid make thought-provoking reading. 135 aircraft took part: there were 60 Wellingtons, 36 Blenheims, 20 Hampdens and 19 Whitleys, carrying a total of around 640 young aircrew man and something like 450 tons of bombs. Only 56 crews claimed to have found and attacked the individual targets. The Germans reported bombs dropping not only in Gelsenkirchen but also in the adjacent towns of Buer, Horst and Hessler. How many of the bombs

---

[61] Sergeants C. A. Smith (pilot), S. H. Burley, L. D. Norman, A. W. Astle, and V. Tarrant. All are buried in Mook cemetery, south of Arnhem.

actually hit Gelsenkirchen itself is not recorded, but is seems unlikely to
have been many – only one person was killed in that town. The Whitley
claimed by Eckhardt was the only RAF loss that night. There is no record
of damage to oil plants. The results of this attack were not untypical for
the period.

The first kill by Lent's *Staffel* was, of course, encouraging, but Lent and
his men still felt discouraged by their apparent lack of progress. They
had been operational for twelve weeks, and they only had one kill to
show for the many times they had been sent into the air. Other units were
doing better. The total shot down by the *Geschwader* now stood at sixty,
against which 6./NJG 1's single victory looked rather pathetic. Thirty-
three of the victories scored by the *Geschwader*, however, had been
claimed by the *Fernnachtjäger*, the long-distance intruders attacking
Bomber Command over its home bases. The 6./NJG 1 pilots were still
learning the frustrating trade of night fighting, and just then their more
experienced comrades in other *Staffeln* were not, in fact, having much
greater success. During the twelve weeks of 6./NJG 1's operational
career, for example, 1./NJG 1 and 4./NJG 1 had each shot down only
three bombers, while 2./NJG 1 had only scored twice. The nature of
night fighting was such that luck played a great part when it came to
being in the right place at the right time to see and attack an RAF
bomber, and luck did not seem to be with Lent or his pilots. Lent himself
was young, ambitious and keen to make his mark   and he perhaps felt
even more depressed with the state of things than did his subordinates,
because as *Staffelkapitän* he should be encouraging his men by example,
which meant that he, particularly, should be tasting success.

Despite his contemporary lack of success as a night fighter, Lent, with
his seven victories as a *Zerstörer* pilot and his reputation as an outstanding
pilot, was looked up to and admired by both aircrew and ground crew.
One wireless operator, Otto Karl Dombrowsky, welcomed it when the
opportunity to fly with Lent arose – but after he had done so he was
disappointed. Most of the pilots, it seemed, left all communication with
the ground to the *Funker*, but Lent preferred to do it himself.
Dombrowsky writes:

> At Deelen in 1940 we were still flying *Helle Nachtjagd* in cooperation with the
> *Flak*. You flew to a radio beacon and played ring-a-roses, flying round and
> round the beacon until the controller on the ground vectored you on to the
> enemy bomber. We got behind the bomber and reported '*Otto Otto*', which
> meant 'Target in searchlight', and then we went into the attack.
>
> I was *Funker* for *Oberleutnant* Uellenbeck, who was a *Staffelkapitän*. One day
> Uellenbeck was Duty Operations Officer, a duty that *Staffelkapitäne* did quite
> often. *Oberleutnant* Lent came to me if I would care to fly a mission with him.
> His *Funker*, Kubisch, was sick or on leave. I felt proud, because *Oberleutnant*
> Lent was already something of a legend and he had more kills to his name
> than we had.
>
> When I was flying with Uellenbeck I was used to talking with the ground
> station on the R/T, getting bearings and doing the navigation myself, and I

expected that it would be the same with *Oberleutnant* Lent. But no sooner had I made contact with the ground station than I heard on the intercom, 'Good, I'll do all the rest. Keep a good look out astern and keep an eye on the sky.' We didn't score that night. And so the trip was a disappointment for me. It just didn't feel right, and I wanted to play my part. I found out later that *Oberleutnant* Lent had a reputation for doing everything himself and that he made it his business to know everything there was to know.

To this day I am proud to have flown with *Oberleutnant* Lent.

There was another victory for the *Staffel* on 15 February when *Feldwebel* Kalinowski shot down a Wellington at Barchem, between Apeldoorn and Enschede. The Wellington, Y8247 LS-R, captained by Pilot Officer C. B. Dove, was from No. 15 Squadron, based at Wyton. Its target had been another Ruhr oil refinery, this time at Sterkrade. Two of the crew of five survived and became prisoners of war. Following this victory, 6./NJG 1 did not score again until the month of May, while other units on NJG 1 achieved no fewer than 57 victories and the *Fernnachtjäger,* by now redesignated II./NJG 2, claimed about thirty victories over England.

Helmut's lack of success led him to request an official interview with his *Geschwaderkommodore, Major* Wolfgang Falck, who writes:

I first met Helmut Lent when he was a brand-new *Leutnant* when I./ZG 76 was formed at Fürstenwalde in Spring 1938 and I was *Kapitän* of the Second *Staffel.* Of the new junior officers posted in to us, Lent stood out immediately. He was a *Leutnant* of athletic, wiry, elegant, slim appearance, self-confident and with outstanding composure, both inward and outward. His sense of humour and his occasional roguish grin could disarm any superior officer when Lent, in his own light-hearted way, expressed criticism or made suggestions. He was a young officer of high ethical professionalism, an outstanding pilot and, within the framework of his own self-discipline, a daredevil.

Lent had been a *Staffelkapitän* since January 1940, and he now held that position with 6./NJG 1. It was the beginning of the great battle, not only against incoming aircraft but also against weather and technology. There was, in practical terms, still no radar control from the ground, not to mention radar within the aircraft itself, and the R/T was very prone to breaking down. Unserviceability caused by icing, plus all the other problems of weather and technology in the field of blind flying, which was not very well developed, had to be overcome. And one needed an element of luck to find enemy bombers in the darkness.

At first this flier's luck, which Lent more or less took for granted, was conspicuous by its absence. Various members of his *Staffel* had already been able to score kills, but so far the *Staffelkapitän* himself had not seen a single enemy. He had come to the conclusion, as he put it, that he was not suited to night fighting, and he wanted to be posted back to a *Zerstörer* unit. This request gave rise to a long discussion with Lent, whom I had come to know very well in the past years, both personally and as a pilot. I told him that I completely understood his request, but I asked him to give Fate, himself, and me as a young *Geschwaderkommodore,* a chance. If he did not get a kill within the next four weeks I would support his application for a transfer. On 12 May Lent

scored his first night kill – the ice was broken!

Early 1941, riding 'Lady Grey'.

It is likely that in fact only two members of Lent's *Staffel*, Eckhardt and Kalinowski, had scored kills when this interview took place, rather than the 'various' that Falck wrote of. But that is splitting hairs. The month of May was already in its second week when there was a dramatic change in the good fortune of Lent's pilots and then of Lent himself. On the early morning of May the 9th, when the RAF carried out attacks on Hamburg and Bremen, *Oberleutnant* Eckhardt and *Oberfeldwebel* Schönherr each destroyed a Wellington, and two nights later *Leutnant* von Bonin, and Eckhardt and Schönherr again, claimed a Wellington, a Whitley and a Blenheim respectively. Then, on the 13th of May, a Monday, Lent wrote home to his Mother again:

> I have a happy piece of news for you, Father and Ulla. During the night from Sunday to Monday, after my little sweetheart had visited me on Saturday and Sunday, I shot two bombers down – my first two night-time victories. Probably Lena's visit had put me in the right mood. Once again God our Father watched over me so faithfully that there wasn't a single bullet-hole in my aircraft.

May 1941. Helmut
Lent at the wreckage
of his first night-
time kill.

An account written immediately after Lent's first kills survives: it is not
known who wrote it, although the style suggests that it was an official war
correspondent:

At last, after a long wait in the readiness room of an airfield in North
Germany[62], comes the order to scramble. At 0035 hours the Me 110, the night-
black bird, lifts off from the ground and flies towards the enemy. After circling
and searching for some time Lent finally sees an enemy bomber caught in a
cone of searchlights. At last he has seen the enemy, at last he's in contact with
the foe!

Helmut dives in pursuit, but the bomber manages to escape from the lights.
But now that he is in touch with the enemy, Lent doesn't let that upset him. He
continues to fly in the presumed direction, and soon, with his excellent night
vision, he recognises the outline of the enemy machine, a pale shadow against
the horizon. 'Stay calm! Aim carefully!' he says to himself. He closes right in,
moves into the most favourable attack position – one press on the trigger and
there are flames coming from the bomber. If falls smoking to the ground.

---

[62] Lent was flying from Schleswig that night. See Chapter 6.

Lfde. Nr. des Fluges	Führer	Begleiter	Muster	Zulassungs-Nr.	Zweck des Fluges	Flug Start Ort	Landung Tag	Tageszeit	Ort	Tag	Tageszeit	Flugdauer	Kilometer	Bemerkungen
89.	Lent	R. Richter	B.F110	G9+CP	Nachtjagd	Schleswig	10.5.41.	01:15	Schleswig	10.5.	02:00	115'		129
90.	"	"	"	"	"		12.5.41.	00:35	"	12.5.	02:20	105'	1,20	130 2 Abschüsse Wellington
91.	"	"	"	G9+GP			10.5.41.	00:15	"	16.5.	01:40	95'		131
92.	"	"	"	G9+CP	Mar.A.Hellflug	"	20.5.41.	13:53	"	20.5.	14:23	30'		
93.	"	"	"	"	Überprüfung		31.5.41.	15:00	Stade	31.5.	15:25	25'		
94.	"	"	"	G9+AP	Zielflug für Flug	Stade	3.6.41.	14:55	"	3.6.	15:40	35'		
95.	"	"	"	G9+CP			3.6.41.	16:40	"	3.6.	17:40	60'		
96.	"	"	"			"	3.6.41.	22:45	"	4.6.	00:15	90'		
97.	"	"	Kleem	A7+CR	Verbindungsflug	"	4.6.41.	17:40	"	4.6.	18:45	65'		
98.	"	"	BF110	G9+CP	Zielflug für Flug	"	4.6.41.	22:45	"	4.6.	23:45	40'		
99.	"	"	"	"		"	6.6.41.	18:45	"	6.6.	14:40	85'		
100.	"	"	"	"		"	6.6.41.	23:40	"	7.6.	01:15	115'		
101.	"	Lütrich	"	"	T.J.-Flug	"	9.6.	15:59	"	9.6.	16:49	50'		
102.	"	"	"	"	Überlandflug	"	12.6.	15:04	Leeuwarden	12.6.	15:52	48'		

Once the first kill has been made, the spell is broken. And so it was with Helmut. Just a few moments later, again hunting in the dark, he sends another British bomber to earth in a column of fire. The first kill in the dark, outside the searchlight cone, has pleased him so much that when he sees the second enemy he positions himself to one side and waits until this one, too, is outside the criss-crossing beams and then finds him with his naked eye and makes his attack.

Lent now had no need – nor, probably, any desire – to go back to *Major* Falck and ask him again to support an application to leave night fighting and return to a *Zerstörer* unit. His *Staffel* now had a total of eleven kills to its credit, of which he himself, their leader, had claimed two. And it is clear from the text of his letter to his mother that his family approved of Lena.

Pages from Lent's logbook showing his first two victories as a night fighter. Entry No. 90 shows Lent taking off from Schleswig at 0035 hrs. on 12 May 1941 with Richter as his *Funker* in Bf 110 G9+CP and landing back there at 0220 hrs. The right-hand column reads, '130. 2 victories, Wellington.' The '130' shows it to be his 130th operational flight.

CHAPTER SIX

May to December 1941
From Staffelkapitän to
Gruppenkommandeur

To explain, in part at least, the sudden change in the operational fortunes of *Oberleutnant* Helmut Lent and his *Staffel* we might go back to early 1941, when, on the 15th of January, the Commander-in-Chief of Bomber Command, Air Marshal Sir Richard Peirse, was directed by the Air Staff that his Command's primary aim until further notice should continue to be the destruction of German's synthetic oil plants. This priority was based on an official assessment that 'the latest reports and analysis on Germany's oil position reveals that the Axis Powers will be passing through their most critical period as regards their oil resources during the next six months'[63], and the directive went on to assert that, 'On the assumption that our present scale of air attack on the enemy's oil plants is maintained, their oil position may be causing them grave anxiety by the Spring of 1941.' There is no doubt that oil supplies were, and would remain, a subject of concern to the leaders of the Third Reich, but even so there does seem to have been a considerable lack of realism in the Air Staff's assumption that Bomber Command's attacks at that time were having a serious impact on production. In any case, oil targets were soon discarded, temporarily at least, in a directive inspired by Winston Churchill himself and dated 9 March 1941, in which the Air Staff instructed Peirse that 'the Prime Minister has ruled that for the next four months we should devote our energies to defeating the attempt of the enemy to strangle our food supplies and our connection with the United States.' This meant, Churchill said, that U-boats and long-range maritime reconnaissance aircraft, their production and their operations, must be targeted to the exclusion of other objectives. A list of specific targets was appended in which such places as Kiel, Bremen, Hamburg and Vegesack (near Bremen) featured. At once Peirse turned his sights towards these northern targets, which meant that there would be many more RAF flights over Holland and hence more opportunities for the German night-fighter units there to attack and shoot down bombers. In

---

[63] Official History Part IV, Page 132.

March Hamburg was visited twice, Bremen twice, Kiel and Wilhelmshaven once each, and in addition the Command went twice to Berlin. In April there were five raids on Kiel, one on Bremen and two on Berlin; and in May five visits to Hamburg, two to Bremen and one each to Kiel and Berlin. There were, of course, many other lesser raids. During this period the pattern of RAF operations was changing. Progressively larger forces were being devoted to individual targets, and bombing was being concentrated into a shorter time-span. Like players at a vast chess board, the Germans reacted to the shift of emphasis in Bomber Command's targeting by the rapid redeployment of their night-fighter units to threatened areas whenever it seemed likely that a raid might be mounted. Between 4 April and 3 May, for example, Lent – and presumably all or part of his *Staffel* – made approximately twenty switches between airfields such as Deelen, Rheine, Schleswig, Jever and Wittmundhafen. It is interesting to note that Lent's logbook also shows him flying three daytime operations during this period, one entered as *'See-Sperrflug'* (sea blockade flight) and two as *'Feindflug'* ('operation' – literally 'enemy flight'). Presumably these sorties were in response to RAF aircraft flying anti-shipping and reconnaissance patrols in the area of the German Bight.

Oberleutnant Helmut Woltersdorf in conversation with Wolfgang Falck at Jever.

From the 3rd until at least the 20th of May 1941, 6./NJG 1 operated from Schleswig. Helmut had been there when, as recounted above, Lena visited him, and it was from there his *Staffel* scored their eleven successes that month, including Lent's two on the night of the 11th/12th, when Bomber Command sent 92 aircraft to attack Hamburg and 81 to attack Bremen. It was a clear night, and considerable damage was caused to both cities, but the large majority of it was to residential and business area, not to industrial targets. Three Wellingtons failed to return to England; in addition to the two that Lent claimed another member of his *Staffel*, *Leutnant* Linke, claimed one. The same night *Leutnant* von Bonin claimed a Blenheim destroyed, bringing the night's claims by the *Staffel* to four. But we are faced with an apparent discrepancy – there were no Blenheims flying operationally that night. One Hampden failed to return from the Bremen raid, but the possibility that von Bonin might have misidentified his victim is ruled out by the fact that the Hampden crashed at Medemblik, on the west shore of the Ijsselmeer, and was positively attributed to *Oberleutnant Woltersdorf* of 4./NJG 1.

Gefreiter Walter Kubisch, Lent's regular *Funker*, was not flying with him at this period, and therefore did not share the satisfaction of success after so long a period of frustration. He had last flown with Lent on 15 February, and would not fly with him again until 9 June. In the wireless operator's position when Lent scored his first night victories was one Richter, who had been flying regularly with him since mid-April. Other wireless operators who flew with Lent during Kubisch's absence were Friedrich Johrden (regular *Funker* to von Bonin), Wengorsch, Hummel and Zwickl. It is possible that Kubisch was away from his unit to participate in an NCO's training course, the successful completion of which was a prerequisite before promotion to *Unteroffizier*: it is, however, also possible that he was in hospital, as is suggested in an unconfirmed contemporary report.

Short Stirling

Almost immediately following their May successes, 6./NJG 1 began   Avro Manchester
another period characterised by frequent shifts from airfield to airfield,
and, at first, only limited results. Flying from Stade, *Feldwebel* Kalinowski
claimed a Stirling in the early hours of the 3rd of June in the course of a
minor raid to Berlin, the first four-engined bomber to have been shot
down by the *Staffel*. Three new heavies were being gradually introduced
into the RAF's bomber force at this period, the Short Stirling, the
Handley-Page Halifax and the Avro Manchester, the first two of which
were powered by four engines, while the Manchester had only two. All
three bombers had been originally designed in the mid-thirties to Air
Ministry specifications calling for aircraft that would carry a greater load
of bombs faster, further and higher than the Hampdens, Wellingtons and
Whitleys. As is now a matter of history, the Stirling was a unsatisfactory   Avro Lancaster

bomber and did not last long in front-line service, the Halifax also had its faults but improved with modification, and the Manchester, after repeated difficulties with its two Napier engines, was withdrawn and replaced by a four-engined version, the Lancaster, which proved to be an outstanding bomber and formed the backbone of the Bomber Command fleet until the end of the war and beyond.

On the 13th of June 1941 *Oberleutnant* Helmut Lent celebrated his twenty-third birthday. Already a successful *Staffelkapitän* and fighter ace, he had his foot on the ladder to enduring fame in the world of military aviation. Nine days later the *Führer*, in an unparalled act of political and strategic misjudgement, launched *Barbarossa*, the invasion of the Soviet Union. On the 30th of the month he wrote home again. It was a letter of no little interest:

> After a short pause for rest I am able to report new successes. During the night of 27/28 June I succeeded in shooting down a Whitley and probably a Wellington as well. So far, however, the latter one hasn't been found. Then, on the night of 29/30 June, there were three more, three 'Short Stirlings', a new kind of bomber. I saw two of them go down in flames myself, so there's no doubt about them. The first one was a very tough opponent. Although I had set his port-inner engine on fire, he flew on into the Flak fire over Bremen, where I couldn't follow him, and crash-landed later southwest of Bremen. Thank God, the prisoners said that it was a Messerschmitt 110 that shot them down, so the Flak can hardly claim it. The third bloke shot one of my engines

30 June 1941. The official confirmation of the destruction of a Short Stirling by *Oberstleutnant* Helmut Lent. It has taken just under a year for the confirmation to be issued by Berlin. This was Lent's 4th victory by night and his 11th overall. In all likelihood the aircraft was a Stirling Mk. 1 of No. 7 Heavy Bomber Squadron, N3664 (MG-Z), which was destroyed during an attack on Hamburg with the loss of all its crew.

PLUMSTEAD FLYING HERO NOW REPORTED KILLED.

NEWS OF HIS DEATH COMES FROM GERMANY.

The many friends of Flight-Sergt. Dennis H. Poole, D.F.M., of 10, Gatling Road, Plumstead, will regret to learn that he has been reported missing believed killed in action over Germany.

Mrs. K. Stevens, who has brought Dennis us from a child, has received information that notification of his death on June 30th

FLIGHT-SERGT. D. POOLE, D.F.M.

was sent in an official German report to the International Red Cross Committee at Geneva. The report also stated that he had been buried at Zeven, in Germany.

Flight-Sergeant Poole, who was twenty years of age, was an air gunner and wireless operator, having joined the Royal Air Force six months before the outbreak of war. He was a former scholar of the Plumstead Central School, and at one time was employed in Woolwich Arsenal.

We announced the award of the D.F.M. to him in February, and he received the medal in March for his service during flights over Germany.

out, and as a result I made a smooth night-time belly landing. Nothing happened to me or my old *Funker*. My successes are, of course, due to my little fiancée, who visited me on Saturday and Sunday, just as she did in Schleswig. On the 1st of July, I'm sorry to say, I have to take over a new, bigger *Staffel*. I'm giving up my 6th *Staffel* very unwillingly. In a certain way it's my child. With it I've been able to get eighteen kills. But the Lord has mercifully spared me, and my trust in Him continues...

The night of 27/28 June, when Lent claimed a Whitley and possibly a Wellington too, had seen an RAF raid of moderate strength – 75 Wellingtons and 35 Whitleys – against Bremen. Weather conditions for the bomber force were very bad, and it seems that many of the bombs destined for Bremen fell on Hamburg, 100 kilometres away, while very few hit Bremen itself. For the first time, Bomber Command records refer to 'intense night-fighter attacks', and eleven Whitleys and three Wellingtons

(Left) Flight Sergeant Denis Poole, DFM, wireless operator of Stirling N3664, shot down by Lent on 30 June 1941. That night Lent claimed three Stirlings, but only two were confirmed. Fourteen men, including Poole, died in the two bombers with which Lent was credited.

(Right) Newspaper article reporting the death of Flight Sergeant Poole, DFM, a victim of Lent.

failed to return. The Whitley that Lent claimed was confirmed, but not so the Wellington. It was Whitley V T4297, DY-?, of No. 102 Squadron at Topcliffe, one of four aircraft that the squadron lost that night. Very unusually, all five members of the crew survived to become prisoners of war. Sergeant Brian Booth, the rear gunner, said later:

'We set off from Topcliffe with the 'met' officer forecasting good weather conditions on the way. As it turned out we ran into an unpleasant front as we approached the enemy coast. This gave icing conditions at about 8,000 feet which meant that we were unable to climb above or into cloud and were 'stooging' along, beautifully silhouetted against the cloud – a sitting duck. It was not long before we were caught in the cones of searchlights and a fighter came straight in. That was the end; smoke and the smell of cordite and the old Whitley flying at all angles, even upside down! Fortunately Jimmy Cullen[64], our pilot, was an experienced Skipper and he did a great job getting the old kite to fly straight and level long enough for us all to get out by parachute. There were no serious injuries apart from poor old Mike Featherstone, the second pilot, who got a bullet in his bum![65]

A belly-landed Bf 110 of the *Staffel* that Lent took over in 1941, 4./NJG 1. The all-black paintwork shows that this was a very early example of the night-fighter version, as does the '*Spanner*' infrared target-seeking device forward of the cockpit.

Bremen was again the main target two nights later, on 29/30 June, but in addition a small force, interestingly made up principally of new-generation machines – there were thirteen Stirlings, six Manchesters, two Halifaxes and seven Wellingtons – went to Hamburg, where they caused not inconsiderable damage. Four Stirlings and two Wellingtons failed to return. Only two of the three Stirlings that Lent claimed were subsequently confirmed as his. It is quite possible that Lent's first victim, shot down at 0140 hours on the 30th, was N6001 of No. 7 Squadron, Oakington, captained by Squadron Leader W. T. C. Seale, and virtually

---

[64] Chorley gives the pilot's name as Sergeant J. R. Culley.
[65] From 'It's Suicide but it's Fun'., by Chris Goss.

certain that his second was N3664, MG-Z, also from No. 7 Squadron, which was captained by Flying Officer V. R. Hartwright, DFM. All of Hartwright's crew perished, including the twenty-year-old wireless operator Flight Sergeant Dennis Poole, who had been awarded the Distinguished Flying Medal just three weeks earlier for service with No. 151 Squadron. *Hauptmann* Ehle, *Kommandeur* of II./ NJG 1, shot down the fourth Stirling that did not return.

Helmut's letter is also of interest because he refers to Lena as *'meine Braut'* – 'my bride', translated here as 'my fiancée'. A more suitable translation might perhaps be 'bride-to-be'. But the message is clear – Helmut and Lena were going to marry.

The new *Staffel* that Lent was to take over on 1 July 1941 was 4./NJG 1. It was stationed at Leeuwarden in Friesland and already had 27 victories to its credit, making it by far the most successful *Staffel* of NJG 1. Among its pilots were several who were destined to become household names in the world of night fighting: *Oberleutnant* Helmut Woltersdorf (24 victories,

Oberfeldwebel Paul Gildner. Seen here as an *Oberleutant*, with the *Ritterkreuz*

Major Wolfgang Falck, *Kommodore* NJG 1, in conversation with Helmut Lent, probably in July/August 1941.

killed in action June 1942); *Leutnant* Ludwig Becker (44 victories, killed in action February 1943); *Leutnant Prinz* Egmont *zur* Lippe-Weissenfeld (51 victories, killed in a flying accident in March 1944); *Leutnant* Leopold Fellerer (41 victories, survived the war); *Oberfeldwebel* Paul Gildner (46 victories, killed in action February 1943) and *Unteroffizier* Siegfried Ney (12 victories, killed in action February 1942). When Lent assumed command there were already four recognised aces in the unit, Gildner with eleven victories to his credit, plus two he had scored on *Zerstörer;* Lippe-Weissenfeld with seven; *Feldwebel* Hans Rasper with six; and Woltersdorf who, although he had so far only shot down two by night, had an impressive record of eight kills on *Zerstörer*. Nonetheless Lent, with seven *Zerstörer* victories to add to the five that he had scored with 6./NJG 1, had no reason the feel overawed.

The reputation enjoyed by Lent's new *Staffel* rested not only on its operational successes but also on the part it had played, and was still playing, in the development of night-fighting techniques and tactics. It had been at Leeuwarden since December 1940 and unlike Lent's former *Staffel*, 6./NJG 1, had concentrated its efforts on finding and destroying British bombers without the aid of searchlights. *Helle Nachtjagd*, it was recognised, was unsatisfactory and would need to be replaced by something that offered more potential for success.

In the search for a more efficient means of destroying the RAF bombers there were two fundamental problems that needed to be resolved: firstly the fighter pilot had to be brought in close enough to the bomber to give him a reasonable chance of attacking it, and for the final stages of the interception he needed help to get within firing range: all experience gathered so far showed that by night the human eye could not be relied upon to see another aircraft at anything more that minimal distance. Radar would seem to offer solutions.

The Germans had two operational radars that might be adapted to provide a solution to the problem of bringing a night fighter into close proximity to its target, the *Freya* and the *Würzburg*. *Freya* was the early warning search radar that had been used to good effect in the Battle of the German Bight in December 1939 and in Wolfgang Falck's night-fighting experiments at Aalborg in April and May 1940. *Würzburg* was a radar designed to control searchlights and anti-aircraft guns, and it had a height-finding capability, which *Freya* lacked. One of the Signals officers who had been involved in Falck's earlier experiments was *Leutnant* Hermann Diehl, who conceived an ingenious modification to the *Freya* called '*A/N Peilung*'. The 'picture' on the CRT (Cathode-Ray Tube) of the modified *Freya* enabled a controller to deduce the relative positions of bomber and fighter and so to pass instructions and information to the fighter pilot, directing him into the vicinity of the target aircraft and making it possible, sometimes, for him to obtain visual contact and carry out an attack. Information on the altitude of the enemy machine was provided by a *Würzburg*. 4./NJG 1 had conducted satisfactory trials with the system, which became known as *Dunkle Nachtjagd*, or 'Dark Night Fighting', sometimes abbreviated as *Dunaja*.

Despite these very positive steps forward, there still remained the problem of getting the fighter to within firing range of the bomber: in the vastness of a dark night sky, even if there was moonlight, chance played a great part when it came to seeing another machine, even when one was in fact quite close. When 4./NJG 1 had originally been formed, however, it had inherited a small number of experimental night-fighter aircraft in the form of Dornier 17s and Dornier 25s, some of them equipped with an infrared night-vision device known as *Spanner*. Flying one of these machines from Deelen on the 18th of October 1940, *Leutnant* Ludwig Becker had made the first *Dunaja* kill of the war. At this early stage of night-fighter experiments communication between aircraft and ground station was by means of Morse W/T (wireless-telegraphy), but Diehl brought Becker so close to the Wellington that he did not need to resort to *Spanner*.

4./NJG 1 had moved from Deelen to Leeuwarden in December 1940. Leeuwarden's geographical location meant that it was literally in the front line of the air defence of the Third Reich. Ahead of the airfield, in a vast sweep following the coastline from the Scheldt estuary to the Danish border, a number of adjacent so-called 'Dark Night-Fighting Areas' (*Dunkelnachtjagd-Gebiete*) were progressively set up: a more appropriate equivalent might be 'Radar Control Areas'. They had names of animals, birds, fish and so on. Leeuwarden itself was in the centre of *Löwe* (Lion), while ahead, on the coast itself, was *Tiger*; to the southwest were *Hering* (Herring) and *Hamster*, and to the north and east *Languste* (Lobster) and *Wolf*. Each area had a radio beacon to which fighters would be despatched to 'hold' while awaiting the approach of bombers, as well as *Freya* and *Würzburg* radars. Later the *Würzburg Riese* (*Würzburg* Giant), an enlarged and more powerful version, would be introduced. Then there was a control room, from which the Fighter Control Officer would communicate with the fighters allocated to him. Set back inland along a line roughly Kiel – Bremen – Arnhem – Louvain – Mons was the searchlight belt that the RAF crews soon christened the 'Kammhuber Line'. It was to this quite sophisticated night-fighting environment that Lent came on 1 July 1941.

Given the successes of 4./NJG 1, both operational and developmental, one might reasonably wonder why Wolfgang Falck had seen fit to remove its *Kapitän*, particularly when it also meant separating Lent from his own *Staffel* just at a time when it seemed to be flourishing after its early period in the doldrums. Possibly the reason lay partly in the fact that *Oberleutnant* Hans Röderer, whom he was to replace, had not yet scored a single victory, but there are also indications that under Röderer discipline on the *Staffel* was lax. At about that time the *Hauptfeldwebel* (Sergeant Major) of the *Staffel*, Künstler, had been moved. Horst Diener, the Clerical NCO of the *Gruppe*, writes[66]: 'After Paul Künstler left the 4th *Staffel*, discipline in the *Staffel* ceased to exist. At that time, as *Gruppe* Clerk, I was writing out more charge sheets than combat reports, which is saying something! *Oberleutnant* Lent's presence was a great spur to the *Staffel* in every respect.' It is fair to assume that Falck moved Lent from the 6th *Staffel* to the 4th not only because of his operational record but also because of his clear potential for a command and leadership.

Helmut Lent flew into Leeuwarden from Stade in a Ju 52 to take over his command. One wonders what thoughts passed through his mind as he flew towards the Dutch airfield. He was just twenty-three and a junior officer of comparatively recent seniority. Slim, blond-haired and fair-skinned he looked even younger than his years, so much so that he still had the nickname *'Bubi'* ('Nipper'), and here he was, under orders to take over the most successful *Staffel* in the night-fighter force. He would have to command men with established reputations, who might well bear a grudge at the removal of the *Staffelkapitän* under whom they had largely established those reputations. He had, it was true, himself shot down five enemy night bombers – including two as recently as the preceding night – but, as the long period devoid of success that he had suffered before he had opened his score told him, luck paid a large part in these things, and he might easily begin his new job with another run of bad fortune. It was not a prospect that anyone – even someone as inherently self-confident as he was – could face without some apprehension. Röderer hadn't made his mark in combat, and Röderer had been replaced – might the same fate await Lent? Yet determined as

---

[66] *Jägerblatt*, the magazine of the *Gemeinschaft der Jagdflieger*.

he was to make a success of his new appointment and to justify Wolfgang Falck's faith in him, even Lent could not have foreseen the extraordinary way in which the month of July 1941, his first weeks with 4./NJG 1, would develop.

★   ★   ★

Lent began his flying with the new unit immediately: on the 2nd July he did a number of familiarisation flights on a Dornier 215, the first one with *Leutnant* Woltersdorf at the controls and the subsequent ones solo. The following day, the 3rd, he did some more local flying, this time in a Bf 110, G9+FM, and at 0117 hours the following morning he was scrambled in the same aircraft against a small force of incoming Hampdens and Wellingtons returning from an attack on Bremen. Among them was Wellington 1C R1492 of No. 301 (Polish) Squadron, and Lent shot it down at Exloërmond at 0034 hours, just seventeen minutes after taking off. He had made a good start in his new field of responsibility. There was another operational scramble on the morning of the 5th, but he made no contact with the enemy in a flight that lasted just under two hours. In the evening, however, he took off at 2351, and at 0056 hours on the 6th he had a further success, destroying a Whitley that came down a few miles to the west of Coervorden, close to the Dutch/German border.

At this point the sequence of events becomes rather difficult to reconstruct, because there are errors of date in Lent's logbook. In addition there are no entries between 9 and 24 July[67]. When one cross-checks with other documentary and published sources, however, an accurate picture emerges. Just before midnight on the 6th July Lent's comrade *Oberleutnant* Woltersdorf shot down a Vickers Wellington into the sea off the island of Texel, but in doing so he himself was shot down. Woltersdorf managed to ditch his Do 215 successfully, although both of his crewmen were injured. Reportedly Woltersdorf and his crew were rescued 'a few hours later' by the German Air-Sea Rescue Service, but Lent, according to his log-book, flew searches for a missing aircraft – presumably the wreck of the Dornier – over the sea on the 7th, 8th and 9th of July in a Klemm KL 35 low-wing two-seater monoplane and a Bf 110. Whether the wreck was found is not known.

On the 8th of July Lent wrote home, 'I haven't told you anything about my new field of activity yet, and it's about time I did. Fit and cheerful and safe in God's hands, I can report to you three further successes in my new *Staffel*. Last night my eighth night kill went down, that is my fifteenth victory. I'm enormously pleased that I've been able to get off to such a good start in my new *Staffel*.'

Lent's eighth night-time victim was a Whitley Mark V from No. 77 Squadron stationed at Topcliffe in Yorkshire. Its captain was Flight Lieutenant C. R. Petley, while the other four members of the crew were

---

[67] The missing entries do appear, but not until February 1942, out of sequence and without any explanation.

Taken shortly before the war, this photograph shows members of the Civil Air Guard at Maylands aerodrome, Romford. Reg Luce is wearing a raincoat and trilby hat.

sergeants. The bomber was heading for Osnabrück to bomb rail targets, and its route took it over Holland and within reach of IV./NJG 1. Petley's machine had lifted off from Topcliffe at 2230 hours on the 7th of July.

The Whitley's wireless operator was Sergeant Reg Luce. Before the war Luce had been learning to fly with the Civil Air Guard, a voluntary force aimed at providing pilots for the RAF, but when war came he elected to join the RAF as a trainee wireless operator, which afforded a more rapid route to operational flying. He already had about thirty operations to his credit and should soon finish his first tour.

Lent took off from Leeuwarden at 0010 hours and he shot the lumbering Whitley down 45 minutes later. Luce's recollections of Lent's attack are understandably imprecise. His first intimation that something was wrong was when he became aware that the other members of the crew were bailing out: he had not heard anything to suggest that they had come under attack, nor had he heard an order from the pilot to abandon the aircraft, possibly because he had been working his radio and was therefore not on the intercom circuit. He left his seat and was clipping on his parachute pack when the aircraft was raked with a burst of cannon fire. One shell hit him in his left hip and, as it later transpired, passed right through his body. Somehow or other, in a semiconscious state, he managed to escape from the aircraft via the escape hatch in the roof, and his descent came to an end when he struck a tree and his harness became entangled in its branches. All was darkness, and he had

no means of telling how high he was above the ground. He remained
suspended there throughout the night until he saw, by the first light of
dawn, that he was in fact only a very short distance up. He activated the
quick-release box of his parachute harness and fell to the ground. He was
in woodland and unable to move because of his terrible injuries. Drifting
in and out of consciousness he remained in that position all that day and
the following night until, at about 9 o'clock on the morning of the 9th of
July, he was found by three Dutch forestry workers. Luce was unable to
move, and so the Dutchmen brought a German officer to the scene. The
injured crewman was taken to a nunnery and thence to a Dutch hospital,
where he was operated upon by a German surgeon. During the rest of
his internment Luce was in a series of prison camps and hospitals until,
in 1943, he was repatriated under the auspices of the Red Cross as unfit
for further military service. The remainder of his crew perished.
Unaccountably, according to Dutch eyewitnesses, none of their
parachutes had opened, suggesting that they had bailed out of their
aircraft at too low a level.

In 1943, after a series of
surgical operations, Reg
Luce was repatriated
from Germany as no
longer fit for military
service. To this day he
suffers the effects of his
near-fatal wounds. Here
he is seen (centre, with
moustache) with other
repatriates at the RAF
Hospital, Halton, after
his return to England.

Although there can be no doubt that it was on the 8th of July that Reg
Luce was shot down, the victory is incorrectly entered in Lent's logbook
as having taken place on the 7th, and there are also omissions and errors
in the course of the following couple of weeks. Following his victory over
Luce's Whitley, for instance, there are only three entries in Lent's
logbook until 22 July, yet it is certain that he flew and scored during that

time. There is an explanation for his failure to keep his logbook up to date, which is revealed in a letter that he wrote to his parents on the 12th of July:

> Two days ago I scored my tenth night victory, my seventeenth[68] altogether. It was the hardest one so far. In the course of it my wireless operator and my flight mechanic were wounded. I myself was grazed on the arm by a splinter. Some other splinters, very little ones, caused a few very small wounds. But I'm in very good spirits. I will probably fly again tonight. I feel very, very sorry for my comrades, but they will both recover.

For the sortie to which this letter refers Lent was flying a Dornier 215, which carried a crew of three as opposed to the two that the Bf 110 carried. The third member of the crew was a flight mechanic (*Bordmechaniker*), and on this occasion the unfortunate man was *Feldwebel* Matschuk. Walter Kubisch suffered severe head wounds, and for some time it seemed that he would lose his sight completely. He did not fly again with Lent until October. What became of Matschuk is not known.

The aircraft that Lent shot down, but which almost brought his brilliant career to an end, was in all probability a Wellington 1C from No. 40 Squadron, piloted by Flying Officer G. C. Conran and on its way back from taking part in a minor attack on Osnabrück: 57 Wellingtons took part in that raid, but no bombs at all fell in the target area. Two German civilians were killed in nearby villages, and two Wellingtons, including the one piloted by Flying Officer Conran, failed to return. From the two crews lost, unusually, only three men died, the other nine becoming prisoners of war.

Despite his wounds Lent took off again only five days later, at 0020 hours on the 13th July, against a force of thirty-three Hampdens and twenty-eight Wellingtons heading for Bremen. He was flying Bf 110 G9+FM and in the wireless operator's seat usually occupied by Walter Kubisch was one Fuchs. Again Lent accounted for a British bomber, this time a Hampden from No. 50 Squadron, the captain of which was Pilot Officer E. D. Vivian. The air gunner's name, as it appeared on the crew list, was Sergeant H. Jackson: in reality his name was Israel Jacobovitch. It was thought advisable for aircrew with recognisably Jewish names to use an English alibi when flying over Germany in case they should be taken prisoner. Israel Jacobovitch, however, did not need to make use of the subterfuge: this was his last flight ever, as it was for all four men in the crew.

July was still not half-way through, and Lent had already added four kills to his own score and that of 4./NJG 1. If anyone on the *Staffel* had doubted his fitness to lead them, that individual's doubts were, one might conjecture, fading. But there was yet more to come. At 0014 hours on the morning of the 15th July Lent, with *Obergefreiter* Meissner as his *Funker*, destroyed Wellington Mk. II W5513 (EP-P) at Veendam in Holland, killing Pilot Officer W. G. Rowse and all his crew. The

---

[68] In fact it was his 9th night victory, and his sixteenth overall.

Wellington reportedly went down in flames after two attacks. His final kill in his first month as *Kapitän* of 4./NJG 1 came at 0354 hours on the 25th , when he shot down another Wellington in a ball of fire at Boazum, a mere nine miles or so the southwest of Leeuwarden. No one could doubt Lent's ability as a night-fighter pilot, nor his determination, nor his bravery. In less than four weeks he had accounted for seven enemy bombers, and in the course of so doing he had been wounded but had not allowed either the wounds themselves nor any psychological effect that the experience might have had on him to deter him from continuing to fly and to fight.

The entries missing from, and the errors in, Lent's logbook have a simple explanation. Lent himself did not maintain the book, but delegated that responsibility to his *Funker*, as is clear from the several styles of handwriting that appear. When Kubisch was wounded Lent did not have a 'regular' *Funker* until *Oberfeldwebel* Reinthal joined him on 22 July and took over the task. Somehow the wireless operators flying with Lent during the interregnum had neglected to maintain the logbook correctly.

After the stirring events of July, August passed at a lower level of excitement. Of the seventeen victories that the *Staffel* had scored in July, Lent had claimed seven. Now, in August, the *Staffel* shot down only eleven bombers, of which Lent's personal tally was but two. It was as if Lent, having established his credentials as leader of the *Staffel*, and hence his authority, was pausing to consolidate his position. He did, however, continue to fly operationally, taking off against Bomber Command on twelve nights of the month. His two successes, a Whitley from No. 51 Squadron and a Hampden from No. 49 Squadron, occurred on the 15th and the 29th of the month respectively: he shot down the former in a Bf 110, G9+MM, the latter in a Do 215, G9+PM.

Since being awarded his first decoration, the Iron Cross Second Class, on 21 September 1939 while fighting in Poland, Lent had received a number of further honours and awards. In October 1939 had come the Sudeten Commemoration Medal with Clasp (*Sudeten-Erinnerungsmedaille mit Spange*), in May 1940 the Iron Cross First Class (*Eisernes Kreuz 1. Klasse)* and in January 1941 the Narvik Shield (*Narvikschild*). June 1941 saw him receiving the Fighter Pilot's Operational Mission Clasp in Gold (*Frontflugspange für Jäger in Gold*)[69] and the Goblet of Honour for Special Achievement in the Air War (*Ehrenpokal für besondere Leistung im Luftkrieg*)[70], and July the Wound Badge in Black (*Verwundetenabzeichen in Schwarz*)[71]. Now, on 30 August, he joined the select band of servicemen to

---

[69] The *Frontflugspange* (Operational Mission Clasp) was awarded in three grades – Bronze after 20 operational flights, Silver after 60 and Gold after 110.
[70] In the First World War the silver *Ehrenpokal* (Goblet of Honour) had been awarded to fighter pilots after their first kill. In the Second World War the award was the personal discretion of Hermann Göring.
[71] The Wound Badge came in three stages, Black, Silver and Gold, after one, two and three wounds respectively.

A comrade adjusts
Helmut Lent's Knight's
Cross.

receive the *Ritterkreuz*, the prestigious – and, one might add, much
sought-after – Knight's Cross of the Iron Cross. The citation read:

> To date *Oberleutnant* Helmut Lent, born on the 13th June 1918 in Pyrehne
> in the District of Landsberg/Warthe, has destroyed two enemy aircraft on the
> ground as well as shooting down seven by day and thirteen by night. In the
> Polish Campaign and the occupation of Norway he proved himself a
> courageous and enthusiastic fighter pilot, and as a night fighter he has faced
> the enemy night after night in indefatigable combat readiness. His score of
> thirteen enemy bombers in ten weeks is the current result of his heroic
> operational dedication.

Heinz Huhn, a junior member of the flying personnel of IV./NJG1,
recalls Helmut Lent from this period:

> When I joined the *Nachtjagd* at Leeuwarden in 1941 Lent was still a
> *Staffelkapitän* and in ongoing competition with Paul Gildner as to who had the
> most kills. I flew with Gildner myself later. Helmut Lent was what one might
> describe as 'soldierly' in both bearing and behaviour, as well as in his inner
> principles. He was a disciplined, fair-minded but also ambitious leader of men
> both then and later, when he became a *Gruppenkommandeur*.
>
> I went to Leeuwarden as a simple corporal, and by chance I developed a
> special relationship with Lent. During the nightly periods at standby in the

rather cramped readiness room that also served as operations room at that time all the crews were crammed together into a small space. Because both he and I were lovers of classical music, however, the two of us often sat together by the radio while the rest of the aircrew were playing cards or reading. It goes without saying that we observed the formalities of our different rank. He sometimes used to question me to see if I was familiar with the composers or the operas. In this way I soon realised that behind his hard military façade there was hidden a musical and sensitive human being. When we talked about Polish and Russian music it was quite clear that he was just the opposite of chauvinistic. I was deeply touched by his death just before the end of the war.

In September 1941 Lent again enjoyed only comparatively modest success in the air, with just three additions to his score, a Whitley in the early morning of the 7th and two Wellingtons just over twenty-four hours later, between four and five o'clock on the morning of the 8th. The first of Lent's two victims in the early morning of the 8th of September was a Wellington 1C from No. 9 Squadron at Honington in Lincolnshire piloted by Sergeant Saich, DFM, which was on its way back from an attack on Berlin. The all-sergeant crew of six lost their lives. Lent's combat report read:

Confirmation of Lent's destruction of Wellington 1C Z8845, WS+?, of No. 9 Squadron on the morning of 8 September 1941, the day he began his marriage leave.

A b s c h r i f t

Der Reichsminister der Luftfahrt   Berlin, den 27.6.42
und Oberbefehlshaber der Luftwaffe
Az.29 Nr.   88809/42 (LP 5 VII)
_____

Bezug: Abschussmeldung vom 11.9.41

            An 4./N.J.G. 1
      der 4./N.J.G. 1

      wird der Abschuss einer Vickers-Wellington

                        am 8.9.41 gegen 04.04 Uhr

      durch Oblt. L e n t in Zusammenarbeit mit 10./Ln.Rgt.201

      als sechsundsechzigster Abschuss der Staffel anerkannt.

                              gez. Unterschrift

      F. d. R.
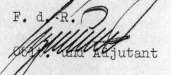
            Oblt. und Adjutant

Lent, Oberleutnant, In the field. 8.9.1941
4./Night-Fighter Geschwader No. 1.
Combat Report

On a night victory by Oblt. Lent – Ofw. Reinthal
on 8 September 1941 ca 0404 hours.

On 8.9.1941 I took off as last wave in Bf 110 G9+FM for Dunkelnachtjagd in the Raum near Leeuwarden. Shortly after reaching my waiting position I was vectored on to an outbound enemy aircraft by means of Seeburg Table. After a few minutes I recognised an outbound Wellington about 800 metres ahead and at an altitude of 4,800 metres. I attacked with several bursts of fire from astern and below, in the course of which the rear gunner was put out of action. The aircraft went down steeply with a long smoke trail and hit the ground near to Drachsterkompagnie.

(Signed) Lent.

Copy of letter translated above.

It is interesting to note that it was not until June 1942, nine months or so later, that Lent's victory was confirmed by Berlin.

There was a very good explanation for Lent's failure to shoot down more than three bombers that month. For once something more important than night fighting intervened. On Tuesday the 9th of the month, the day after he scored this, his 16th nighttime victory, he began three weeks' leave. But it was a very special leave, and it is entered in his *Soldbuch* as

The marriage of Helmut Lent and Helene 'Lena' Senokosnikov, 10 September 1941.

Helmut and Lena Lent following their marriage.

'*Hochzeitsurlaub*' – 'Wedding Leave'. He and Lena Senokosnikova were married in Wellingsbüttel, the suburb of Hamburg in which Lena lived, on the tenth day of September.

All German officers had to obtain official permission to marry, but usually such permission was little more than a bureaucratic formality. In Lent's case, however, there was a complication. Lena was of Russian origin, and when she and Helmut had first met she was not a German citizen. On the 15th of March 1941, however, she had been granted German citizenship, presumably having applied for it with a view to marriage. As one might expect, citizenship had not been granted without a thorough investigation of her racial antecedents, as is evidenced by a letter from the Headquarters of the Commander-in-Chief of the *Luftwaffe* containing the following paragraphs:

Lent's marriage
certificate.

Heiratsurkunde

(Standesamt **Hamburg-Wollingsbuttel** — — — — — — — Nr. 61 — — — —

Der **Oberleutnant Helmut Johannes Siegfried L e n t** — — — — — —,

evangelisch — — —, wohnhaft **im Felde,Feldpost Nr. L 28748** — — — —,

geboren am **13. Juni 1918** — — — — — — — — — — — — —

in **Pyrehne** —

(Standesamt **Döllensradung** — — — — — — — — — — — — Nr. **11/1918**), und

die **Korrespondentin Helene Senokosnikow** — — — — — — — — — —

griechisch katholischohnhaft **in Hamburg-Wellingsbüttel,Barkenkoppel 16**

geboren am **24. April 1914** — — — — — — — — — — — — — —

in **Moskau** —

(Standesamt — — — — — — — — — — — — — — — — — Nr. — — — —),

haben am **10. September 1941** — — — — — — — — — —

vor dem Standesamt **Hamburg-Wollingsbüttel** — — — — — — — — — —

die Ehe geschlossen.

Vermerke: —

— — — — — — — — — — — — — — — — — — — —

— — — — — — — — — — — — — — — — — — — —

— — — — — — — — — — — — — — — — — — — —

Hamburg, den **2. Juni** — — — — — 19**42**

Der Standesbeamte
In Vertretung

(Siegel)

With reference to letter D.R.d.L.u.Ob.d.L. L.P.Nr.58894/41 (5,VI),
concerning permission to marry for *Oberleutnant* Lent, attached are the
Certificates of Genealogy of *Oberleutnant* Lent's bride, *Fräulein* Helene
Senokosnikova, to be returned to *Oberleutnant* Lent.

We are informed by the *Reichssippenamt*[72] – No. 16S 107/41 of 8.9.41 – that
there is no objection to the assumption that *Fräulein* Senokosnikova is of
German or generically related blood.

It is accepted that Helene Senokosnikova is of Aryan descent.

The 'Certificates of Genealogy' mentioned included a legal document dated
January 1938 concluding that Lena 'has no Jewish ancestors on either her
paternal or her maternal side and is therefore of pure Aryan descent.'

Back from his honeymoon leave, Lent resumed operational flying on

---

[72] Literally *'Reich* Office of Genealogy'.

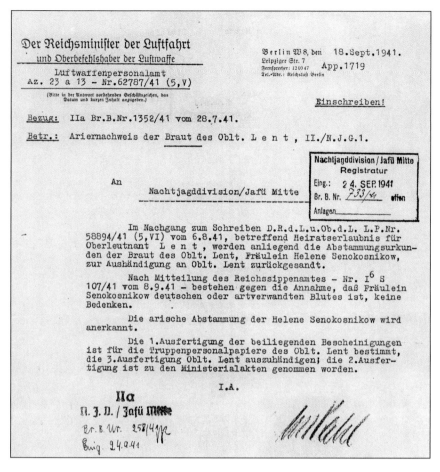

Letter from the office of the Commander-in-Chief of the *Luftwaffe* to the Night Fighter Division / Fighter Leader, Central Germany, certifying that Helene Senokosnikov is of Aryan blood and that there is therefore no objection to her marriage to Helmut Lent.

the 7th of October. The entries in his logbook for the remainder of the month show him apparently flying operationally rather less frequently but making a number of short visits to airfields in the NJG 1 area. It is likely that these visits were directly connected with a new field of responsibility for which he had already been earmarked but had not yet been promulgated. On the night of 12/13 October, however, he shot down two more aircraft, a Wellington and a Hampden, and he wrote home to tell his parents about it:

> Through God's loving kindness and with his protection I shot down two more Englishmen the night before last. The *Staffel*, too, were not idle. After the battle we had an enjoyable time. We had a few English prisoners in our mess. Some of them made a very good impression. It really is a cause for regret that we have to fight against such men.

In addition to Lent's two kills, from which there were no survivors, Paul Gildner, Siegfried Ney and Leopold Fellerer of his *Staffel* each claimed a victory.

The 12th/13th October had been a very busy, if not at all successful, night for Bomber Command with 152 aircraft aiming for Nuremberg, 99 for Bremen and 90 for a chemical factory in the village of Hüls on the western fringe of the Ruhr area. Of the 373 aircraft despatched (there were also minor raids), the biggest force of the war thus far, thirteen were lost. Clouds interfered with accurate bombing, but even allowing for that the results were abysmal. Only a few bombs fell in the main target city, Nuremberg, where one person was killed and six injured. Bombs that were intended for the main target, Nuremberg, wrought greater damage in the villages of Lauingen, sixty-five miles south of the target, and Lauffen, ninety-five miles to the west. The other attacks, on Bremen and Hüls respectively, caused only very minor damage. Of the thirteen bombers lost, night fighters claimed nine. Fifty bomber crewmen died. Leopold Fellerer's victim was a Halifax from No. 76 Squadron, operating from Middleton St. George. It crashed at Wons, a small coastal village just twenty miles west-southwest of Leeuwarden, and of the eight-man crew only the pilot, Flight Sergeant E. B. Muttart, RCAF, died, the remaining seven being taken prisoner. The rear gunner, Sergeant John Duffield, was one of the RAF crewmen entertained in the Leeuwarden officers' mess, as mentioned by Lent in his letter home. Duffield's aircraft had been a victim of *Leutnant* Leopold Fellerer, and he had been injured slightly. From the mess he was taken into the sick quarters at Leeuwarden where, the following day, he was visited by a tall, good looking German officer who introduced himself as Helmut Lent. Duffield describes how Lent visited him every day for the five or six days he stayed in sick quarters. On one occasion it was very hot in the room. Duffield continues: 'The nurses refused to open the window, and when Helmut Lent arrived and asked if there was anything I wanted I told him I would like a window open, to which he laughed and said, "They think you are trying to escape". He had words with the nursing staff and a window was opened.'

There survives an interesting published story concerning this period, probably based loosely on fact but impossible to confirm or refute. According to the story, Lent was returning to Leeuwarden after an operational sortie and was on his landing approach. There was heavy drizzle and the danger of icing. Lent's aircraft was in radio contact with the airfield, when suddenly communication was broken off. The Bf 110 came in and landed. Lent was alone in the machine, and the cockpit canopy had been jettisoned. The *Funker* had baled out at an altitude of 300 feet without being instructed to do so. The story has it that the wireless operator in question was Reinthal, but a study of Lent's logbook makes that seen extremely unlikely.

Helmut Lent had only been *Kapitän* of the 4th *Staffel* for four months, but during that short time his personal score had increased by fourteen. The Wellington and the Hampden that he claimed on the night of 12/13 October were destined to be his last successes with 4./NJG 1. During October there had been considerable activity within the higher echelons of NJG 1 and the Night-Fighter Corps. A reorganisation was afoot which was to have its effect on Lent's career, and the planning had culminated in a series of recommendations, beginning with one from Wolfgang

Falck, *Kommodore* NJG 1. It was succinct and to the point:

Operations Centre, 28.10.41

A young officer imbued with genuine military tradition and possessed of an unusual degree of daring and enterprise, who is in every regard far above the average.

Oberleutnant Lent is well suited for the position of *Gruppenkommandeur* and promotion to *Hauptmann*.

(Signed) Falck.

It was not unusual in wartime for an appointment to be made and for the formal paperwork to lag behind, which is clearly what happened in this case. On the 4th of November Lent told his parents in a letter home:

I have a welcome piece of news for you. On 1 November I became the *Kommandeur* of a night-fighter *Gruppe*. It is a great honour, but the responsibilities are also very great. Yet I know that without God's help I would never have got as far as this. Trusting in His grace I will master my new task. I will be remaining at the same location. My new command will to a large extent develop from my old *Staffel*.

Oberleutnant Helmut Lent became *Kommandeur* II./NJG 2 on the 1st November 1941. The appointment was on an acting basis, but so strong were the recommendations from his superior officers that there could be no doubt that it would be confirmed, as would the concomitant recommendation that he should be promoted to *Hauptmann*. *General* Kammhuber, for example, wrote:

Commanding General,
Corps Operations Centre,
12th Air Corps (Night-Fighter Corps.
3 November 1941

Oberleutnant Lent is one of the most successful pilots of the Night Fighter Corps. He is a young officer of a maturity far beyond his rank and age, of impeccable bearing and sense of duty, imbued with great enthusiasm for his profession and his Service.

By reason of his drive, his enthusiasm for operational flying and his tally of victories he is a shining example for his comrades and his subordinates. He has proved himself outstanding as a *Staffelkapitän*.

Oberleutnant Lent's natural abilities, achievements and personality fully guarantee his suitability for the proposed appointment of *Gruppenkommandeur*.

I request that he should be appointed *Kommandeur* of II./NJG 2 and that he should be given accelerated promotion to the rank of *Hauptmann*.

(Signed) Kammhuber.

As a Commander of a *Gruppe* Lent would lead a fighting force of three *Staffeln*, each of which would have a nominal establishment of twelve aircraft. In addition there would be a Staff flight of three machines, bringing the total number of aircraft that he might expect to have under his control to thirty-nine. The aircrew to man these machines, with a prudent reserve, would number perhaps seventy, to which would be added the members of ground crews and the usual administrative personnel.[73]

Lent's *Staffel*, 4./NJG 1, was to form the nucleus of a *Gruppe* that would be integrated into another *Geschwader*, NJG 2, as part of the ongoing expansion and rationalisation of the night-fighter force and its adaptation to meet the changing threat posed by the enemy, not only in Europe but also in the Mediterranean area and now, since June, on the Russian front. NJG 1 was a compact and closely-knit *Geschwader* firmly located in Holland and North Germany, but NJG 2 had a somewhat complex and confusing history. In the most general of terms, it had originally been formed to fly long-range intruder missions against the RAF over the North Sea and the British mainland, in which function it had performed well. At that period the *Geschwader* had comprised only one *Gruppe*, I./NJG 2. In October 1941, arguing that claims of kills over the sea and England could not be confirmed and that what the German people wanted to see was enemy aircraft being shot down over Germany, Hitler ordered the intruder missions to be discontinued. I./NJG 2 was transferred to Catania in Sicily and Lent's new *Gruppe*, II./NJG 2, was formed. The *Geschwader* Staff was in Gilze-Rijn, and its *Kommodore* was *Major* Karl Hülshoff. With the formation of II./NJG 2 the *Geschwader* would have one *Gruppe* in Holland, led by Lent, flying alongside NJG 1 and defending Germany against the night attacks by Bomber Command and one *Gruppe* in the Mediterranean for convoy-protection duties and participation in the siege of Malta.

During November and December 1941, his first two month as *Kommandeur*, *Oberleutnant* Lent – he had not yet been promoted to *Hauptmann* – shot down only one more bomber. To some extent this was due, no doubt, to his flying less frequently because of the great deal of administrative work that he now had to cope with as *Gruppenkommandeur*. Difficult winter weather, too, played its part. Additionally, as explained below, Bomber Command was forced to reduce its effort from the middle of November onward.

Lent's first kill as *Gruppenkommandeur*, and his last in 1941, came during the night of Friday the 7th to Saturday the 8th of November. He took off from Leeuwarden at 0045 hours on the 8th, and at 0121 hours he shot down a Wellington 1C heading for Berlin that came down at Akkrum, about fifteen miles south of Leeuwarden. The six-man crew of the bomber, X9976 of No. 75 (New Zealand) Squadron, all died. This was Lent's twentieth night-time kill, and an announcement to that effect appeared in the *Wehrmachtsbericht*, the 'Armed Forces' Report', which, as its name implies, was an overt information bulletin issued regularly by the Headquarters of the *Wehrmacht*. To be named personally in the *Wehrmachtsbericht* counted as an honour and was entered in the 'Orders and Decorations' section of one's Service Record Book. That same night other pilots of Lent's *Gruppe* – Lippe-Weissenfeld, Fellerer and Becker – claimed two Wellingtons, a Stirling, and a Whitley respectively. These

---

[73] It is stressed that these figures are not hard and fast. They represent standard establishments, but in practice they were subject to considerable variations.

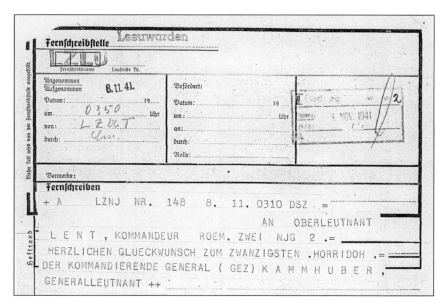

8 November 1941. *General* Kammhuber congratulates *Oberleutnant* Helmut Lent, *Kommandeur* II./NJG 2, on his twentieth night-time victory. Lent also had seven daytime 'kills' to his credit, so that his total score was twenty-seven.

successes were the subject of an article written by an official War Correspondent, Hans Kreten. Such reporters (*Kriegsberichter*) were full-time members of the armed forces serving with military units, and in the *Luftwaffe* they often flew operationally to gather material for their published reports.

The 20th Kill.
Oberleutnant Lent scores his 20th night-time victory. 27 British bombers shot down in night raids'. In the West, 10 November 1941.

In the *Gefechtsstand*[74] tonight we again see the smoothly functioning, well-organised work of the raid-reporting service. They report many British aircraft heading towards Germany. The British machines have hardly reached German airspace when they are detected and the defenders are ready to receive them. Our night-fighter crews stand prepared, ready to take off a second's notice, and the Tommy is granted no reprieve. He is located and he is overcome.

The first victory report from our *Staffel* comes in. *Leutnant* Fellerer has picked up a four-engined bomber, and he attacks the British aircraft with dogged determination. Five, six times he approaches the huge British machine, and then the Englishman is on fire. They see the crash, which causes a huge column of flame. Among us the young *Leutnant* from Vienna has a reputation as a *Viermot*[75] specialist. He is warmly congratulated on his kill. The *Kommandeur* of our *Gruppe*, *Ritterkreuzträger*[76] *Oberleutnant* Lent, is also in contact with the enemy. After a few moments he reports, 'Have attacked successfully.' Thus he has tonight scored his 20th night kill. It might well have been more, but a second one got away.

Our *Staffelkapitän*, *Oberleutnant* Lippe, also has hunter's luck. In a dashing

---

[74] *Gefechtsstand* – Operations Room.
[75] *Viermot* – Vernacular expression for a four-engined aircraft.
[76] *Ritterkreuzträger* – holder of the Knight's Cross.

attack he destroys an enemy bomber, and when a second Wellington passed in front of his guns, that too went down. In another daring attack he pursued a third machine at great height for some time and forced it to lose altitude, but he wasn't able to destroy it positively, although he was certain that he had hit it hard and damaged it. He finally lost sight of the British aircraft, not knowing that it had crashed and lay in a heap of wreckage somewhere in the occupied zone. When *Oberleutnant* Lippe landed and reported his two victories, his comrades were able to congratulate him on his third as well.

Then came another opportunity. This time it was the calm *Oberleutnant* Becker, a man who was like a teacher to the *Nachtjagd*, who was in contact with the enemy. It rankled with him that a few hours previously a Tommy had slipped through his fingers. This time he did not let the enemy escape, and the British machine, torn apart and broken into pieces, dived down to the ground.

In the early hours of the morning that night's victors sat down together. It was a matter of pride for all the men of our *Staffel* that despite sometimes very bitter resistance the victory was such a big one. This night's victors in our one *Staffel* alone have 20, 14, 8 and 4 kills respectively to their credit. The enemy lost six machines to our *Staffel*, and a total of 27 altogether were destroyed.
Kriegsberichter Hans Kreten.

Kreten's figures were inaccurate, but that was more a result of confusion in gathering data than intentional misrepresentation. The total number of kills by the *Nachtjagd* was nine, while the number of bombers that did not return was in fact thirty-seven, many of them not as a result of enemy action. The operations that night had an effect on the way in which the bomber offensive developed, and so are worth looking at in some detail.

Despite a pronounced 'head in the sand' attitude on the part of the Bomber Command leadership in general, a strong tendency by bombers crews to exaggerate the accuracy of the bomb-aiming and a readiness by debriefing and intelligence officers to accept the crews' biased reporting, it was becoming increasingly clear that the results being achieved were, greatly to understate the case, less than satisfactory. In August 1941 a detailed investigation into Bomber Command's operations in June and July that was carried out by a civil servant, D. M. Butt, had concluded that on average only one crew in four had dropped its bombs within five miles of its target. Results were slightly better on moonlit nights, but on nights when there was not a moon the results were considerably worse, the figure on German targets rising to one crew in twenty bombing within a five-mile radius. In the meanwhile losses of machines and men were increasing as the *Nachtjagd* grew in size and potency.

On the night of 7/8 November the Commander-in-Chief, Air Marshal Sir Richard Peirse, possibly in an attempt to counter the implications of this report, had decided to mount the biggest effort of the war so far, with Berlin as the principal target, sending out a total of 392 aircraft: he had done so even though extremely adverse weather conditions were forecast, with thick storm clouds, icing and hail affecting the North Sea and northern areas of Germany, and he had overruled objections to his operational plan made by some of his Group Commanders. The final order of battle included 169 bombers to Berlin, seventy-five to Cologne and fifty-five to Mannheim, and there were a large number of minor raids. Bombing results on the three major targets were lamentably poor, and the overall loss of thirty-seven aircraft was double the previous highest figure for one night. The force detailed to attack targets in Berlin incurred the majority of losses, twenty-one or just over twelve percent of those taking part. The overall percentage loss for the night was just under ten, well above the 'acceptable' figure. A large number of the losses were not caused by the enemy but by the weather, with a high proportion of the missing RAF machines coming down in the North Sea.

As a direct result of this disastrous night, the Prime Minister summoned Peirse to a meeting at Chequers the following day. On 13 November the Air Ministry informed Peirse that only limited operations were to be carried out until such time as the future of Bomber Command had been decided.

Helmut Lent took Christmas leave from the 22nd December 1941 to the 4th January 1942, spending it partly with Lena's family in Hamburg and partly, together with Lena, with his own family in Pyrehne. He finished the year as the *Luftwaffe*'s third most successful night-fighter pilot: only Werner Streib (22 kills) and Paul Gildner (21) were marginally ahead of him, but his overall tally, including his seven victories by day, exceeded both of theirs.

In November Lent had made rather an cryptic observation in one of his letters home: 'It is to be hoped that soon more and more people will realise that it is only with God that this war can be won.' Hitherto Lent's frequent references to the Almighty had been expressions of his belief that he enjoyed God's favour and His protection. Now he seemed to be calling for others to share his faith. The sentence quoted survives out of the context of the letter in which it was written, but one cannot help wondering whether it reflects a hint of doubt in his mind as to the prospects of ultimate victory.

CHAPTER SEVEN

January to September 1942
The Oak Leaves and a Daughter

HELMUT Lent, Acting *Kommandeur* II./NJG 2, was promoted to the substantive rank of *Hauptmann* on 1 January 1942, when he had served only eighteen months as an *Oberleutnant* as against the three years in that rank that was necessary for automatic promotion. Still six months short of his twenty-fourth birthday, he was the youngest *Gruppen-kommandeur* in the *Nachtjagd* – albeit still on an acting basis – responsible not only for the many aspects of bringing his new *Gruppe* up to full strength and efficiency, but also for leading it in the air in the escalating battle against the seemingly indiscriminate bombing of Germany by the Royal Air Force, whose aircrew were understandably called '*Terrorflieger*' by the civilian population, although the night-fighter crews tended to refer to them rather more tolerantly as '*Die Kollegen von der anderen Feldpostnummer*'[77].

While stationed at Leeuwarden Lent's former unit, 4./NJG 1, had, in addition to the operations that it flew from that airfield, also controlled small operational detachments of three or four aircraft (*Aussenkommandos*)[78] at Bergen aan Zee on the west coast of Holland and at Wittmundhafen, to the west of Wilhelmshaven in Germany. In November 1941 each of these two detachments became the nucleus of a *Staffel* of the newly-formed II./NJG 2. In due course the officer in charge of the Wittmundhafen detachment, *Oberleutnant* Rudolf Schoenert, became *Staffelkapitän* 4./NJG 2; *Oberleutnant* Prinz Egmont *zur* Lippe-Weissenfeld, who had commanded the detachment at Bergen, took over 5./NJG 2; and *Oberleutnant* Ludwig Becker became *Kapitän* 6./NJG 2. To bring the new *Gruppe* up to strength the necessary flying and ground personnel were posted in. Lent's three *Staffelkapitäne* were all experienced and successful night-fighter pilots and men of proven qualities of leadership, so that the future for the new *Gruppe* augured well. Neither Becker nor Lippe-Weissenfeld, who scored 44 and 51 victories respectively, would survive the war, but Schoenert was destined to see the

---

[77] 'Our colleagues from the other Field Post Office Number'. German units on active service had a Field Post Office Number as their official address.
[78] '*Aussenkommando*' - literally 'External Command'. Sometimes also referred to as a '*Sonderkommando*' (Special Command).

end of hostilities with the rank of *Major* and 64 kills to his credit.

The *Dunkle Nachtjagd* fighter-control system introduced and largely developed by 4./NJG 1 had by now taken on a form that was to become standardised throughout the *Nachtjagd* and which had come to be known as '*Himmelbett*'.[79] Central to the system, both figuratively and literally,

were the *Freya* and *Würzburg* radars. Two *Würzburgs* and one *Freya* were located within each of a multiplicity of so-called '*Himmelbett Räume*' or '*Himmelbett* Areas', the radius of which was dictated by the range of the *Würzburg* radars, at first a little over 20 miles[80]. The *Freya*, which had a range of up to 70 miles dependent upon the altitude of the bomber, picked up the approaching target aircraft and tracked it into the *Himmelbett Raum*, where it was taken over by one of the more accurate *Würzburgs*, the so-called 'Red *Würzburg*'. In the meanwhile – or possibly some time earlier – a night fighter had been scrambled to wait in the *Raum*, in the centre of which was a radio beacon on which the pilot could home and around which he would orbit while awaiting further instructions. The second, or green[81], *Würzburg*, was focused on the

Telegram from *Major* Wolfgang Falck, *Kommodore* NJG 1, to Helmut Lent on his promotion to *Hauptmann*. It reads, 'To *Hauptmann* Lent II./NJG 2 Leeuwarden, the youngest *Gruppenkommandeur*, my most sincere congratulations on your promotion. *Sieg Heil!*

---

[79] '*Himmelbett*' means 'four-poster bed' or 'honeymoon bed'. Presumably the codeword was selected at random.
[80] Later an improved version, the *Würzburg Riese* (*Würzburg* Giant), with a range of about 30 miles, was introduced.
[81] Sometimes also referred to as the '*blauer Würzburg*', or 'Blue *Würzburg*'.

Prinz Egmond *zur* Lippe-Weissenfeld, seen here as a *Hauptmann* and wearing the *Eichenlaub*. Lippe-Weissenfeld was fated to die in a flying accident when his score of bombers destroyed had reached 51.

fighter, and the position of each aircraft reported orally by land-line to a separate plotter in the fighter-control centre. These two plotters, positioned beneath a so-called *Seeburg Tisch* (Seeburg Table) and using red and green light-pointers to identify the target and the fighter respectively, marked their positions on the under-surface of a large translucent plotting table, which was overlooked by the fighter control officer (*Jägerleitoffizier*)[82], whose task it was to broadcast instructions to the fighter to bring it into contact with the enemy bomber. The plots that the controller saw on the table were, of course, a short time out of date, but the relative positions of fighter and bomber were reasonably correct. With great rapidity overlapping *Himmelbett* areas were set up wherever there was a threat of Bomber Command attacks.

Such was the situation at the beginning of 1942. In terms of personnel Lent's *Gruppe* had the makings of a dedicated and powerful force, and *Himmelbett* promised great opportunities for the fighters to find and destroy the enemy. It was Lent's responsibility to see that their potential was fully realised. The *Nachtjagd* had cured itself of the lack of enthusiasm that had been present in its formative days: instead the crews now saw themselves as members of an élite force and were proud of the job they were doing. Their task was clear-cut and unequivocal, just as that of the RAF pilots had been in the Battle of Britain and during the

These two photographs, of Lent on the telephone and playing cards while on standby, are from a series posed for publicity purposes.

---

[82] Abbreviated '*JLO*' which was sometimes used as a word in its own right, pronounced 'Eelo'

'Blitz'. Their Germany was under direct attack from the air and it was their job to shoot down the bombers that were attacking the *Heimat* – the homeland. Every British bomber destroyed was one fewer that could come back again with another cargo of bombs, every member of a bomber crew killed or captured was one less to man the machines that dropped the high-explosive and incendiary bombs that killed and maimed their women and children.

Lent returned to Leeuwarden from Christmas leave on the 5th of January. On the night of the 10th/11th *Oberleutnant* Schoenert, operating from Wittmundhafen, claimed a Wellington during an attack on Wilhelmshaven. A new recruit to Lent's *Gruppe*, *Unteroffizier* Kurt Zipperlein, also flying from Wittmundhafen, tasted success at 2215 hours on the night of the 15th when he shot down Whitley MH-R of No. 51 Squadron, from Dishforth in Yorkshire, near Drachten in Friesland in the course of an raid on Emden, killing three of the crew. The Pilot,

Telegram from Kammhuber to Lent congratulating him on the 100th victory of 5./NJG 2 and adding a special congratulation to the pilot responsible for the victory, *Oberleutnant* Schoenert.

Sergeant E. J. Richards, survived and was taken prisoner, as were the remaining two crewmen. Zipperlein's kill that night was his first, but it was also his last. He and his *Funker*, Werner Schunter, died when their Bf 110 crashed into the sea, shot down by the rear gunner of the 51 Squadron Whitley that Zipperlein had just destroyed.

Despite the demanding responsibilities that went with his command, Lent himself flew operationally whenever possible. His first kill of 1942 came on the night of 17/18 January, when, flying Bf 110 R4+AC[83] he accounted for a Whitley V in the vicinity of the island of Terschelling. In common with the aircraft that Zepperlein had claimed a couple of nights before, Lent's victim came from No. 51 Squadron and it too was probably returning from Emden. It was the only aircraft claimed by the *Nachtjagd* that night. Then, four nights later, another Whitley fell to Lent's guns, yet again from No. 51 Squadron and again on its way back from an attack on Emden. This one came down in the sea some thirty miles west of Terschelling. There were no survivors from either bomber.

On the night of 26/27 January 1942 *Oberleutnant* Rudolf Schoenert shot down another British bomber, probably one of the two Whitleys lost from a force of 32 that once again went to the much-bombed – possibly 'much targeted' would be more accurate – town of Emden, the 100th RAF bomber shot down by II./NJG 2 since its formation in its previous identity, 4./NJG 1. This achievement was officially marked by Helmut Lent's second mention in the *Wehrmachtsbericht*.

Just like their counterparts in the RAF, the great majority of *Luftwaffe* men would, if asked, claim to be Christians, but very few would claim to have a Christian faith as strong and uncompromising as that of Helmut Lent. On the 13th January, in a birthday letter to his father, he wrote, 'What better can we Christians ask for than, "God give us the strength to fulfil our earthly tasks and bring us ever closer to Thee"?' Lent's main 'earthly task' was to shoot down bombers and hence to kill other men. In two other letters home later in the month, apparently written in reply to worries about his safety on the part of members of his family, he again referred to God as his personal benefactor. The first one, written on 30 January, read:

> But you don't need to worry so much about me. I cannot but be ever thankful to our Lord for granting me so much that is wonderful, especially through my Lena. When all is said and done we must be thankful, even when things are difficult. It all has just one purpose – to bring us nearer to Him.

The second of the two letters, dated the following day, was to his mother:

> Dear *Mutti*,
> After I got your letter yesterday, the postman brought me another today. Very many thanks – I was very pleased to get it, but you needn't worry too much about me. You surely know what a strong shield I stand under. If it is not God's will, nothing can happen to me. You see, that is what distinguishes us

---

[83] 'R4' indicated NJG 2, 'A' the *Kommandeur* and 'C' the II./*Gruppe*.

Christians from other folks, that we feel ourselves safe in God's strong hands, safer than anywhere in the whole world. Unless he wants it, not a single one of my hairs will be harmed, even if there are bullets striking to left and right.

Helmut Lent's next kill did not count towards his score as a night fighter. It took place during the afternoon of Friday the 6th of February, when Bomber Command sent a force of 46 aircraft to lay mines off the Friesian

A mechanic stands in front of the rudder of Lent's Bf 110, which carries thirty victory icons. Lent's 30th victory was a Hampden 1, which he shot down by daylight in 6 February 1942.

Islands. When the raid-reporting service picked up the bombers Lent, although his unit was not on standby and had no orders to scramble, took off on his own initiative together with another three aircraft. The four joined up into a day-fighter formation of two pairs with Lent in the lead, reminiscent of his days as a *Zerstörer* pilot. There was thick cloud at low level, but despite this Lent sighted a Hampden just after three o'clock in the afternoon and went in to the attack, shooting it down into the sea. Describing the incident in a family letter, he wrote, 'As you can imagine, it caused a great stir here when I, a night fighter, shot one down by day.' The War Correspondent Kreten, in the final paragraphs of an article headed 'Ready for Action Round the Clock!'[84], reported:

---

[84] *'Zu jeder Minute einsatzbereit!'*

Our aircraft are back. This taste of day fighting has gripped and excited the night-fighter men. With obvious pleasure the *Hauptmann* accepts his comrades' congratulations. He has just relived the old times when he took part in the victorious battle for Narvik, scoring his victories in bitter combat and once flying his Me 110 back on one engine from Narvik to Trondheim. He speaks words of appreciation to the comrades that took off together with him. His words of thanks to the technical personnel are especially sincere: today they have shown that they can have everything ready within a few minutes, even when they are not on standby. And there is pride in their eyes, because this victory belongs to them as well.

Our night fighters, who have so often hit the Tommy with devastating force when he attacks by night, have shown that they, in common with the rest of the German defences in the west, are at all times ready for action and able to strike annihilating blows against the British Air Force.

The comparative lull in bomber operations against Germany was coming to an end. On 8 January 1942 Peirse had been removed from the position of Commander-in-Chief of Bomber Command and replaced on a temporary basis by Air Vice-Marshal J. E. A. Baldwin. On 14 February a new Directive to Baldwin, tacitly acknowledging that attempts to strike at pinpoint targets were unrealistic, informed him that, 'it has been decided that the primary object of your operations should now be focussed (sic) on the morale of the enemy civil population and in particular, of the industrial workers.'[85] Portal, Chief of the Air Staff, in a note on the Directive the following day, commented, 'I suppose it is clear that the aiming points are to be the built-up areas, *not*, for instance, the dockyards or aircraft factories where these are mentioned. This must be made quite clear if it is not already understood.'

The following week, on the 22nd of the month, Air Chief Marshal Sir Arthur Harris assumed the leadership of Bomber Command. His force comprised a miscellany of about 550 aircraft, the majority of them twin-engined machines such as the Blenheim (56), the Boston (22), the Whitley (54), the Hampden (112) and the Wellington (221). Of these the Wellington was by far the most efficient bomber. There were also just under a hundred new-generation aircraft – Stirlings, Halifaxes, Manchesters and Lancasters – and their numbers were increasing rapidly. A new and promising navigation aid was on its way too, TR 1335, later to be known as *Gee*. Despite the radical nature of the damningly adverse Butt Report, Bomber Command now had a new lease of life, a new and unequivocal *raison d'être* plus a new opportunity to prove itself – and, very importantly, a new leader.

During the first months of his tenure Harris gradually applied his own concepts of strategic bombing to the directive that he had inherited – one main target in a night when conditions were favourable, the improvement of navigation, the increased use of incendiary bombs both

---

[85] Official History, Volume IV, Page 144.

(top) Leeuwarden, first half of 1942. *Hauptmann* Helmut Lent, *Kommandeur* II./NJG 2, entertains senior officers in the Officers' Mess. To his left is *Generalleutnant* von Döring, while to his right is *Generalleutnant* Josef Kammhuber, Commanding *Fliegerkorps*XII.

(bottom) *Hauptmann* Helmut Lent delivers the after-dinner speech. Kammhuber is to his right, von Döring to his left.

to spread the destruction that the bombers caused and to illuminate the target for following aircraft, and the concentration of each attack within a shorter space of time. The growing build-up of the bomber attack and the increasing intensity of the night fighters' battle against the bombers is clearly evident from the number of RAF aircraft claimed each month by the night fighters: from only 5 in February (all, incidentally, shot down by pilots of II./NJG 2) the figure went up to 41 in March, 46 in April and 59 in May, while in June, July and August the tally reached over a hundred per month.

In the meanwhile, there was small diversion of effort for both Bomber Command and the *Nachtjagd*, although it did not bring the two forces into direct contact with each other. On the 12th of February the German capital ships *Scharnhorst*, *Gneisenau* and *Prinz Eugen* left Brest for their historic dash through the English Channel to North Germany

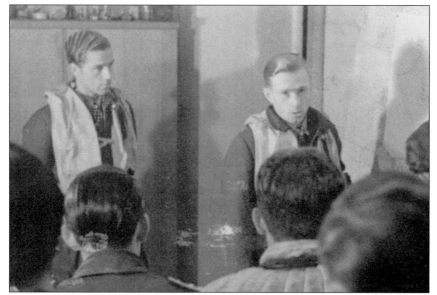

These two photos, in all probability part of the product of a photocall, were taken at Leeuwarden during 1942. They show, or purport to show, members of II./NJG 2 at an operational briefing. While Gildner and Lent may be seen in front of the seated group, there is uncertainty as to the identity of the aircrew in the larger group, but probable names are (left to right) Kleinhans (*Funker*); Walter Kubisch (Lent's *Funker*); Leopold Fellerer; Rudi Müller (*Funker* to Gildner); Hermann Greiner and fnu Bruk.

(Operation *'Donnerkeil'*)[86]. Night fighters, including some from II./NJG 2, formed part of the daytime escort for the vessels, although Lent himself did not fly on the operation. In a series of abortive daytime attacks on the enemy ships (Operation *'Fuller'*) Bomber Command lost sixteen machines. In a minor raid on Kiel on 26/27 February, however, *Gneisenau* suffered a direct hit that killed 116 of her crew and effectively ended her career as a naval fighting unit.

The Hampden that Lent shot down by daylight, AE308 UB-L of No. 455 Squadron, proved to be his only success in the month of February. His appointment as *Kommandeur* II./NJG 2 was confirmed on the 27th of the month. March seemed set to be another unproductive period for him. It began with a heavy and well-publicised attack on a target in France, the Renault factory at Billancourt, and then Harris turned his attention to the Ruhr steel town of Essen, mounting six major attacks on the city, experimenting with the *Gee* equipment to see whether it might be used as a blind-bombing device. Optimism that such might be the case proved to be misplaced. Lent did not fly between the 14th and the 25th of March – possibly he was away on duty or on leave – but in the meanwhile his *Gruppe* had not been without its kills, *zur* Lippe-Weissenfeld, Becker and Gildner adding to their scores. Then, on the 25th, *Kommandeur* Lent scrambled just before midnight. Harris had despatched 254 aircraft to Essen, and 181 returning crews reported excellent visibility and claimed to have bombed visually and accurately. A large number of them said that they had hit the Krupp steel works. In fact only nine high-explosive bombs hit the entire city, one house was destroyed and two were badly damaged. Casualties in Essen were slight, two killed and eleven injured, while about fifty RAF aircrew died in the nine bombers shot down, one of which, a Manchester from No. 61 Squadron, was accounted for by Lent at 0032 hours.

The following night, 26/27 March, the RAF's target was again Essen, and once more the bombing results were very poor. Lent scrambled but failed to score, but nevertheless II./NJG 2 enjoyed a very successful night. *Oberfeldwebel* Paul Gildner shot down three bombers, two Hampdens and a Blenheim intruder in a clear, starlit sky, so bringing his personal score to 28, but the best performance was by *Oberleutnant zur* Lippe Weissenfeld, who destroyed a Wellington after three attacks, a Manchester that exploded when his first burst of fire struck home, another Wellington that went down and crashed with its starboard motor pouring smoke, and finally yet another Wellington. Then, in the night of 27/28 March, a small force comprising fifteen Hampdens went to lay mines off the northwest German coast. Lent claimed two Hampdens and the Wittmundhafen *Staffelkapitän, Oberleutnant* Schoenert, claimed another. A fourth Hampden was credited to a member of Schoenert's *Staffel, Oberfeldwebel* Ney. Bomber Command records, however, show that only three Hampdens, all from No. 408 Squadron, were lost that night, so one of the

---

[86] *Donnerkeil* (poetic) - 'Thunderbolt'.

four claims must have been erroneous. There were also two other aircraft lost over Holland, a Blenheim intruder and a Whitley from 138 Squadron that had dropped a secret agent by parachute at Steenwijk, to the north of Zwolle. The Blenheim crashed near Utrecht, while the remains of the Whitley were not found. There is, however, a note in the records of No. 138 Squadron that Whitley T4166 'crashed into the sea at Den Helder'[87]. It is extremely likely that this Whitley, not a Hampden, was the bomber shot down by Ney. An eye-witness on the ground at St Maartensbrug, south of Den Helder, saw tracer ammunition, presumably from a fighter attacking a bomber, followed by an enormous explosion and pieces of the bomber falling into the sea. A very short time later Ney's Bf 110 R4+AN, probably damaged in the explosion, crashed near the hamlet of Petten, a few miles to the south. Both Ney and his *Funker*, *Unteroffizier* Josef Buhler, perished. There is an interesting point here. As Ney and his wireless operator both died, the probability is that they would not have had time to report the type of aircraft that they had destroyed, and because the other three RAF bombers destroyed that night were Hampdens, and because there was no wreckage to examine, it was assumed that Ney's victim was also of that type.

The raid that Harris mounted on the night following these events demonstrated the down-to-earth, clinical rationality of the new Commander's interpretation of his brief. He had been ordered to focus on the morale of the German population and that meant, as the Chief of the Air Staff had emphasised, bombing built-up areas. Experiments with *Gee* over the Ruhr having proved that it could not be used as an accurate aid to blind-bombing, Harris chose a target that was comparatively easy to find by conventional methods of navigation and had the added advantage, as far as the implementation of the new bombing policy was concerned, of being more vulnerable to concentrated bombing than most cities. In addition to striking at the inhabitants' morale, Harris saw the attack as an opportunity to see whether a target might be hit in such a way as to make aiming at it easier for a follow-up force. The unfortunate town chosen for Harris's experiment was the ancient Hanseatic port of Lübeck on the Baltic, characterised by its many picturesque, but highly inflammable, half-timbered buildings. After the war Harris, describing his calculated decision to bomb Lübeck, wrote in the following terms:

> It was not a vital target, but it seemed to me better to destroy an industrial town of moderate importance than to fail to destroy a large industrial city. However, the main object of the attack was to learn to what extent a first wave of aircraft could guide a second wave to the aiming point by starting a conflagration.[88]

Lent was scrambled against the bomber force attacking Lübeck, but did

---

[87] 'Agents by Moonlight', by Freddie Clark, published 1999 by Tempus Publishing Ltd.
[88] Quoted from 'Bomber Offensive' by Sir Arthur Harris, published in 1947 by Collins of London.

The much-publicised but controversial 'glove in rudder' photograph. Did it really happen, and if so when? Or was it just a propaganda exercise?

not score. He finished the month of March with one more kill the following night, taking off from Leeuwarden at 2147, shooting down a mine-laying Manchester off Terschelling at 2200 and landing back at Leeuwarden at 2212 hours. Lasting just 25 minutes, this was the shortest successful operational flight of his night-fighter career. His kill was of indirect and academic interest.

The achievements of Helmut Lent, the Germans' leading night-fighter ace, in defence of his country were frequently the subject of reports in the press, on the radio and in news films in the cinema, and of course any genuine material so used could only be published with the approval of the censorship authorities. Many reports for public consumption, however, were either greatly embellished or completely invented by Joseph Goebbel's Ministry of Propaganda. An interesting example of the latter survives in the form of a photograph of Lent holding his dog 'Peter' and standing in front of the port fin of his Bf 110, on which are 34 victory icons. Apparently trapped between the fin and rudder of the aircraft is a large glove. Entitled, 'A glove is caught in the rudder', the photograph was published in the German press, probably in the *Berliner Illustrierte Zeitung*, date unknown. The caption to the photographs reads:

> I have crept up on a Tommy from above and positioned myself very close astern of him, and I open fire. I can see my tracer disappearing into the fuselage of the Stirling, when the Tommy explodes in pieces like a shell. Pieces of aeroplane rain around my aircraft like shrapnel. I dive away thinking to myself, 'That's my lot!' but my machine flies bravely on, though my rudder

feels as if it is pulling hard to one side. It is sticking, and I can hardly move it. When I have landed I go to inspect the damage. Like a dead man's hand there is a heavy English electrically-heated glove hanging there. Some bizarre twist of fate has torn it from the pilot's hand when the bomber exploded and whirled it into my rudder.' *Hauptmann* Lent, to whom this unusual 'hunter's yarn' relates, is a *Gruppenkommandeur* in the most successful night-fighter unit, which has already achieved more than 500 victories.

Photograph of Lent with his dog Peter in front of a Bf 110 with 34 kills marked on the port fin.

This photograph has been printed many times since the end of the war with widely differing attempts to date the event. Several authors, for example, say that the incident took place when Lent made his 60th kill (in May 1943); one report says that it was when he destroyed 'his first and last Stirling from Leeuwarden' on the 4th or 5th of May 1943. Neither of these dates can be correct. Lent's rank is given as *Hauptmann*, which is confirmed by the photograph, and Lent was promoted to *Major* on 1 January 1943. It is interesting to note that in the picture Lent is wearing the *Ritterkreuz* but not the *Eichenlaub*, awarded to him 6 June 1942. As he was promoted *Hauptmann* on 30 August 1941, the photograph was presumably taken between approximately September 1941 and June 1942. During that period, however, Lent did not claim a single Stirling.. There are thirty-four victory badges on the fin, beginning correctly with one Polish victim followed by two RAF and one Norwegian. Lent's 34th victory overall is recorded as having been scored on 29 March 1942, which would be consistent with the latter possibility. In his logbook, however, Lent identifies his victim that night as a Manchester. Mistakes in identification are not uncommon, but it would be strange for Lent to enter 'Manchester' in his log and talk to reporters about a Stirling.

There is another picture of Lent with Peter the dog in front of a Bf 110 with 34 victories marked on the port fin. At first sight one would think that this photo was taken on the same occasion as the 'glove' one, with the same aircraft, but close inspection gives rise to a thought-provoking discovery: the position of the whole 'block' of symbols differs slightly from one aircraft to the other with reference to the edge of the fin and the swastika, that on the 'glove' picture being lower than that on the other. It would presumably be unlikely that Lent had *two* aircraft marked with his personal score, which would strongly suggest some sort of 'fixing', although it is hard to say in what particular way.

In April 1943 Lent had only two kills from ten scrambles, and in May only one from four starts. April was marked, however, by the award of another decoration for gallantry, the German Cross in Gold (*Das deutsche Kreuz in Gold*).[89] Meanwhile, Harris was continuing his experimental approach to the problem of maximising the effect of the bomber force. Fire raids on Rostock – there were five attacks in all – were carried out with results that, taken overall, were encouraging. Other coastal towns were attacked, as were major towns inland, with the proportion of four-engined bombers in the force, and hence the total weight of bombs, gradually increasing. Then, on the night of 30/31 May 1942, Harris sent more than a thousand bombers against a single German city.

With the future of Bomber Command still in the balance, Harris had conceived the idea of mounting a raid of unprecedented magnitude against a major German city. If successful, he believed, such an attack, in addition to its effect on the enemy, would not only boost the morale of the bomber crews but would also demonstrate to those directing the war effort that bombing could make a unique and valuable contribution to ultimate victory. Further, in his own words, 'the result of using an adequate bomber force against Germany would be there for all the world to see, and I should be able to press for the aircraft, crews, and equipment we needed with far more effect than by putting forward theoretical arguments.'[90] Churchill was consulted and gave his enthusiastic support to the plan, and Cologne was the first-choice target. The frontline strength of Bomber Command was less than 500, but aircraft and crews from Conversion Units and Operational Training Units were pressed into service to make up the headline-catching figure

---

[89] This decoration was more usually awarded after the recipient had earned the Iron Cross but before he had been awarded the Knight's Cross. Lent was already a holder of the Knight's Cross when he received the German Cross.

[90] 'Bomber Offensive'.

of 1000. In addition to the psychological aims of the operation, which was aptly code-named 'Millennium', Harris perceived and planned the undertaking as an experiment in overwhelming the German defences, the Flak and the night fighters, by sending all the bombers along the same route and giving them strict individual bombing times within a short period and thus achieving concentration in both space and time. *Gee*, although it had been proved unsatisfactory as an aid to blind-bombing, enabled the navigators in the early stages of the attack to attain a much more accurate standard of dead-reckoning navigation than hitherto, and the use of a high proportion of incendiary bombs would serve to mark the target for the bombers following up. It was realised by the Air Staff, by Harris himself and by the Prime Minister, that the experiment represented a considerable gamble and that, if the planners had miscalculated the risk posed by the night fighters, Bomber Command might incur prohibitive casualties. Churchill let it be known that he would be prepared to accept the loss of 100 bombers. The final choice of target lay between Cologne and Hamburg, and Cologne was chosen on the basis of more favourable weather conditions at the relevant time.

The raid was not only a huge publicity and morale-boosting success in England, but it was also by far the most devastating raid against the Fatherland to date and effectively removed the doubts as to the viability and future direction of the Command, and it set the general pattern for future attacks on cities. Only 49 bombers were lost, so supporting the Air Ministry experts' assessment that *Himmelbett* system had a fundamental weakness. In simple terms, only one fighter, or at the most two, could

Leeuwarden 1942. *Hauptmann* Lent, *Kommandeur* II./NJG 2, monitors his fighters' R/T. Probably a posed publicity photograph.

A leaflet dropped by the RAF over Germany in June 1942. It recalls the first thousand-bomber raid on 30 May and the second one on 1 June, and it promises heavier raids in the future, especially when the American Air Force joins in the attacks.

> „Wir werden von nun an Deutschland in immer grösserem Maßstab mit Bomben belegen, Monat auf Monat, Jahr auf Jahr, bis das Naziregime entweder von uns ausgerottet ist, oder — besser noch — bis ihm das deutsche Volk selbst den Garaus macht."

CHURCHILL:
14 : VII : 1941

Am 30. Mai 1942
Der erste Angriff
mit über
1000 Bombern
Der zweite folgte am 1. Juni

Nach diesem Angriff erklärte Churchill

„ Diese beiden grossen Nachtangriffe kennzeichnen den Beginn einer neuen Phase der britischen Luftoffensive gegen Deutschland. Und diese Offensive wird bedeutend an Wucht zunehmen, wenn erst — wie das bald der Fall sein wird — die amerikanische Luftwaffe an den Angriffen teilnimmt.

„ Deutsche Städte, Häfen und kriegswichtige Industriegebiete werden einer so schweren Prüfung unterworfen werden, wie sie noch kein Land, weder an Dauer, Wucht oder Ausmass erfahren hat."

operate under close control in each circular *Raum*. If the bomber force were tightly concentrated, it would only pass through one *Raum* at a time, so that while the single fighter was devoting its attention to a single bomber, many other enemy aircraft would pass through the *Raum* unmolested. Further, fighters manning areas that were not penetrated would not come into contact with bombers, so that the maximum potential of the *Nachtjagd* was not achieved. It would, however, take a considerable time before the *Luftwaffe* accepted the limitations of *Himmelbett* and replaced it with a more effective system.

Harris used his nominal 'thousand force' against two more targets before disbanding it, striking at Essen on the night of 1/2 June and Bremen on the 25th/26th of the same month. Neither attack was as dramatically successful as that against Cologne, but the precedent had now been set. Losses of bombers, 31 for the Essen raid and 48 for that on Bremen, again were tolerable.

Lent had taken off against the bombers heading for Cologne at the end of May, but had not added to his single victory that month. Operating in the *Himmelbett* areas around Leeuwarden, II./NJG 2 did not come into contact with the bombers stream, which crossed into Holland well to the south, roughly over the Scheldt estuary, and headed almost directly for Cologne, quitting Holland by a close parallel route when the attack was completed.

June 1942 was a momentous month for the young *Gruppenkommandeur*. In terms of bombers destroyed it was the most successful of his whole career. Previously the largest number of enemy aircraft he had shot down in a single month had been six in July 1941, just after he left 6./NJG 1 and took over as *Staffelkapitän* of 4./NJG 1, and then he had scrambled thirteen times to reach that score. Now, in June 1942, he took off operationally just ten times and he claimed nine bombers. His first success came against the second 'thousand force' raid, when Essen was targeted, a Hampden that crashed near Medemblik, and a further kill – a Halifax from No. 76 Squadron – followed the following night when Bomber Command sent a comparatively small force of 170 aircraft to Bremen at a cost of eleven missing. The next day he wrote home:

> Yesterday and the day before yesterday we were kept quite busy. I scored my 31st and 32nd night victories, and thus my 40th altogether. Once again God mercifully looked after me when I was in action. The 40th was a hard, four-engined nut to crack. Praise be to God, he didn't succeed in dropping his bombs on Germany. He was forced to jettison them, and I was able to see just what the monsters can carry. Down below a path of high explosives and incendiaries a kilometre long flared up.

Another bomber force of comparatively moderate size attacked Essen on the night of the 5th/6th of June. For the RAF it was yet another failed raid on the steel-producing town. Lent and Kubisch took off from Leeuwarden a few minutes into the morning of the 6th, and they landed back there at 0137, having shot down two Wellingtons. The same night the aircraft of *Oberleutnant* Heiner Petersen of 6./NJG 1 was in collision with a Stirling from No. 149 Squadron. Against all the odds not only Petersen and his *Funker* but also the complete crew of the Stirling survived, although Petersen was badly injured. After recovering in October 1942 he went to Leeuwarden and became Helmut Lent's adjutant.

Later that morning Lent made the half-hour's flight to

Wittmundhafen in Do 17 R4+ZC, returning to Leeuwarden in the afternoon: then, after breakfast on Sunday the 7th he flew to Zwischenahn, again in the Do 17, and onwards to Hamburg-Fuhlsbüttel, and he remained there until the following Wednesday before returning to Leeuwarden. It was his twenty-fourth birthday on the 16th of June, and once again he wrote home.

This photograph of Lent pistol-shooting was probably taken at Leeuwarden. Lent is wearing the *Eichenlaub*, which he received on 6 June 1942.

This very birthday on which I enter a new year of life causes me to look back with a heart full of thankfulness. How greatly God has blessed me during the past year. He has not only given me military successes and decorations, but also a wonderful wife, and now a delightful baby daughter as well. And He has mercifully watched over and protected mother and child in times of danger. But in addition to all the times when His mercy and his protection are self-evident, how often has He protected us all, and especially me myself when I'm flying on operations! For that I cannot thank Him sufficiently!

Lent's daughter, Christina, had been born on the 6th of June, and the flight to Hamburg on the 7th and the short stay there that followed were doubtless to see mother and child: and probably the earlier trip, to Wittmundhafen on the 6th, was not unconnected with the birth – Wittmundhafen is no great distance from Hamburg, and there were

Hauptmann Helmut
Lent, *Kommandeur*
II./NJG 2, wearing the
Eichenlaub awarded to
him on 6 June 1942. A
formal portrait.

always light aircraft to be had on a *Luftwaffe* base, particularly when the *Kommandeur* had a good reason to fly a short distance on personal business.

On the 8th of June, while Lent was still in Hamburg with his wife Lena and his new daughter Christina, another gratifying item of news reached him: the *Führer* had awarded him the Oak Leaves to the Knight's Cross – the *Eichenlaub*. He was the first night fighter ever to receive this prized award, and only the 98th member of the *Wehrmacht* – the entire armed forces – to be so honoured. The official date of the award was the 6th of June – the very day on which his daughter had been born.

Lent resumed command of his unit on the 10th of June, and early on the 21st he scored his next kill, a Hampden of No. 420 Squadron

A less formal photograph of *Hauptmann* Helmut Lent, *Kommandeur* II./MJG 2, wearing the *Eichenlaub*.

heading for Emden. That day his name appeared for the fourth time in the *Wehrmachtsbericht* with the announcement of this, his 35th night time victory. Under the headline 'Victory in the Night Sky' the official war reporter Josef Kreutz described it as follows:

Hauptmann Lent reaches his aircraft, which is standing ready for take-off, by jumping over a number of wire fences on to the grass. An airman throws his parachute over his shoulders, two elastic straps are fastened, and the *Eichenlaubträger* is in position at the controls. The motors roar, the aircraft moves forward, races with rapidly increasing acceleration along the runway. It lifts off, pulls up and disappears in the night.

Back in the Operations Room, the expectancy is tense. R/T contact is functioning well. Now the *Eichenlaubträger* is already reporting that he has made contact with then enemy. A British bomber has crossed the flight path of the searching night fighter. The range is growing shorter and shorter. Will the enemy crew see the fighter? But there is not a single shot. The Tommy is now

Another formal portrait
of Lent with the
Eichenlaub.

within attacking range. The guns are loaded and set to 'fire'. One press on the button, and all hell will be let loose. But still the *Eichenlaubträger* holds back. He wants the first attack to blow the enemy to pieces. He wants to make quite certain that his target is right in his sights. Another slight adjustment of position – then it is time. The cannon hammer out in short bursts, then there comes the lighter rattle of the machine-guns. His aim is good! A flurry of bright fragments from the aircraft swirls through the air, and there are already flames emerging from the vast fuselage of the British bomber. *Hauptmann* Lent pulls his aircraft away – the bomb-load could explode at any moment and endanger his own machine. But the *Eichenlaubträger* does not take his eyes off his victim – there, a brilliant glow! All around night turns to day. Fragments fly

Nose art from Wellington III X3713 (WS-J) of No. 9 Squadron, RAF, shot down by *Oberleutnant* Egmond *Prinz zur* Lippe-Weissenfeld of II./NJG 2 as his 27th victory. Lippe's *Gruppenkommandeur*, Helmut Lent, also claimed a bomber the same night. The nose art was retained as a trophy in the officers' mess at Leeuwarden.

about like flaming torches, and then the mighty enemy colossus, many tons in weight, crashes into the earth with tremendous force. The bomber continues to burn for a long time. The instantaneous destructive effect of German night fighter's dashing attack gave the enemy crew no chance of escape.

This was the 35th aerial victory of our most successful night-fighter pilot, the first holder of the *Eichenlaub* in this new arm of the *Luftwaffe*.

In the early hours of the morning of the 24th Lent accounted for two mine-laying Wellingtons, both from No. 303 (Polish) Squadron, to the north of the island of Terschelling. His final two kills of the month followed during the night of the 25th/26th June, when Harris sent out his third thousand-bomber force to Emden. The *Nachtjagd* enjoyed a fruitful night, claiming 39 kills from the 48 RAF aircraft reported missing, and Lent's *Gruppe* was the most successful with fifteen victories to its credit. The month finished on a high note for Lent. He wrote home, 'Just now, on the 28th and 29th of June, I was at the *Führerhauptquartier* and with the *Reichsmarschall* to collect my decoration. I had the honour to be invited to have supper with them both.'

For a young officer to be decorated by the *Führer*, Adolf Hitler himself, and to be personally received and entertained to dinner by him and the popular Commander-in-Chief of the *Luftwaffe*, Hermann Göring, was indeed a very great honour and no doubt, no matter how modest that officer might be, a source of considerable pride as well. For Helmut Lent it was the climax to what had, from the personal and professional viewpoint, been an extraordinarily propitious month. But there was another side to the coin. During the same month of June a serious

problem that had existed for some time within the close Lent family brought Helmut Lent into direct conflict with the security apparatus of the Third Reich.

Both Joachim and Werner Lent, Helmut's elder brothers, had followed the family tradition and become Evangelical ministers. Both were members of the *Bekenntniskirche* (Confessional Church), a movement within the Protestant Church outspokenly opposed to the Nazi concept of a *Reich* Church that supported the Nazi *Weltanschauung* (View of the World) and the doctrines of Aryan superiority and the *Führerprinzip* – the 'Leader Principle', or the concept of the supreme authority of the *Führer*. Members of the clergy of the Confessional Church underwent great persecution at the hands of the Nazis, and many paid for their faith and outspokenness with their life. Included among those who suffered were Helmut Lent's brothers. Surviving documents are unfortunately very few, but there does exist a copy of a letter that Helmut wrote in June in support of his brother Joachim:

> On Active Service, 15 June 1942.
> To the Head of Section IV of the *Reichssicherheitshauptamt*
> Berlin, Prinz Albrechtstrasse 8.

Lent receiving the *Eichenlaub* from the *Führer*, 28/29 June 1942. The officer to Lent's left is *Oberleutnant* Heinrich Setz of 4.JG 77 (day fighters), who had scored 76 victories. Setz finished the war as a *Major* with 138 victories.

On 8 June 1942, in recognition of my operational record in this war, the *Eichenlaub zum Ritterkreuz des Eisernen Kreuzes* was awarded to me by the *Führer*. A soldier's pleasure at receiving such a high decoration is quite naturally very great. Unhappily, my pleasure has been greatly overshadowed by the fact that since the 2nd April 1942 my brother Joachim, *Pastor* in the parish of Hochzeit, *Kreis* Arnswalde, has been imprisoned by the *Gestapo* office in Schneidemühl. After careful enquiries, it seems that the following are the facts of this matter:

In his sermons on Heroes' Remembrance Day my brother made use of two sentences from the 'Mölders Letter', which is now known to have been a forgery. The report about this appeared in my brother's newspaper on the Saturday before Heroes' Remembrance Day. However, because the paper was not delivered to his home until the Monday following Heroes' Remembrance Day, my brother knew nothing of the forgery. This fact, which is in favour of my brother, can be corroborated by a number of witnesses. In the course of interrogation my brother himself has also drawn attention to this fact, which proves his innocence. Unfortunately, however, only the opposite has been believed of my brother. In the interests of an objective examination it would be advisable to accept the word of these witnesses and to reach the appropriate conclusions. In two letters to the Head of the *Gestapo* in Schneidemühl I have already attempted to clarify the matter. Quite politely, I received a reply to my first letter by return of post, but I have already waited in vain for three weeks for an answer to my second letter.

I am now turning to you to request that you should be good enough to release my brother again. As a front-line soldier who has been in continuous action since 1 September 1939 it is intolerable for me to know that this is my reward for my front-line service. I am not begging for mercy, but I am requesting justice for my family. My brother's wife is expecting her third child at the beginning of July following a miscarriage, and as she is deeply upset by the arrest of her husband her concern for him could have a catastrophic effect on her and the new baby.

I hope that, now that I have presented the facts, I am not asking for anything impossible, and I request an early reply.

Heil Hitler!

(Signed): Lent, *Hauptmann und Gruppenkommandeur.*

Lent must have thought carefully about the risks he might be running by going over the heads of the local *Gestapo* office to complain about his brother's arrest and imprisonment, and presumably he had decided that his reputation and his record were such that his intervention would carry weight without jeopardising him personally.

In the context of the Christian religion in the Third Reich in general, and of Helmut Lent's Christianity in particular, the Mölders Letter is of real interest and therefore, although complicated, worth summarising here. Werner Mölders was a national hero, a highly decorated, widely publicised and outstandingly successful fighter pilot: he held the office of *General der Jagdflieger* and was the most highly decorated soldier in the *Wehrmacht* when he met his death in a flying accident in November 1941. Like Helmut Lent he was a dedicated Christian, although he belonged

Oberst Werner Mölders.

to the Catholic, rather than the Evangelical, Church. In 1942 a letter
written by Mölders to one of his former Catholic mentors came into the
possession of Sefton Delmer, before the war a German-speaking British
journalist and during the war a leading member of the highly secret
Political Warfare Executive, an organisation charged with conducting
subversive operations, including 'black' propaganda, against the enemy.
The letter gave Delmer an idea for a 'dirty tricks' operation. Aware of the
Nazi Party's fundamental opposition to organised religion and of the
anti-religious persecution campaigns spear-headed by the *Gestapo*, he
conceived a scheme aimed at fomenting internal dissent in Christian
circles in Germany. From the clandestine radio station that he controlled,
call-sign '*Gustav Siegfried Eins*'[91], Delmer made a series of broadcasts

---

[91] *Gustav Siegfried Eins* was located in England, but purported to be a clandestine
transmitter in Germany run by a secret anti-Nazi group.

Officers of II./NJG 2 at Leeuwarden in summer 1942, possibly to celebrate Lent's award of the *Eichenlaub* (6 June). Rear row, left to right: *Leutnant* Denzel; *Leutnant* Kuthe; *Oberleutnant* Gardiewski; *Oberleutnant* Sigmund; *Oberleutnant* Schauberger; *Oberleutnant* Greiner; *Leutnant* Köstler. Centre row, left to right: *Leutnant* Völlkopf; *Oberleutnant* Fellerer (*Kommandoführer*) Bergen; *Hauptmann* Siebeneicher (Commanding *Stab* Company); *Hauptmann* Ruppel (Area Controller); *Hauptmann* Schürbel (On attachment from *Division*); *Oberinspekteur* Rhinow (Administration); *Leutnant* Richter (Liaison Section); *Doktor* Schreiber (Medical Officer). Front row, left to right: *Oberleutnant* Gildner; *Oberleutnant zur* Lippe-Weissenfeld; *Hauptmann* Helmut Lent; *Oberleutnant* Becker.

claiming that Werner Mölders' aircraft had been shot down by 'Himmler's Bolshevik scum' simply because Mölders was a devout Roman Catholic. To add verisimilitude to the deception, Delmer arranged for a number of copies of a letter apparently written by Mölders, but in fact a complete forgery, to be dropped by RAF aircraft over Germany. The letters, which were typewritten, were on forged *Luftwaffe* signals forms to give the impression that they had been scattered by an anti-Nazi pilot. Very soon copies of the letter, in which Werner Mölders apparently attested to the supreme importance of his Catholic faith in his life – by implication placing it above his allegiance to the National Socialist Party – were being duplicated and circulated among the population, so drawing attention to the government's anti-Christian policies. Many clerics, of both convictions, read out the letter or part of it from the pulpit – as did Helmut Lent's brother Joachim – or nailed copies of it to the doors of their churches, and were arrested and imprisoned by the *Gestapo*. The German security services rapidly, and correctly, established that the letter was a complete forgery, but they failed to recognise that it was an ingredient in a British disruption operation, convincing themselves that the culprits were within either the Catholic or, possibly, the Evangelical Church in Germany.

Lent's other brother, Werner, was also a target of the secret police, as it is convenient to record here even though it is jumping slightly ahead of the chronology. On 31 July 1942 Werner had a notice of penalty from the *Gestapo* office in Frankfurt/Oder requiring him to deposit the sum of 1,000 *Reichsmarks* in a special account because of his 'anti-State conduct'. Should he not 'behave faultlessly from the political point of view' until October 1945 the money would be forfeited to either the National Socialist People's Welfare Organisation or the Winter Relief Fund.

★　　　★　　　★

Lent flew back from Hitler's Headquarters near Rastenburg in East Prussia – the notorious 'Wolf's Lair'[92] – on 29 June, sandwiching a call at Staaken near Berlin between two overnight stops that night and on the 30th at Hamburg/Fuhlsbüttel and arriving back at Leeuwarden on the 1st July. In the early morning of the 3rd of the month he shot down a Wellington heading for Bremen. The Bomber Command force, 325 strong, lost 13 aircraft, all of which were accounted for by the *Nachtjagd*. Lent's II./NJG 2 claimed six, including three destroyed by *Prinz zur Lippe-Weissenfeld*. Just under a week later, during the night of 8/9 July, when Wilhelmshaven was the target for 285 machines, II./NJG 2 destroyed three – the only night-fighter claims that night – out of a total of five that failed to return to their bases in England. *Hauptmann* Lent shot down a Wellington, *Oberleutnant* Sigmund got a Halifax, while Paul Gildner, who already had the Knight's Cross and had been promoted from *Oberfeldwebel* to *Oberleutnant* in June in recognition of his outstanding record of victories, destroyed a Lancaster, his 36th victory.

Promotion from NCO to officer was a very rare honour. Presumably Lent, as Gildner's *Kommandeur*, had either recommended him for the promotion or, if the recommendation had come from a higher level, had supported it. Yet shortly before Gildner became an officer he had, it seems, been involved in a breach of discipline which would almost certainly have disqualified him – and Lent had in all probability known about it.

The *tableau* seems to have broken up in disarray. Lent and Gildner are hoisting *Oberinspekteur* Rhinow on their shoulders, while the other officers look on in amusement. The reason for their boisterousness is not known.

---

[92] 'Wolf's Lair' has become the accepted English-language version of *Wolfsschanze*, the name of Hitler's operational Headquarters. A more literal translation would be 'Wolf's Redoubt' or 'Wolf's Dugout'.

Possibly the same occasion. Lent in conversation with *Hauptmann* Ruppel. Others who are recognizable are (from left to right) Lippe-Weissenfeld, Becker, Richter, Greiner and Fellerer.

Horst Römer was a *Funker* with II./NJG 2 at Leeuwarden at that time and his rank was *Gefreiter*, the equivalent of Leading Aircraftman in the RAF. He recalls:

Shortly before Gildner was promoted to *Oberleutnant* there was fog all over Holland and so all flying was cancelled, which meant that we could go into town. We had a good old celebration in a pub in the town called the '*Gröne Weide*'. On the way back home Gildner and I swapped uniform jackets, so that he became a *Gefreiter* with the Knight's Cross and I became an *Oberfeldwebel* with the German Cross. We were all extremely drunk. The streetlights annoyed Gildner, so he took out his pistol and fired at them. We had to drag my room-mate, *Feldwebel* Hemmen, along the road because he couldn't walk. Suddenly, standing in front of us, we saw a *Major* from the airfield, and he demanded our names and ranks. He grabbed me by the arm, and then Gildner fired again and I was able to pull myself loose and run away. We dragged our drunken comrade along with us and put him to bed, and then we continued the celebration in our quarters.

The following day *Hauptmann* Ruppel was duty officer, and at the morning weather briefing *Major* Lent asked him for the previous day's report. He had, he said, had a report from a *Major* on the permanent staff of the airfield about drunken aircrew who had been shooting at the streetlamps, among them a *Gefreiter* with the Knight's Cross and an *Oberfeldwebel* with the German Cross. When *Hauptmann* Ruppel replied that all flying had been cancelled at 2030 hours, Lent simply tore up the report and threw it into the waste-paper basket.

Horst Römer recalls Helmut Lent as an officer who was always approachable and who would listen carefully to anything that even the lowliest ranks had to say. He was one of the few officers who set little store by rank and decorations. Although for the higher echelons of the

Luftwaffe and the Nazis he was the type of Nordic soldier who fitted well into their ideological concept, he was in fact more the traditional Prussian officer who did his duty and did not court the limelight. He was above all a human being, despite his brilliant career.

Römer adds that Lent's *Funker*, Walter Kubisch, was a retiring individual who did not mix a great deal, but who was, like his pilot, unassuming and modest. He obviously had a special comradely relation with Lent, the sort of relationship that was fundamental to success in the field of night fighting.

The short summer nights during this period meant that Bomber Command's targets were by and large restricted to the North German coast, the Ruhr and the Rhineland, and until the 26th of July there had only been five attacks that month in which more than 200 aircraft took part. Harris was digesting the results of his experimental raids, including the three 'thousand force' attacks, and formulating plans for the future. Bombing results were mixed: moderate damage was inflicted on Bremen on 2/3 July but little damage on Wilhelmshaven on 8/9 July. Attacks on Duisburg on 21/22, 23/24 and 25/26 achieved marginally more encouraging results, but overall the damage caused seemed disproportionately slight compared with the effort deployed. Then, on 26/27 July, Harris sent a major force of 409 bombers to Hamburg, and despite cloud and icing conditions there were clear skies over the target and bombing was heavy, if widespread, causing much damage to

1942, exact date not known. Lent, an enthusiastic hunter, shows off his bag.

Lent in flying kit.

Helmut Lent, *Kommandeur* II./NJG 2, with Lippe-Weissenfeld (left) and Ludwig Becker. The officer to Lippe's left is not known.

residential and commercial districts but little to industrial premises and the extensive dockland areas. More than 14,000 people were rendered homeless, but surprisingly only 337 were killed and just over 1,000 injured, a tribute to the widespread practice in Germany of living in huge blocks of flats: these flats had very substantial cellar-systems, which had been converted to serve as air-raid shelters. The *Wehrmachtsbericht* the following day reported, 'Following ineffective daylight nuisance raids on West German territory, Hamburg and its surroundings were bombed

by the British Air Force on the night of 26/27 July with high-explosive and incendiary bombs. The civilian population suffered heavy casualties. Very many buildings, mostly in residential areas, were destroyed or damaged. Night fighters, anti-aircraft guns, naval guns and light marine craft shot 37 of the attacking bombers down.' The actual number of RAF bombers missing that night was 29, but even so it represented, at about seven percent of those despatched, a heavy toll. The night-fighter units claimed eighteen victories, including a Halifax and a Wellington destroyed by Lent. Once again II./NJG 2 was the most successful night-fighter *Gruppe*, with seven kills to its name.

On balance, one might cautiously describe the attack against Hamburg in the small hours of Monday 27 July as successful: by contrast the next attack, mounted three nights later by 256 aircraft, would have to be called a failure. The force became scattered by bad weather and only 68

Air Vice-Marshal Donald Bennett, CB, CBE, DSO.

machines from the 256 sent out reported having bombed within the target area. Thirteen German civilians were killed, twelve of them either patients or nurses in the Eppendorf hospital. Thirty-six RAF aircraft, carrying in total over two hundred men, failed to return.

Lent took leave for almost the complete month of August 1942, dividing it between Hamburg and Pyrehne. II./NJG 2 continued to enjoy steady success in his absence. During August there were two developments within Bomber Command that had an effect on the way the offensive developed, a minor one and a major one. Firstly, the Germans succeeded in jamming *Gee*[93]. the RAF's new navigation radar. For the short period that *Gee* had been in operation the bomber navigators had been able to fix their position very precisely after setting course and so to calculate the velocity of the prevailing wind with a high degree of accuracy as long as they were in *Gee* cover, which was of great help to them in maintaining concentration for the remainder of their flight to and over their target. The second development was the formation of a target-finding and marking force, with an original strength of five squadrons, under the command of an outstanding aviator and officer, Donald C. T. Bennett. Bennett, a substantive Wing Commander, was given the rank of Acting Group Captain for his new job – he was a Squadron Commander when selected – and was destined to end the war as an Air Vice-Marshal. Commander-in-Chief Harris, strangely, was at first opposed to the concept of a special, élite force within his command, but once it was in being he gave it his full support, naming it 'Pathfinder Force', or 'PFF' in its abbreviated form. PFF's task was to fly ahead of Main Force (another term introduced simultaneously) and to locate targets and mark them accurately with specially designed and constructed flares of easily-recognised colours, at which the bomb-aimers in the Main Force machines would aim instead of, as had been the case until now, at miscellaneous objectives on the ground. The official date of the formation of PFF was 17 August 1942, and the following night Bennett sent 31 of his aircraft to lead a Main Force of 87 bombers in an attack on the Baltic port of Flensburg. The initiative was a complete failure, but it was the introduction of a technique that was used with steady improvement to the very end of the war and which undoubtedly considerably increased the potency of Bomber Command.

Back at Leeuwarden at the end of August, Lent began a busy month's flying. Operationally, he flew five sorties on three nights and destroyed a Lancaster – his first – on the night of the 4th/5th September and a Wellington on the 13th/14th, the hard-pressed city of Bremen being the RAF's target on both nights. The Lancaster can be readily identified as R5682 (QR-R) of No. 61 Squadron, RAF Syerston, from which four crew-members survived as prisoners of war, but it is not possible to say which of the fifteen Wellingtons lost on the 13th/14th September was Lent's victim.

---

[93] In strict terms *Gee* was not radar, because the aircraft did not carry a transmitter. The airborne receiving equipment received transmissions from ground stations.

German records state simply that Lent shot down his Wellington at 0502 hours on the 14th to the northwest of Terschelling. From the time given it appears that it was on its way back to England, probably after having bombed the target. British records show eight Wellingtons as either 'Presumed lost over the sea' or 'Lost without trace'.[94] The life of a conscientious unit commander was a busy one, as is evidenced by a summary of Lent's flying pattern during the month of September, when over and above his operational flying he took off twenty-seven times, and flew four different types of aircraft, the Bf 110, the Do 215, the Fieseler 156 *Storch* high-wing communications machine, and – interestingly – the Focke-Wulf Fw 190 single-engined fighter. His duties as *Gruppenkommandeur* took him to Moenchengladbach and Wittmundhafen in Germany, to Saint Trond in Belgium, and to Gilze-Rijn and Soesterberg in Holland. In the Bf 110 he flew air tests and made operational sorties; in the Do 215 cross-country flights, operational sorties (without success), a weather flight and an air-sea rescue flight; and in the Fieseler *Storch* a 'special flight' and a reconnaissance mission, of which no further details are available. All his trips in the Fw 190, twelve in number, were during the daylight hours, and they included 'conversion to type', air-firing and, at 0657 hours on the morning of the 14th September, less than an hour after he had landed his Bf 110 R4+AC from the night-fighting sortie in which he had destroyed a Wellington, a 'live' but unfruitful scramble. In addition to this busy flying programme, of course, Lent was responsible for the man-management, command and representational duties that went with his Command.

It is believed that a few other pilots of II./NJG 2 in addition to Lent flew the single-engined FW 190 fighters, but very little is known about their presence at Leeuwarden, which seems to have been very short-lived and unproductive. Probably it was an to defend against daylight mining operations and anti-shipping sweeps by the RAF off the Friesian Islands. Apart from an air test of eight minutes' duration on 2 October, no further flights in the Fw 190 appear in Lent's logbook.

With effect from 1 October 1942, II./NJG 2 was part of yet another reorganisation of the *Nachtjagd*, being taken back into NJG 1 as a fourth *Gruppe*, and *Hauptmann* Helmut Lent became *Kommandeur* IV./NJG 1. With an overall tally of 53 kills - 45 by night and 8 by day - to his credit, he was firmly established as the leading night-fighter pilot of the *Luftwaffe*.

---

[94] 'Royal Air Force Bomber Command Losses of the Second World War, 1942' by W. R. Chorley.

CHAPTER EIGHT

October 1942 to July 1943
Kommandeur IV./NJG 1.
The Ruhr and Hamburg

A N OFFICER who knew Helmut Lent well, if not intimately, was Hermann Greiner, who served under him in both II./NJG 2 and IV./NJG1 – in fact the same unit – which, as explained in the preceding chapter, was transferred from NJG 2 to NJG 1 and renamed accordingly in October 1942. When the then *Leutnant* Greiner was posted to Leeuwarden as an untried night-fighter pilot Lent was already a *Hauptmann* and holder of the *Ritterkreuz*, the rising star of the *Nachtjagd* with approaching forty victories to his credit, and the gulf between them in terms of rank, status and esteem was great, even though Greiner was only two years younger than Lent. Greiner was himself destined ultimately to become *Kommandeur* IV./NJG 1, but not until the late stages of the war. There was a far greater observance of difference in rank in the *Luftwaffe* than, for example, there was in the Royal Air Force, and over and above that Lent was inherently an officer in the Prussian tradition, which meant that he did not form close friendships with subordinates, even though he was universally greatly admired and respected by them. Greiner is, however, an objective observer of character, and his comment on the man who was his commanding officer over a period of about twenty months is of great relevance:

In February 1942 I met the then *Hauptmann* Helmut Lent, at that time *Kommandeur* II./NJG 2, for the first time. After the completion of *Unternehmen Donnerkeil*, for which I was attached as a member of the airborne escort of the German warships, I was posted from I./NJG 1 to II./NJG 2 at Leeuwarden. My first impressions were of a mature, self-controlled, composed and intelligent young man, likeable, sensitive and educated, a good representative of his elite origins. At first he was rather distant, but I put that down to his being an introvert, so that every new acquaintance needed time to establish itself. Sensitivity is a characteristic that merits close consideration, a psychological theme that deserves to be studied more closely. From my own experience I believe that, as was quite apparent in Lent, sensitivity, in a perceptible but healthy form, always indicates basic mental strength, particularly when it comes to ethical and moral strength, which he had in abundance, and its use

Georg Hermann Greiner – during the war he was known as Hermann – seen here as a *Hauptmann* with the Knight's Cross. By the end of hostilities he had added the Oak Leaves, had shot down 51 bombers and was *Kommandeur* IV./NJG 1.

in the sense of human spiritual responsibility.

Months passed, and by then my picture of him was almost complete. I would describe it as exemplary. Clearly apparent in this picture were the characteristics and properties of the Teutons and the Balts, probably inherited from his forefathers.

In him we find a composed yet highly alert, impressive Commander of a flying unit. He gave the impression of being an intellectual and he was clearly looking for reactions, which indicated high intelligence, astuteness, logic and discrimination. He was a master of self-control. His unshakeable faith, his iron will, his reliability and his constant striving to set an example and to expect and demand similar achievements of his men could only result from the input of considerable energy. In Lent we see a Christian imbued with deep faith who, in his manner and philosophy of life, let himself be guided by moral principles of the highest value. In him his approach to life and his way of thinking can be seen as a direct consequence and result of his responsibilities: all in all a synthesis of characteristics that combined to make a genius. In heroes and creative personalities such as Lent everything must be in tune and harmony.

We aircrew at that period had a saying,. 'Breakfast is the best season.' During the ample breakfast that we enjoyed we were able to observe the *Kommandeur* more closely and longer than usual in a relaxed atmosphere. His official responsibilities when operational flying was being planned – maintaining the war diary, correspondence with the Ministry and the Technical Trials office, dealing with disciplinary matters, just to give a few examples – provided us with few opportunities to observe the *Kommandeur*. In the relaxed atmosphere of breakfast however we came to know, to our surprise, an open-minded, approachable, obliging and talkative *Hauptmann* who was also inclined to cheerfulness and practical jokes. As undoubted *primus inter pares* he could let himself relax and motivate his pilots. When he did so no jewel fell from his crown: he remained a born leader and an outstanding *Kommandeur* of his *Gruppe*, and in return his *Gruppe* afforded him the proper respect that was his due.

Helmut Lent, *Kommandeur* IV./NJG 1, presents awards to NCOs. Adjutant Reiner Petersen is in the foreground.

The first few months of Helmut Lent's command of IV./NJG 1 coincided with a period of comparatively low-level activity on the part of Bomber Command, largely due to seasonally adverse weather conditions. Harris

was still in what he later described as his 'preliminary phase'[95], working to overcome the inadequacies in both equipment and operational capability of the force that he had inherited, and he was aiming to begin his main offensive in the Spring of 1943. On the German side *Himmelbett* seemed to be working well, and Kammhuber was continuing his policy of setting up new close-control radar areas wherever there seemed to be a threat of attack by Bomber Command. Within each these circular *Räume* the two basic *Würzburg* acquisition radars had long been superseded by their bigger cousins, the *Würzburg Riesen*. By this time, too, virtually all the *Luftwaffe* night fighters in the northern defence areas were equipped with the *Lichtenstein* B/C air interception radar and results were, from the German point of view, very encouraging. In the months of June, July and August 1942, for example, out of a total of 531 RAF bombers that had failed to return to England the *Nachtjagd* had accounted for no less than 349. As post-war studies were to show, at that time the RAF statisticians were grossly underestimating the proportion of their bombers that were shot down by night fighters as compared to those destroyed by anti-aircraft fire[96], but despite that the increasing potency of the *Nachtjagd* was evident to Harris and was causing him some concern. In his book 'Bomber Offensive' he wrote: 'In the autumn of 1942 I was being continually pressed to attack Berlin as soon as the nights were long enough to bring this objective within range... But in 1942 I refused, however much I was urged, to attack Berlin. I knew that at this time we could do little damage there and I declined to risk the very heavy casualties that could be expected... Berlin was the target which the night fighter force was bound at all costs to defend.' In the same context he wrote: 'A new and deadly tactic of the enemy fighters was first observed in March 1942. The fighter climbed steeply until it got under the tail of the bomber, opened fire at close range, and continued to fire and to climb yet more steeply until it stalled.' Although the tactic as described might have been used occasionally by individual pilots, what returning bomber crews were reporting was the so-called *'von hinten unten'* ('from astern and below') approach, not quite as dramatic as that described by Harris – the fighter did not stall – yet very effective. Taking advantage of the fact that when approaching from a lower altitude his aircraft would be very difficult for the bomber crew, and in particular the rear gunner, to pick out against the dark landscape below, the fighter pilot would come in behind and below the bomber, gradually creeping up on it in a shallow climb until he felt that he was in a favourable position for an attack. Then he would pull up and open fire simultaneously, giving quite a long burst and 'spraying' the enemy machine, hoping to eliminate the rear gunner in the process of destroying the bomber. He would then dive away to one side or the other

---

[95] 'Bomber Offensive'.
[96] In the second six months of 1942, for example, Air Ministry estimated that 169 of their losses had been caused by night fighters, whereas the *Nachtjagd* claimed 373 kills.

into the cover of the dark landscape. This tactic is believed to have been devised and taught by Lent's subordinate in both II./NJG 2 and IV./NJG 1, Ludwig Becker, who was known by the self-explanatory cognomen *'Professor der Nachtjagd'*. *'Von hinten unten'* was not, of course, to be recommended when the bombers were flying above a covering of cloud, when the fighter would appear as a dark silhouette that would probably be seen by the rear gunner.

The creation a fourth *Gruppe* of *Nachtjagdgeschwader* 1 consolidated the night-fighter defence of the Dutch, Belgian and North-West German area under Wolfgang Falck's command. When II./NJG 2 had been formed at Leeuwarden eleven months earlier it had in all probability been part of an experiment to see whether the number of *Gruppen* in

Oberleutnant Ludwig Becker, 'Professor of Night Fighting'. He was lost in daylight action against American bombers on 26 February 1943 when his score stood at 44.

Oberleutnant Hans-Joachim Jabs was a successful *Zerstörer* pilot with II./ZG 76 before transferring to night fighting. Here he is seen with *Hauptmann* Groth at Jever in October 1940 after both had been decorated with the Knight's Cross.

NJG 1 might usefully be increased from three to four, and the outstanding performance of II./NJG 2 under Lent's command had confirmed that to do so would be a good move. *Major* Wolfgang Falck (he was promoted to *Oberstleutnant* on 1 January 1943) commanded the *Geschwader* from his Headquarters at Deelen. Of the other three *Gruppen*, I./NJG 1 (*Hauptmann* Werner Streib) was stationed at Venlo, ll./NJG 1 (*Hauptmann* Walter Ehle) at Saint Trond in Belgium, and III./NJG 1 (*Hauptmann* Wolfgang Thimmig) at Twente. In accordance with the standard procedure, the three *Staffeln* of *Oberleutnant* Lent's new Fourth *Gruppe* were numbered 10.NJG 1, 11.NJG 1 and 12.NJG 1, and Lent appointed *Oberleutnant* Rudolf Sigmund (who had replaced *Oberleutnant* Schoenert as *Staffelkapitän* preparatory to the latter's posting), *Oberleutnant* Egmont *zur* Lippe-Weissenfeld and the 'Night-Fighter

Lent's confidential
fitness report on Rudolf
Schoenert.

Beurteilungsnotizen

über den

Oberleutnant	d.R.	1.9.41	Rudolf Schoenert
(Dienstgrad)	(d. R. z. V. - o. ä.)	(R. D. A.)	(Vor- und Zuname)

27.7.1911	Glogau	Flugzeugführer(Einflieger)	verh.	Bremen II
(geb. am)	(zu)	(Beruf)	(led., verh.)	(zust. W. Bez. Rdo)

Zeitdauer der Verwendung von bis	1.11.1941 - 30.9.1942
Art der Verwendung	Staffelführer
Grund des Abgangs	Versetzung
Versetzt zu	I./N.J.G. 3
Beurteilung (Persönlichkeits- wert, Bewährung vor dem Feinde, dienstliche Leistung, Körperliche, Eignung)	Oblt.Sch.ist eine mittelgroße,schlanke,blonde,gut ausse- hende Erscheinung mit durch und durch ehrlichem,aufrich- tigen Wesen.Innere Geschlossenheit,zielbewusstes Denken und klare Entschlusskraft stempeln ihn zu einer Persön- lichkeit.Er besitzt eine überdurchschnittliche Begabung, die Gabe zum Improvisieren und steckt voller Iniative. Bei der Gruppe fand er als Staffelführer Verwendung.Er hat es verstanden trotz seiner geringen militärischen Vorbildung(Sch.ist Res.-Offz.)eine Staffel zu führen,dere Einsatz sowohl wegen ihrer Selbständigkeit, als auch de Aufgabe des Einsatzes nicht leicht war.Seine nachtjägeri- sche Passion hat er versucht auf seine ganze Staffel zu übertragen. Besonders liegen seine Fähigkeiten auf fliege- rischem Gebiet.Trotz kurzer Einweisungszeit gelang es ihm bisher 23 Nachtjagdsiege zu erringen. Seine Einsatz- freude und seine Tapferkeit fanden durch die Verleihung des Ritterkreuzes eine würdige Anerkennung.Die Führung der Staffel in truppendienstlicher Hinsicht wurde befrie- digend durchgeführt.Seine besonderen Interessen und Fähig keiten liegen auf fliegerisch-technischem Gebiet.Im Krei- se des Offizierkorps ist er beliebt und geachtet,Bei Un- tergebenen geschätzt und geehrt.Seiner Ernennung zum Staffelkapitän stehen keine Bedenken mehr entgegen.Er steht fest auf dem Boden der nationalsozialistischen Welt anschauung.
Eignung für	Staffelkapitän.
	(Unterschrift)

Professor' *Oberleutnant* Ludwig Becker, all of whom had served with him in II./NJG 2, as *Staffelkapitäne*. On 15 October, *Oberleutnant zur* Lippe-Weissenfeld left IV.NJG 1 on being appointed to command 1./NJG 3 at Vechta, and his position as *Staffelkapitän* was assumed by *Oberleutnant* Hans-Joachim Jabs. 'Achim' Jabs, an experienced *Zerstörer* ace who had flown in the Battle of Britain and was a holder of the Knight's Cross, had been serving as a *Staffelkapitän* with II./ZG 76 in November 1941 when it was absorbed into the *Nachtjagd* as III./NJG 3, at which time he already had 19 *Zerstörer* victories to his credit. With III./NJG 3 he had scored two night kills, so that he arrived at Leeuwarden with a total score of 21.

Lippe-Weissenfeld's departure from Leeuwarden was followed almost immediately by that of Rudolf Schoenert on posting to I./NJG 3. In a confidential fitness report Lent spoke of Schoenert on the following terms:

Oberleutnant Sch. is of average height, slim, blond and of good appearance. His personality is thoroughly honourable and honest. Inner determination, focused thinking and clear decisiveness mark him out as an individual. He has an above-average gift for improvisation and possesses great initiative. In the *Gruppe* he was employed as *Staffelführer*[97]. Despite his limited military training (Sch. is a Reserve Officer) he proved capable of leading a *Staffel*, which was, by reason of the type of operation it was engaged in coupled with its independent role, no easy task. He attempted to communicate his own passion for night fighting to the whole *Staffel*. His abilities in the field of flying are particularly marked. Despite only having a short period of preliminary training he has so far succeeded in scoring 23 victories by night. His readiness for operations and his bravery have found worthy recognition in the award of the Knight's Cross. His leadership of the *Staffel* in military terms was carried out satisfactorily. His particular interests lie in the field of aviation technology. In the officers' social circle he is much liked and admired, and by subordinates he is highly regarded and honoured. There are no objections to his appointment as *Staffelkapitän*. He is firmly grounded in National Socialist world philosophy.

Rudolf Schoenert was destined to end the war with the rank of *Major*, having been awarded the *Eichenlaub* and scored 64 victories. His most important achievement, however, lay in his having sponsored a new weapon within the *Nachtjagd* that made a great impact in the relentless struggle against the bombers.

As his adjutant to IV./NJG 1 Helmut Lent coopted *Oberleutnant* Heiner Petersen, who had been a member of 6./NJG 1 but had been severely injured when his Bf 110 collided with a Short Stirling in June 1942 and was no longer fit for operational flying duties. Petersen was an able

Helmut Lent, Adjutant Heiner Petersen and Hans-Joachim Jabs on the tennis court at Leeuwarden.

---

[97] *Staffelführer*: The operational leader of a *Staffel*. The *Staffelkapitän* coupled this role with administrative command of the *Staffel*.

A Dornier Do 215 night fighter. When this photograph was taken at Leeuwarden in Spring 1942 this aircraft was on the strength of II./NJG 2 and carried the identification number R4+DC. When II./NJG 2 became IV./NJG 1 it was renamed in the C9 (=NJG 1) series.

administrator, and he would remain with Lent until the latter's death.

Lent's first operational flight as *Kommandeur* IV./NJG 1 was on 13 October, when the RAF attacked Kiel. He scrambled in Bf 110 G9+AF at 2037 hours, but he landed 64 minutes later without having scored. He did not fly again operationally until 9 November, this time in a Dornier 215, G9+DF, when he was more successful, shooting down a Halifax near the island of Ameland at 2038 hours. Halifax II W7864, DY-F, of No. 102 Squadron had taken off from its Yorkshire base of Pocklington just before six o'clock in the evening, piloted by Flight Sergeant T. R. N. Fetherston and carrying an extra man, probably a 'Second Dickie', a pilot newly arrived on the squadron and flying to gain operational experience. There were no survivors. Ludwig Becker claimed a Wellington. The RAF's target that night had been Hamburg, but extremely bad weather meant that the majority of the bombs dropped by the 200-plus participating aircraft fell well wide of the city, where only comparatively slight damage was caused. Fifteen British machines failed to return, but the Nachtjagd claimed only four victories.

Lent's next two successes against Bomber Command, the last he scored in 1942, came during the night of 17/18 December, when IV./NJG 1 claimed five of the thirteen bombers destroyed by the *Nachtjagd* from a force of 104 sent to attack miscellaneous minor targets over a wide area, of which eighteen failed to return – a daunting overall loss-rate of 17.3 percent. The entry in Lent's logbook recording these two kills claims a Lancaster and a Halifax, but no Halifaxes were operating that night, and it is virtually certain that both his victims were Lancasters. The first,

ED355 (KM-D) of No. 44 (Rhodesian) Squadron, Waddington, is readily identified, while the second was in all probability ED333 OF-B, from 97 Squadron, Woodhall Spa. All the men on board both aircraft perished.

From mid-November until mid-December 1942 Lent's wife Lena was with him at Leeuwarden, but whether she was accommodated in official or private quarters is not known. On the 20th December Lent wrote home to Pyrehne:

> Since the day before yesterday I am once again a grass widower. After a wonderful five weeks with Lena we each now have to live alone again. In fact

Helmut on his promotion to *Major* on 1 January 1943.

during this period I tasted something of true marriage for the first time. And during the whole time that she was here Tommy didn't give us much trouble – right until the last night. And then I shot down another two four-engined bombers. I was very pleased to strike a blow against those people who say that married soldiers are cowards! If the Tommies stay quiet on Christmas Eve I will be thinking of you. The memories of the Christmas Eves that I spent at home will enhance the evening this time. And what is more, we Christians have something above all that others haven't got – we have a Christ the Lord. And even if we are alone on our Lord's birthday we will not let that detract from our happiness.

Major Helmut Lent (right) in conversation with *Major* Werner Streib, *Kommandeur* I./NJG 1. Both officers wear the *Eichenlaub*. Taken in early 1943.

Lent was only without Lena for few days, because they spent Christmas 1942 with Lena's family in Hamburg, and he returned to duty at

Leeuwarden on the 6th of January 1943 with the rank of *Major*: his promotion had been promulgated on the first day of the New Year. Writing home about his elevation to senior rank, Lent said,

> I'd like to thank you especially for your congratulations on my majority. It's quite incredible, being a Major at twenty-four! But I can't do anything about it – I consider myself completely blameless! I feel certain that you, and above all Lena, are more proud than I am myself!

It did not take the newly-promoted *Kommandeur* IV./NJG 1 long to score his next kill. On the night of 8/9 January small forces of bombers were sent to attack Duisburg and to lay mines off the German and Danish coasts respectively. Five Lancasters did not return, all shot down by night fighters, three by IV./NJG 1: Lent, Becker and Jabs were the successful pilots.

The Duisburg raid was one of a series of trials mounted by Harris at this period to test a remarkable new device, *'Oboe'*, by means of which bombs could be aimed with a degree of precision hitherto unequalled. The nature of *Oboe* was such that each aircraft carrying it had to be controlled separately from ground stations on the English mainland, which meant that it was unsuitable for general use by the bombers in the main stream, and in addition its range was limited by the optical horizon – the higher an *'Oboe'* aircraft flew, the deeper into Germany it could penetrate and still be seen by the ground radar in England. Fortunately for Bomber Command – but not for the Germans – Mosquito aircraft could fly high enough to bring targets in the Ruhr area within range, and it was a logical step for them to drop not bombs but pyrotechnic target markers at which the heavy bombers flying lower down could aim their

De Havilland Mosquito Mk IV

incendiary and high-explosive cargoes. Also under development and test at this period was a revolutionary new airborne radar, codenamed *H2S*, designed to improve navigation and blind bombing. The first *H2S* sets went to the Pathfinder Force, but it was intended that eventually all Bomber Command machines would be equipped with the device. *H2S*, which operated on a wavelength in the 10 centimetre band, employed a rapidly rotating aerial in a blister beneath the fuselage of the bomber which transmitted radio energy downwards all around the aircraft and received such energy as was reflected from the ground: the strength of the reflected signals varied according to the nature of the surface from which they came, and they were displayed on a cathode-ray tube – rather like a very rudimentary television screen – in the navigator's 'office' in the form of a primitive map of the ground over which the bomber was flying[98]. Together with for example *Freya, Würzburg* and *Lichtenstein* by the Germans, the introduction of *Oboe* and *H2S* – not to forget the earlier *Gee* – by the RAF were symptomatic of the increasing extent to which science-based technology was shaping the aerial battle between the night bombers and the night fighters. Harris was still planning for, and working towards, what he called the 'Main Offensive'.

On the night of Thursday the 21st to Friday the 22nd of January 1943, 82 Bomber Command aircraft visited Essen, while a further 70 flew mine-laying operations off the Friesian Islands. From the latter force four Wellingtons and two Halifaxes were lost, one of the Wellingtons falling victim to *Major* Helmut Lent in the sea north of the island of Schiermonnikoog at 2011 hours. It was Lent's 58th confirmed victory overall, and his 50th by night, and as such the subject of much publicity in Germany. Lent was the first night fighter to shoot down fifty enemy aircraft in the hours of darkness. War Reporter Walter Dölfs described the occasion as follows:

Leeuwarden, probably January 1943. Lent is congratulated on his 50th night-time victory. (Left to right): Hans-Joachim Jabs; Holst, Base Commandant; Area Controller Heinrich Ruppel; Adjutant Heiner Petersen.

---

[98] How *H2S* got its name has been the subject of much discussion and dispute over the years. The most widely aired theory is that in its early days someone or other, unimpressed by the device, said of it, 'It stinks!' which led to it being endowed with the formula of the foul-smelling substance hydrogen sulphide. A more likely explanation, since *H2S* was based on the anti-submarine device ASV (Air to Surface Vessels), would seem to be that *H2S* stems from 'Height to Surface'.

During the night of 21/22 January 1943 *Eichenlaubträger Major* Lent scored his 50th night-time victory. Just as during the most recent attack on Berlin on 17 January, when the British lost *25* bombers, most of them four-engined, the Tommies came up against determined resistance on the part of our air defences when they made a weak thrust against North-West Germany. Night fighters and flak once again destroyed a proportionately high percentage of the British bombers involved, thereby inflicting a new defeat on the Royal Air Force. The *Nachtjagdgruppe* led by *Eichenlaubträger Major* Lent played its part in this outstanding tally of victories. With the destruction of a Wellington the *Kommandeur* scored his 50th night-time victory.

'It was my hardest combat!'

When *Major* Lent returned from his victorious aerial combat he said, 'That was my most difficult engagement. There was a full moon, and the night was bright. The Tommy could see our night fighters attacking in good time and open fire at them, so that there were bitter combats that called for the highest degree of skill on the part of our night fighters.

When *Major* Lent was crossing the sector allocated to him that night he came into contact with a Wellington. *Major* Lent pulled his nimble aircraft round and headed for the enemy. But in the course of this manoeuvre the Tommy must have seen the danger. The Wellington immediately went into a dive and attempted to escape at low altitude.

But *Major* Lent refused to be shaken off. Flying with great skill, he stayed with the enemy, and a nerve-racking combat developed. Shimmering threads

Leeuwarden, 1943. *Major* Helmut Lent is interviewed for the radio.

of tracer flashed to and fro. The fire from our night fighter struck home in the centre of the Wellington's fuselage. But the expected results didn't come. The Wellington clung on tenaciously and refused to catch fire. *Major* Lent went in close to the bomber, which by this time was desperately attempting to escape by means of wild turns and heavy defensive fire. Then eventually the Wellington burst into flames under the hail of bullets that hammered into him for minutes on end. The bomber went down vertically. *Major* Lent had brought his most difficult combat to a successful conclusion, and in doing so he had reached his fiftieth night victory.

In a letter to his mother Lent himself spoke of his victory in less dramatic terms:

> Yes, as you heard on the wireless, I got my fiftieth night-fighter kill yesterday evening. It was only a Wellington, but we had quite a tough scrap. But when it was all over he was down on the ground. The number fifty is a small milestone. But above all I feel bound to thank God from the depths of my heart for his protection and for his favour. Shooting down an enemy is not always a simple matter, but sometimes a hard fight. But He has endowed me with the necessary physical and spiritual strength to do it. Admittedly, a number of enemies are sent to the other side every time, but on the other hand, how many Germans' lives do I save?

At this time there was a significant development in the Allied bomber offensive against the Third Reich: American heavy bombers stationed in England flew their first attack against a target in Germany. There had been a steady build-up of Boeing B-17 Flying Fortresses and Consolidated B-24 Liberators of the United States Eighth Air Force on bases is East Anglia since the arrival of the first of the heavies there in July 1942, and they had been flying operationally since August against targets in France. Now, on 27 January, a force of B-24s headed for the submarine-building yard at Vegesack, just to the north of Bremen, so initiating what came to be known as the 'Round the Clock' offensive, with the USAAF bombing by day and Bomber Command by night. It was an inauspicious beginning to what was to develop into a prolonged onslaught of terrible magnitude and ferocity: Vegesack was cloud-covered, so the B-24s bombed alternative targets at Wilhelmshaven, but without achieving notable accuracy, and one B-24 was shot down by single-engined fighters. The bombers approached and left the target area over the North Sea, and Lent's logbook shows that he scrambled at nine minutes past twelve and landed an hour later. His flight is shown as *'Einsatz'* – 'Operation' – so it seems likely that he took off to intercept, or simply to investigate, the American raid.

Lent took leave from the 3rd to the 26th of February 1943, spending it in Hamburg and at Langen in the Tyrol. The leave is shown in his pay book as *Erholungsurlaub* (Recuperation Leave) and he probably spent it partly at one of the several *'Luftwaffenerholungsheime'* (*Luftwaffe* Recuperation Homes) located in Southern Germany and Austria. These were requisitioned luxury hotels in winter sports resorts at which aircrew recovering from wounds or injuries or assessed as suffering from battle strain could spend a short period – usually a fortnight – relaxing, receiving therapeutic treatment and taking part in winter sports – all at *Luftwaffe* expense.

The day after Lent left Leeuwarden to begin his leave another force of American bombers, this time B-17s, attacked targets in the Ruhr town of Hamm, well known for its vast railway marshalling yards, and eight Bf 110s from IV./NJG 1 in four *Rotten* (combat pairs) led by *Oberleutnant* Jabs, *Kapitän* of the 11th *Staffel*, took off from Leeuwarden to intercept. The night-fighter Bf 110s, hampered in terms of speed as they were by their *Lichtenstein* aerials and overwhelmingly outgunned by the combined fire-power of the B-17s, were at a considerable disadvantage, yet they pressed their attacks home with great gallantry and managed to shoot down three B-17s, *Oberleutnant* Jabs, *Oberfeldwebel* Grimm and *Unteroffizier* Naumann destroying one each. There were no fatal casualties on the German side, but three men were wounded. Two of the Messerschmitts had to crash-land, and not one of the others returned to base without combat damage.

On 26th February, the final day of Lent's leave, Jabs again led twelve aircraft of IV./NJG 1 against a force of American heavies, this time B-24 Liberators flying on a westerly heading north of the Friesian islands on the way back from an attack on Emden. *Oberleutnant* Rudolf Sigmund

Lent, Becker and an unidentified officer, Leeuwarden 1943.

and *Unteroffizier* Georg Kraft each destroyed one American bomber, but of the twelve night fighters that took off one failed to return, that of *Oberleutnant* Ludwig Becker, *Staffelkapitän* of 12./NJG 1, who had 44 confirmed victories to his credit. The 'Professor of Night Fighting' was posthumously promoted to *Hauptmann* and awarded the Oak Leaves to the Knight's Cross of the Iron Cross.

Over and above their success against the Americans, the pilots of Lent's *Gruppe* acquitted themselves well by night during the period of his absence by shooting down thirteen Bomber Command machines. Jabs in particular distinguished himself, destroying three Stirlings, all from No. 15 Squadron, within a short space of time during the night of 19/20 February to add to the B-17 he had claimed on the 4th of the month.

Back from his leave, Lent flew twice on 1 March, doing forty minutes local flying in the afternoon in G9+EF, presumably to familiarise himself after four weeks' absence from the controls, and then operationally that evening in the same machine, taking of from Leeuwarden just before eight o'clock against a force of RAF bombers heading for Berlin. He shot down a Halifax – probably DT641, VR-R of No. 419 Squadron – north of the island of Ameland at twenty minutes past nine. Losses to the 302-strong bomber force, at 5.6 percent, were heavy but just on the margin of acceptability, and of the nineteen aircraft that were lost night fighters claimed seventeen, five of them falling to Lent's *Gruppe*.

Harris had not attacked the German capital at all during 1942, although the directive that he had inherited when taking over as Commander-in-Chief had included the city as a low-priority target, specifying that 'your operations should be of a harassing nature, the object being to maintain the fear of attack over the city and to impose ARP measures[99]. By January 1943, however, it seems that Harris had felt that his force was by then strong enough and well-enough equipped to visit the 'Big City', and on the night of the 16th to the 17th of the month he had sent 201 Lancasters and Halifaxes to Berlin on an experimental raid using only four-engined bombers, with the Pathfinder Force dropping specially designed target indicators in an attempt to concentrate the bombing. The results were disappointing: without electronic aids – Berlin was well beyond *Gee* and *Oboe* range and *H2S* was not yet available – and in conditions of cloud cover and haze both on the way to and above the target the navigation by both Pathfinder and Main Force aircraft was very poor, so that bombing was widely scattered. On a happier note, only one aircraft, a Lancaster of No. 61 Squadron captained by Squadron Leader E. D. J. Parker, GC, DFC, failed to return[100]. Harris had repeated his Berlin experiment the following night:

---

[99] Official History. Part IV. Page 144.

[100] Earlier in the war, in June 1940, Squadron Leader Parker, then a Pilot Officer with No. 49 Squadron, had been awarded the Empire Gallantry Medal for rescuing his wireless operator from their burning Hampden after it had crashed near Lincoln in the course of an operational sortie: he had later exchanged his EGM for the George Cross, which was introduced in September the same year.

again the results were poor, but this time the debit side of the account was ominous. Of the 187 four-engined bombers dispatched, 22, or 11.8 per cent, were shot down, mostly by night fighters. Lent himself had scrambled but had failed to score.

The results of the third Berlin raid, on 1 March, when Lent claimed his 59th victory overall, were somewhat better than those achieved in the two earlier experimental attacks, but still far from satisfactory. By this

time the Pathfinder machines were carrying *H2S*, and first results against targets further west had been encouraging. Over Berlin, however, *H2S* proved very difficult to use. The size of the city and the density of its built-up areas were such that it was almost impossible to distinguish individual features, such as lakes and rivers, suitable for use as reference points for navigation and bomb aiming. Later, the introduction of a version of the device operating on a much shorter wavelength would make things somewhat easier, but Berlin would never be an 'H2S-friendly' target.

March 1943. Helmut Lent pays a visit to Deelen. Here he is seen with *Oberstleutnant* Friedberg (left) and *Hauptmann* Thimmig.

H2S had first been used operationally by No. 8 (Pathfinder) Group to mark targets in Hamburg in the early hours of the 31 of January 1943: three nights later it had been similarly employed against Cologne: in the course of that attack a Stirling of No. 7 Squadron equipped with the revolutionary radar set had been shot down near Rotterdam by *Oberleutnant* Reinhold Knacke of I./NJG 1. The equipment was fitted with an automatic self-destruction device, which however failed to

Another photograph taken on the same occasion. Left to right: Streib; Friedberg; Lent; Thimmig; Frank. *General* von Döring is in the foreground, right.

Deelen, March 1943. Left to right: Thimmig; Streib; Frank; Friedberg (?), Lent.

function, with the result that the little-damaged set, which the Germans then named the *'Rotterdam Gerät'*[101], fell into their hands and was sent to the Telefunken works in Berlin for investigation. During the raid on Berlin on 1/2 March the set, which was in the course of being reassembled and evaluated, was completely destroyed when the factory in which it was being inspected was hit by RAF bombs, but the very same night another British aircraft, Halifax II TL-O of No. 35 Squadron, was shot down over Holland by *Leutnant* August Geiger of III./NJG 1 and another almost intact *H2S* set recovered from it. The German scientists were able to build a set, install it in a German bomber and test it from the

[101] A *Gerät* is a device, a piece of equipment, a gadget, an instrument etc. Hence *'Rotterdam Gerät'* may be translated 'Rotterdam Device'.

air. The knowledge that they thus gained enabled them in due course to
take counter-measures, the most important of which was the
introduction of a device called *Naxos* – twenty-five versions of it were
built! – by means of which a night-fighter pilot could home on to aircraft
transmitting *H2S* signals. Perhaps even more importantly, as the use of
H2S by Bomber Command aircraft rapidly increased, knowledge of the
frequency on which it operated permitted the German signals
monitoring service, the *Horchdienst*, to pick up *H2S* signals emanating
from Britain during pre-operation air testing of the bombers and by so
doing to forecast whether there would be raids that night and, if so, the
likely strength of the bomber force. Once the enemy bombers were on
their way towards their targets, their route could be plotted by means of
the H2S transmissions and the appropriate defences alerted and
deployed accordingly.

Deelen, March 1943.
Left to right: Friedberg
(?); von Döring; Lent;
Streib.

   In microcosm, this mini-history of *H2S* typifies the extraordinarily
rapid way in which the air battle above the Third Reich was becoming
increasingly dependent upon radio technology, with new devices and
concepts being introduced by one side or the other, detected by the
enemy, countermeasures being conceived and introduced, and the
balance of advantage swinging short-term from one side to the other. At
the outbreak of war the perceived nature of air-to-air combat, fighter
versus bomber, had changed little from that which had applied at the
end of the 1914/1918 conflict, except that the aircraft were faster and the
armament heavier. Few, if any, air commanders or pundits had foreseen
the introduction and meteoric development of radar and related devices.
Hermann Göring opposed early requests for the introduction of
airborne interception radar in his night fighters by saying, in effect, 'We

Oberleutnant Reinhold Knacke. He shot down the Stirling from which the Germans recovered their first functional H2S set.

didn't need fancy peep-shows in our fighters in the First World War, and I can't see the need for them now!'

Despite such scornful rejection of the idea of radar-assisted interception and of early scepticism on the part of the crews, it was by now accepted that an extra, and possibly decisive, dimension had been introduced into the battle, and the crews – particularly the *Funker* – had to learn and adapt to new techniques. The importance of the radio-operator in the crew had increased, and great mutual trust and co-ordination between pilot and *Funker* was essential if success was to be achieved. That such trust existed between Helmut Lent and Walter Kubisch, his regular *Funker,* is attested to by their steady record of victories.

This period also saw the occasional, but gradually increasing, introduction into the night-fighter crew of a third man *(Dritter Mann)*, variously referred to as a *Bordmechaniker* (Flight Mechanic), *Beobachter* ('Observer' or 'Look-Out') or *Bordschütze* (Air Gunner), which was

recognition of the fact that the wireless operator's increasing workload made it necessary for him to have help, especially with the task of keeping a visual lookout and manning the rearward facing machine-gun(s), if the aircraft carried them: some pilots had the rear armament removed entirely in order to give the aircraft a slight increase in speed. The bigger night-fighter machines, for example the Do *215s*, already carried a third crew member, a *Bordmechaniker,* as the norm.

March 1943 saw another honour added to the formidable collection that Lent had already accrued, but is was not a decoration or a medal that the recipient wore with his uniform as evidence of gallantry or distinguished service. The honour was entirely at the discretion of the

Helmut Lent, *Kommandeur* IV./NJG 1, sitting next to a *Luftwaffenhelferin,* reportedly in the canteen of the Operations Centre at Leeuwarden.

In the Officers' Mess at Leeuwarden, 1943. Lent's is to the left.

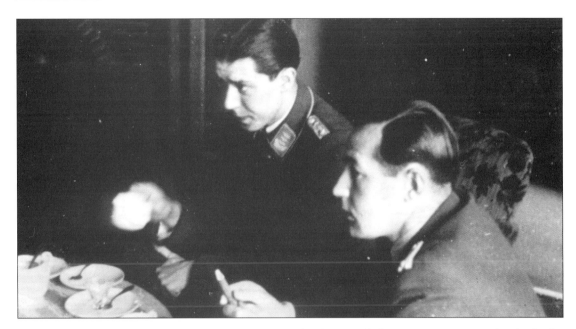

Hauptmann Hans-Joachim Jabs with the Adjutant of IV./NJG 1, *Oberleutnant* Reiner Petersen.

Reichsmarschall, Hermann Göring, and there were no set criteria for its award which, in common with that of more traditional decorations, was entered in the recipient's record of service. Helmut Lent received a portrait of the *Reichsmarschall* in a silver frame.

★　　★　　★

'At long last we were ready and equipped. Bomber Command's main offensive began at a precise moment, the moment of the first major attack on an objective in Germany by means of Oboe. This was the night of March

5th/6th 1943, when I was at last able to undertake with real hope of success the task which had been given to me when I first took over the Command a little more than a year before, the task of destroying the main cities of the Ruhr.'

These are the terms in which Harris describes in 'Bomber Offensive' the beginning of what subsequently became known as 'The Battle of the Ruhr'. The term is perhaps somewhat misleading. During the twenty-one weeks that this phase of the bomber offensive lasted, it is true, there were twenty-four major attacks on targets in and on the edge of the Ruhr industrial area, but there were also rather more than that number against individual targets elsewhere, many of them at long range. Berlin was visited, as for example were Munich, Frankfurt, Nuremberg, Stuttgart and places as far afield as Stettin and Pilsen, and there were raids on targets in France and Italy[102]. Harris adjudged the Battle to have been a considerable success: enormous damage was caused to cities and towns in the industrial complex of the Ruhr by a combination of *Oboe* and Pathfinder techniques. Gee, too, played its part: although the system was heavily jammed by the Germans, and although the navigators in the bombers lost the signals as they approached the Dutch coast, Gee made it possible for them to ensure that they were well on track and on time on the outward journey over the North Sea and to make the calculations necessary to stay on track and on time all the way to the target. The result was a considerable 'tightening-up' of the bomber stream in both space and time, and consequently an increase in the concentration of the bombing.

The was also a considerable increase in the number of casualties on the ground, the vast majority of them civilians, as is strikingly illustrated by one simple comparative statistic: when the battle began the highest recorded number of civilian casualties in any one attack had been about 475 in the 'Thousand-Bomber' raid on Cologne in May 1942, whereas in another attack on Cologne during the Battle of the Ruhr (28/29 June 1943) 4,377 – almost ten times as many – died. To form an idea of the intensity of bombing that Bomber Command could – but did not always – achieve, one might consider that in the same raid more than 10,000 were injured and 230,000 rendered homeless. This was the cold reality of area bombing. Arthur Harris would later write in 'Bomber Offensive': 'But it must be emphasised that in no instance, except in Essen, were we aiming specifically at any one factory during the Battle of the Ruhr; the destruction of factories, which was nevertheless on an enormous scale, could be regarded as a bonus. The aiming points were usually right in the centre of the town"[103]

Essen, which had hitherto proved an extremely difficult objective, largely because of the permanent covering of industrial haze that

---

[102] There was also the remarkable raid on the Möhne, Eder and Sorpe Dams on the night of the 16th/17th May, but this was a unique operation and outside the parameters of the main bomber offensive.

[103] From 'Bomber Offensive'.

With IV./NJG 1, Leeuwarden 1943. *Major* Lent with *Hauptmann* Ruppel, Area Controller. Ruppel had been a pilot on the Western Front during World War One.

obscured ground detail, was the target of Harris's opening move in the battle, and the raid was a signal success. In the space of 40 minutes 360 bombers aiming at markers dropped 'blind' by five *Oboe* Mosquitos and backed up by Pathfinder aircraft created 160 acres of destruction between the Krupp works and the city centre, hitting 53 separate buildings within the Krupp complex and destroying over 3,000 houses and damaging over 2,000 more within the city itself. Fourteen RAF bombers were lost in the attack, ten of them to NJG 1. Of them Lent's *Gruppe* shot down six, of which he himself claimed two: according to a usually reliable list of night-fighter kills he shot down a Halifax at twenty minutes past eight and a Lancaster at twenty-four minutes past ten. His logbook, however, shows quite clearly that he was only airborne for 44 minutes, taking off at ten o'clock exactly and landing at sixteen minutes to eleven, and, moreover, that he logged both his victims as Halifaxes. It seems virtually certain that one of Lent's victims was a Lancaster, despite the 'two Halifaxes' entry in his logbook. Lancaster I W4847 (OL-V) of No. 83 Squadron is logged as being shot down by a night fighter and crashing into the Ijsselmeer off Hindeloopen at 2224 hours: Lent's claim, at that precise time, is recorded as '10 km. east of Wieringen'. Wieringen and Hindeloopen are on opposite sides of the IJsselmeer and so, allowing for a reasonable latitude of error, the two locations agree. Lent's other kill is more difficult to identify, but the probability is that it went down at 2220 hours, not at 2020 hours as is given in the list of kills, and that it was probably a Halifax of No. 76 Squadron or possibly a

Lancaster of No. 49 Squadron, both of which are recorded as lost without trace.

Major Lent and his *Gruppe*, well placed at Leeuwarden to meet and engage bombers approaching over the North Sea and overflying Holland on their way to Germany, were literally in the forefront of the action. As *Kommandeur*, he was frequently the first pilot to scramble and head for the incoming bombers, which is reflected in the number of his kills that took place over the North Sea, before the bombers had even reached the mainland.

On the day following this first strike in the Battle of the Ruhr, Lent wrote a letter to his family in Pyrehne, which, unusually, seems to have contained a slight note of pessimism about the final outcome of the war and the dedication of some of the German population:

The *Reichsmarschall* inspects night fighter at Neuruppin in mid-1943. *Major* Helmut Lent is to his left.

> But I do believe that God will give us victory, even though we will need to use all our strength. Perhaps, through the hardship, the difficulty and the sacrifice that he demands of us, He will erode the discord and the immaturity that is unhappily too widespread among our people, for the great task that awaits us when victory comes.
>
> On the 1st and the 6th of the month I shot down one and then two more Tommies. During these missions God once more looked after me and protected me. They were three four-engined bombers. They were my 60th and 61st victories – a number to be proud of. But I ask God always to make me as modest as possible.

Lent only destroyed one more RAF bomber during March, a Wellington on the night of the 29th/30th, and then he claimed a Lancaster on the very early morning of the 4th of April. He wrote home:

During the moon period we didn't have a great deal to do. The Tommies prefer weather situations in which we are at a disadvantage. Either we couldn't take off because of fog, or we couldn't hunt because of clouds. Nevertheless, we managed to shoot a few down. On 30 March I scored my 54th, and on 3 April my 55th, night-time victory. The flying was more difficult than the shooting down, but God let me overcome all difficulties.

The next claim that the young *Gruppenkommandeur* made marked a notable achievement. His logbook reads: '20 April, took off Leeuwarden 0215 hours. Landed Leeuwarden 0352 hours. Airborne 97 minutes. One kill, Mosquito.' The victory was confirmed and publicised, and Lent went down in history as the first German pilot to destroy a Mosquito by night.

The remarkably versatile twin-engined de Havilland Mosquito, in its night-fighter version, had been an occasional, but increasingly frequent, visitor to the occupied countries during the hours of darkness since about mid-1942. These aircraft, from Fighter Command, went as intruders with the task of destroying any enemy machines they might chance upon, preferably German night fighters, and their activities were concentrated on *Luftwaffe* night-fighter airfields. From December 1942 unarmed *Oboe* Mosquitos of the Bomber Command Pathfinder Force had joined the bomber offensive, with dramatic results. The high speed and the altitude at which these Mosquitos flew made them invulnerable to normal night fighters and night-fighting techniques. Greatly concerned by these developments, the *Luftwaffe* sought, as a matter of urgency, ways in which counter-action could be taken. It is believed that experiments were carried out by Helmut Lent and *Leutnant* Heinz Lübke, the senior controller of *Eisbär,* the *Himmelbett* close-control area centred on Sondel to the south-west of Leeuwarden, into possible methods of intercepting Mosquitos. Lent's kill is recorded in the Nonnenmacher List as having taken place to the west of Stavoren – i.e., over the Ijsselmeer – at 0339 hours on the morning of the 20th April, but there was no Bomber Command activity at all on the night of 19/20 April 1943 and thus no aircraft from that Command recorded as missing. Two Fighter Command Mosquitos flying 'Night Ranger' patrols over Holland, however, failed to return, DZ755 from No. 151 Squadron and DZ694 from No. 410 (RCAF) Squadron, so it is seems likely that Lent's victim was one of them. The crew of the former aircraft, Flying Officer D. A. Sparrow and Pilot Officer V. G. Brown, occupy graves in the cemetery at Onstwedde, south-east of Groningen and near the border with Germany, which rules it out as Lent's victim and leads to the conclusion that the Mosquito that Lent destroyed, which had the doubtful distinction of being the first of its kind to be shot down by a German night fighter, was DZ694, pilot Flight Sergeant W. J. Reddie (RCAF), navigator Sergeant K. Evans (RAF). It had taken off from Coleby Grange, just south of the River Humber in Lincolnshire, at 2230 hours on the 19th, and so was presumably on its way back home when Lent intercepted it.

Dortmund suffered a heavy raid by just under 600 bombers on the night of the 4th/5th May, and there was considerable damage to both industrial premises and residential areas. There were over 1,700 casualties on the ground, of which nearly 700 were fatal, and Bomber Command lost thirty-one machines, the *Nachtjagd* claiming twenty-two. Of these kills, twelve fell to IV./NJG 1. Lent himself shot down two Stirlings within the space of ten minutes. A rare glimpse into the nature and hazards of being a night-fighter pilot emerges from his letter to his parents immediately after the night's events:

> Yesterday – and today – there was a lot of activity here, and for many reasons I have cause to thank God for His goodness and His protection. The *Gruppe* alone shot down twelve of the attackers, of which nine were on their way in and still carrying bombs, and in doing so we gained our 300th night-time victory. I

May 1943. Lent (right) with *General* von Döring at the funeral of *Oberleutnant* Lothar Linke, killed in a flying accident when his score of enemy aircraft destroyed stood at 27.

> managed to shoot down two more four-engined machines. When I was going for a third I had bad luck – my port engine caught fire. Thank God, however, the fire went out and I was able to get back home safely under God's protection. As you can imagine, it was an eventful night. In the moments of danger I had absolutely no feeling that anything would happen to me. I prayed, and I knew that God would shield me. And that is exactly what happened.

The next issue of the *Wehrmachtsbericht* reported:

> In this night the night-fighter *Gruppe of Major* Lent, holder of the *Eichenlaub,*

Oberleutnant Lothar Linke, seen here as a *Leutnant,* and *Kapitän* of the 11th *Staffel* of IV./NJG 1.

who reported their 250th night victory only four weeks ago, scored their 300th night kill. *Major* Lent himself, the most successful night-fighter pilot, shot two down, so increasing his personal tally of victories by night to fifty-eight.

After further victories by Lent on the 13th/14th and the 23rd/24th May respectively, the *Wehrmachtsbericht* reported that his night-fighting score had reached 60. By the end of the Battle of the Ruhr, his tally of kills stood at 71, of which 63 had been achieved at night.

Lent's last kill during the Ruhr Battle took place on the night of 25/26 June, when what was for that period a moderate force of bombers – 214 Lancasters, 134 Halifaxes, 73 Stirlings, 40 Wellingtons and 12 Mosquitos, a total of 473 aircraft – attacked Gelsenkirchen to no great effect, the performance of the *Oboe* Mosquitos being below par and the bombing widely scattered. Thirty RAF aircraft failed to return, and the *Nachtjagd* claimed 29 kills. The importance of IV./NJG 1 in the defensive plan, as well as its effectiveness, is clear from the fact that the *Gruppe* alone made fifteen of the kills. Lent's personal contribution to the night's performance was a Wellington, which he shot down in the Ijsselmeer to the west of Urk. A

Royal Australian Air Force pilot of No. 466 Squadron, Flight Sergeant A. B. R. Airy, had taken off from Leconfield in Yorkshire at eleven minutes to midnight in the Wellington on what was destined to be his last flight. He perished together with the other four men in his crew.

For Harris, the Battle of the Ruhr represented a success, but the price

of that success was not light. For the period 5 March to 24 July 1943 1,000 RAF bombers failed to return from the 23,401 sorties that Bomber Command flew in the dark hours, a loss-rate of 4.3 per cent. In terms of human life, that meant that approaching 7,000 aircrew were missing, of whom the overwhelming majority had doubtless perished[104]. The standard tour of operations for aircrew was thirty, which meant that the odds were markedly against any individual surviving a tour: for Pathfinders the odds against were even higher, because they were committed to flying sixty[105] operations before becoming 'screened'.[106]

The award of the *Ritterkreuz* to *Major* Wilhelm Herget and *Hauptmann* Hans Dieter Frank, Venlo 20 June 1943. Left to right: Streib; Frank; *Generalmajor* Kammhuber; Herget; Lent.

---

[104] During the war approximately 55,000 aircrew of Bomber Command died, while only about 10,000 survived being shot down and became prisoners of war.

[105] Later reduced to forty-five.

[106] Tour-expired. When a member of aircrew had flown the prescribed number of operations to complete a tour he was posted to a non-operational job, frequently as an instructor. An instructor flying with a trainee crew was called a 'screen', hence the expression 'to be screened'.

The performance of the German night fighters during the same period represented, if not a victory, at least a creditable achievement. Exact figures are not available, but a good estimate is that of the 1,000 bombers destroyed the *Nachtjagd* accounted for 770. Nevertheless, there was a growing feeling of dissatisfaction at more than one level in the night-fighter force with Kammhuber's *Himmelbett* intercept control system. When bombers were detected approaching, one fighter would be despatched to orbit the radio beacon of each circular *Raum* in the general area threatened and to wait there until directed on to a bomber by the controller. As Harris's bomber streams became more compact, however, fewer *Räume* were penetrated, which meant that there were always fighters in the air that had little chance of intercepting a bomber, which was fundamentally an uneconomical way of managing one's fighter resources. Further, there was little defence in depth in *Himmelbett*, because when a bomber had passed out of the limited area of a *Raum* he was unlikely to come under fighter attack unless and until he entered another one. There were already voices from senior commanders advocating some method of interception control that would offer both a more flexible and economical way of handling the available fighters together with the prospect of a higher percentage kill rate. There was another aspect of the *Himmelbett* system, too, which was having an adverse effect on aircrew morale, particularly among junior front-line crewmen. It had become usual for the more senior and experienced pilots, such as Lent himself, to be the first to be scrambled, and they would be sent to the *Räume* on the direct track of the bombers. Junior and less experienced pilots would find themselves on operational readiness night after night, more often than not without being scrambled: should they be ordered into the air, however, they would usually be sent to peripheral *Räume*, where they would be destined to wait, circling the beacon, with very little chance of being vectored on to a bomber. Meanwhile they saw the aces adding to their score night after night and often being awarded decorations. Yet despite calls for change, Kammhuber was adamant that *Himmelbett* was the best method of defence against Bomber Command.

There was one *Luftwaffe* officer who had recognised the defensive problems posed by Bomber Command and who had conceived a way in which they might, in part at least, be overcome. Furthermore, he had set about testing his theories in person under operational conditions. Surprisingly, he was a comparatively junior officer and a bomber pilot at that, with no personal experience of flying fighters by either day or night. The newly promoted *Major* Hajo Herrmann was already a legendary figure, having served with the *Legion Kondor* in Spain and flown over three hundred operational missions in Poland, Norway, France and the Low Countries, the Battle of Britain, the so-called 'Blitz' against Britain, the Middle East and the Arctic. In late 1942 he was assigned to a desk job in Potsdam, a move that he accepted under protest, and while there he conceived the idea of using single-seater day fighters, Bf 109s and Fw 190s, to supplement the effort of the

Mid 1943. U-Boat men visit Leeuwarden and are hosted by *Major* Helmut Lent, *Kommandeur* IV./NJG 1.

conventional night fighters, the twin-engined Bf 110s, Do 215s and Ju 88s[107] and so on. In his concept the single-seaters, standard day fighters carrying no sophisticated navigational instruments, would head visually for the target area and hunt freelance, with the flak gunners limiting their fire to specific altitude bands. Despite his comparatively lowly rank, Herrmann was well connected, and he used his connections to borrow aircraft from airfields near to Berlin and take off when bombers were approaching the capital. He gathered a group of pilots, all highly experienced, particularly in night flying, and formed the nucleus of a freelance force, which was dubbed *Wilde Sau*, or 'Wild Boar'[108]. His experiments came to the ears of Göring, who authorised him to form an experimental unit and test it out in live combat. The outcome was that Herrmann led a force of ten single-engined fighters against the Bomber Command attack on Cologne of 3/4 July, and he and his men claimed the destruction of twelve enemy bombers. The claims were strongly disputed by the Cologne *Flak*, which also claimed twelve. Finally, a diplomatic

[107] The Ju 88 was gradually being introduced into the night-fighter fleet, although it was not yet with NJG 1 in quantity.

[108] Not a literal translation, of course, but the equivalent term in hunting circles. From the very early stages of combat flying fighters had been known in the *Luftwaffe* as '*Jäger*' ('Hunters') and fighter operations as '*die Jagd*' (the hunt).

compromise was reached, with *Flak* and *Wilde Sau* being credited with six victories each – although the Cologne *Flak* had never before shot down more than one or two in a night. Immediately after this success, Göring ordered Herrmann to form a Wild Boar *Geschwader*, of which he would be *Kommodore*. The new *Geschwader*, JG 300, it was agreed, should be ready for action by the end of September.

With the Ruhr battle behind him, Harris focused his attention on his next objective, the great seaport and shipbuilding city of Hamburg. Planning for the 'Battle of Hamburg' had been started shortly after the beginning of the Battle of the Ruhr. The second-largest city in the *Reich* was, of course, an important and legitimate target in its own right, but there was another factor that Harris took into consideration when doing his planning. Much of the success of the Battle of the Ruhr had been due to the remarkable accuracy of *Oboe* blind marking, but Hamburg lay outside *Oboe* range. On the other hand its geographical location, on the broad River Elbe and with the distinctive coasts of the North Sea and the Baltic about fifty miles to the north-west and the north-east respectively, made it theoretically an ideal subject for marking by *H2S*, which was by this time installed in most PFF aircraft. Harris, wishing to hit more accurately at targets outside the range of *Oboe*, needed a practical assessment of the capabilities of *H2S* to assist him with his forward planning.

There was another problem that was exercising the mind of the Commander-in-Chief at this time: the increasing success rate of the enemy night fighters. If somehow the enemy radars responsible for this increase could be jammed, RAF losses would decrease. What he found particularly galling was that a simple means of jamming radars was already known, but his repeated requests to use it against the German ground and airborne equipments had consistently met with refusal. The principle of *Window*, as it was code-named (the Germans called it *Düppel*), was known to both sides, but neither had so far dared to use it in case the other side, in retaliating, might gain the greater advantage. *Window* consisted of strips of paper covered in tinfoil which, if dropped in sufficient quantities into the field of coverage of a radar would, by reflecting the transmitted energy, jam the radar completely, making it impossible to differentiate the signals reflected by the bombers from the spurious ones reflected by the silver strips. For optimum efficiency the strips needed to be cut to half the wavelength of the radar that it was intended to jam. *Lichtenstein*, the airborne interception radar in the night fighters, and the *Würzburg Riese*, which was used to show both fighter and bomber in the *Himmelbett* areas, operated on approximately the same frequency, making them both vulnerable to strips of the same length. And there was a great bonus: the *Würzburg Riese* was also used to lay the anti-aircraft guns and to control the searchlights. It was theoretically possible to blot out all the enemy's *Flak*, searchlight, control and airborne intercept radar simultaneously.

At last, in July 1943, clearance was given for the use of *Window* by Bomber Command, and Harris decided that the attacks on Hamburg that he was planning would be a suitable occasion. Harris planned to

A social occasion with
other ranks of IV./NJG
1, Leeuwarden 1943.

make a short series of concentrated attacks on Hamburg by night, and it
was hoped that the Americans would carry out raids by day during the
same period. Harris's aim was simple: in Bomber Command Operation
Order No. 23 of 27 May 1943 he expressed it succinctly and chillingly as,
'Intention. To destroy HAMBURG.' Equally chilling was the choice of
codename for the project, *Gomorrah*.

Whereas the Battle of the Ruhr had lasted for twenty weeks, the
Hamburg 'battle' only lasted for ten days – but then there was only one
main target. The RAF began the battle on 24/25 July, with subsequent
attacks on 27/28 July, 29/30 July and 2/3 August, while the Americans, in
considerably less force, struck by day on the 25th and the 26th of July.

Almost eight hundred bombers, of which about seven hundred were
four-engined, set from out their bases in eastern England on course over
the North Sea at about ten o'clock on the evening of the 24th, each
aircraft carrying a large number of brown-paper parcels each of which
contained thousands of strips of *Window*. Their estimated time of arrival
over Hamburg was from midnight onward, and their planned route
would take them well north of the Friesian islands to a position to the
north-west of Heligoland, where they would begin to drop their *Window*
bundle by bundle, simultaneously turning on to a south-easterly heading
towards Hamburg. This meant that as long as they remained on track
they would not penetrate the *Himmelbett* areas served by IV./NJG 1 at
Leeuwarden. Their homeward route would be roughly similar – north-
west from the target to a dead-reckoning position over the North Sea,
then westerly towards England. Their main danger from *Himmelbett*
would be on the long legs into and out of the target area, when they
would infringe *Räume* occupied by fighters from airfields in the

Schleswig-Holstein region, mainly from NJG 3 with its headquarters at Stade. Nevertheless, some fighters from IV./NJG 1 were scrambled against RAF machines inexplicably flying well south of track. *Hauptmann* Rudolf Sigmund and *Oberleutnant* Greiner each claimed a victim flying a long distance off track, but Lent himself did not take off.

The impact of *Window* on the German defences was enormous. Returning RAF crews spoke of searchlights apparently groping aimlessly about the sky and anti-aircraft fire lacking both accuracy and concentration, while German night-fighter crews reported impenetrable jamming on their Lichtenstein screens. *Würzburg* stations could not see either target or fighter and so could not feed their positions to the fighter controllers. RAF losses that night amounted to only twelve bombers, 1.5 per cent of those taking part, when a loss-rate of about five per cent (which this night would have meant 40 bombers) was the norm at that period. Overall, from the point of view of damage inflicted, the raid might be described as a qualified success. The marking, which was a combination of H2S and visual, was not as accurate as had been hoped, but great damage was caused to the city and about 1,500 people lost their lives. *Himmelbett* had been dealt what was virtually a death-blow.

The following day the Americans sent forces of bombers to strike at two targets in Hamburg, one in Warnemünde and one in Kiel. While the results of the attacks at Warnemünde and Kiel might be described as satisfactory, those at Hamburg, the main objective, were disappointing. Bomb aimers found their task greatly impeded by smoke from fires caused by Bomber Command the previous night, with the result that the bombing was scattered. German fighters, mostly single-engine interceptors, were up in some force, and night fighters, too, were scrambled. The Americans lost a total of nineteen heavy bombers that day, the majority to fighters. Some Bf 110s from Lent's *Gruppe*, IV./NJG 1 – the exact number is not known – attacked a formation of B-17s returning to England, and *Leutnant* Gerhard Dittmann of the 12th *Staffel* claimed his first kill. On the debit side, however, Dittmann's *Staffelkapitän*, *Oberleutnant* Eberhard Gardiewski, was shot down and had to ditch in the North Sea off den Helder. Gardiewski and his *Funker*, *Unteroffizier* Fritz Abromeit, boarded their rubber dinghy successfully, and as they were no great distance from the Dutch coast they waited confidently to be picked up by the German air-sea rescue service. Eventually they were picked up – but by a Royal Navy motor torpedo boat operating in the coastal area. They spent the remainder of the war as prisoners.

That night, the 25th/26th July, IV./NJG 1 were again in action, this time against a heavy – and successful – RAF raid on Essen. Lent's *Gruppe* shot down five of the 23 bombers that the whole *Nachtjagd* claimed from the total of 26 lost that night, which, at 3.7 per cent of the number despatched, was slightly less than the norm for recent attacks on targets in the Ruhr, but it was impossible to say what effect *Window* had had on the fighters' score. Helmut Lent was scrambled but, unlike his subordinates *Hauptmann* Sigmund, *Oberleutnant* Drünkler, *Oberleutnant*

Greiner, *Feldwebel* Kraft and *Unteroffizier* Busch, he had no success. It is interesting to note that on this occasion Lent took off from Stade, near Hamburg, having flown there earlier in the day: he had spent the night of the 24th/25th at Gilze Rijn and flown to Leeuwarden in the afternoon, then on to Stade in the early evening, these movements being recorded in his logbook as '*Einsatzüberführung*' (operational deployment). The tactical deployment of night fighters at short notice was a regular feature in the chess game of air defence. In recent weeks Lent had made an unusually large number of visits to other airfields in the region in addition to Stade, such as Deelen, Venlo, Twente, Saint Trond (scrambling from there on 14 July, when the bombers' target was Aachen), Travemünde and Gilze Rijn, but only two of them are logged as *Einsatzüberführung*, so the likelihood is that he was paying liaison visits to other units, possibly to discuss night-fighting tactics and related matters. In his book '*Nachtjäger, Bomber, Wolken und Sterne*'[109] Fritz Engau, who was stationed at Saint Trond as a member of II./NJG 1, speaks of Lent's visit on 14 July and reports that Heinz Schnaufer, a rising star of the night-fighter force then with II./NJG 1, asked Lent for a transfer to IV./NJG 1 at Leeuwarden, where, he believed, the opportunities to increase his score would be greater than at Saint Trond. At that time Schnaufer's night-fighting kills stood at twenty as against Lent's sixty-three, but Schnaufer had not begun his operational night-fighting career until October 1941, a year later than Lent.

To revert to the Battle of Hamburg: on the 26th July the Americans mounted a further daylight attack on the great port. Only comparatively slight damage was caused, and only three B-17s were shot down. Night fighters were not scrambled. That night Hamburg was left in peace,

This photograph, from the collection of *Oberstleutnant* Jabs, is annotated by him, 'IV./NJG 1, Leeuwarden. Departure of Lent.' It was, however, not until the beginning of August that Lent transferred to NJG 3, by which time several of those depicted were already dead. Left to right, excluding those in steel helmets: Petersen, Linke, Gardiewski; Lent; Jabs; Sips; Sigmund; Kuthe.

---

[109] 'Night Fighters, Bombers, Clouds and Stars', published in 1993 by Hoppe, Graz, Austria.

except for a 'siren' visit by six Mosquitos. Bomber Command's second major attack on Hamburg took place on the night of 27/28 July. The force sent out was similar in strength to that of three nights previously, and the overall plan was the same – Pathfinders marking an aiming point in the centre of the city, this time by H2S alone, and Main Force aiming at the markers dropped by PFF. The markers fell between two and three miles to the east of the aiming point, but the bombing that followed was very concentrated. It was a beautiful, warm, dry summer's night, and the bombers' loads, as was standard practice at the time, included a high proportion of incendiary bombs. On the ground, a firestorm developed, a rare phenomenon only occurring when a certain combination of meteorological and atmospheric conditions prevails: air heated by flames rises rapidly, sucking in further air, the oxygen in which fuels the flames and increases the temperature, triggering off a self-perpetuating process that only comes to an end when all the combustible material in the vicinity is burnt. The holocaust generated in Hamburg that night defies both description and imagination: at a very conservative estimate 35,000 souls perished, the overwhelming majority incinerated or suffocated when hurricane-force winds sucked the air out of their shelters. Night fighters were up in force, still confused and hampered by *Window* but largely abandoning their attempts at formal *Himmelbett* interception and hunting freelance on the basis of a running commentary broadcast by the ground control centres on the location, heading and height of the enemy. The conventional night fighters claimed thirteen kills, while Hajo Herrmann's *Wild Boar* single-seaters, still nominally in the process of preparation but ordered into action by Göring, claimed three. From IV./NJG 1, Helmut Lent and Achim Jabs each shot down a Lancaster, and *Hauptmann* Meurer of I./NJG 1 claimed a Mosquito, possibly one from Fighter Command or possibly the bomber version that failed to return from a diversionary raid to Duisburg. Published Bomber Command losses were seventeen: eleven Lancasters, four Halifaxes, one Stirling and one Wellington. This matches nicely with the list of German claims: ten Lancasters, three Halifaxes, one Stirling and one Wellington – and, of course, one Mosquito. It is probable that the Lancaster and one of the Halifaxes not accounted for were shot down by flak. Although Jabs' victim can be identified, that attributed to Helmut Lent cannot, but it seems likely to have been either EE169 of No. 100 Squadron or ED708 of No. 106 Squadron. Lent intercepted his victim when it was on its way back to England at 0237 hours on the 28th July: he manoeuvred into position and opened fire, but the Lancaster did not begin to burn, so he broke away and made a second attack, only to experience a complete stoppage of his main armament when he pressed the triggers. He broke off and instructed Kubisch to 'talk' him into position for an attack with the rearward-firing MG 15 machine-gun[110]: this Kubisch did, opening

---

[110] Or possibly 'machine-guns'. At this period the rear-facing armament of the Bf 110 comprised either a single MG 15 or twin MG 8Z guns in a flexible mount.

fire when the Bf 110 was in position and destroying the Lancaster with his second burst. Although the kill was credited to Lent, as was usual in such cases, it appeared on the *Gruppe* score-board as 'No. 401. Lancaster. 28.7.1943. Kubisch'.

One wonders what thoughts went through the minds of night-fighter crewmen when they witnessed, as they did night after night, their towns and cities being laid waste by explosion and fire, and what they felt when they learned of the extent of the unprecedented catastrophe that had been inflicted on Hamburg. For those who had loved ones in that city, the mental agony must have been extreme: and Helmut Lent's wife Lena and his daughter Christina lived in the Hamburg suburb of Hohenkirchen. When Lent landed back at Leeuwarden after shooting down his Lancaster it was ten minutes to three in the morning, and we may well imagine that he was desperate for news about his wife and baby daughter. All communications with Hamburg were disrupted, including the telephone lines. Lent's logbook shows him taking off again at just

Feldwebel Helmuth Conradi, IV./NJG 1.

before seven-thirty, this time in Dornier 17 G9+ZF, and flying to Travemünde, arriving at twenty minutes to nine and remaining there until half-past eight that evening before flying back to Leeuwarden and landing there at fifteen minutes to ten. The times in his logbook would be consistent with his having flown to Travemünde when night flying was stood down and having returned to Leeuwarden that evening in time for operational readiness. Travemünde is about fifty miles north-east of Hamburg, so we may speculate that Lent went into Hamburg to assure himself that his loved ones were safe and well. Flying as flight mechanic in the Do 17 with Lent and Kubisch was Helmut Conradi, who writes, 'I remember flying to Travemünde as a young *Obergefreiter* in the early morning of the 29th July 1943 with the "ace of aces" Helmut Lent, and not returning until late in the evening. In my opinion your surmise that Lent went to see his family could well be correct. It was unusual for him to stay away from Leeuwarden for such a long time, and it is only 60 kilometres from Travemünde to Hamburg.'

Back at Leeuwarden, Lent scrambled at twenty minutes past one the morning of the 30th July against the third RAF attack in the series against Hamburg, an attack that caused very considerable material damage in the city without, however, replicating the firestorm of two nights previously. Twenty-eight bombers were shot down, twenty-six of them by night fighters, but IV./NJG 1 only claimed one victory, an unidentified Lancaster destroyed by Lent 25 kilometres north of

Officers of IV./NJG 1 after Lent had handed over command to Jabs at the beginning of 1943. Front row, left to right: Hermann Greiner; Martin Drewes; Heinrich Ruppel; Hans-Joachim Jabs; Sutor; Heinz Schnaufer. Schnaufer, the highest-scoring night fighter of the *Luftwaffe*, joined IV./NJG 3 on 13 August 1943.

Ameland at 0210 hours. Herrmann's *Wild Boars* had a very successful night, shooting down eight bombers, of which Herrmann himself claimed three. There followed a moderate-strength raid by 273 bombers on the small Ruhr town of Remscheid on 30/31 July that was marked by extremely accurate bombing, an estimated 83 per cent of the town being left in ruins. By contrast, the final raid of the Battle of Hamburg, on the night of the $2^{nd}/3^{rd}$ August, was a complete failure. Intense thunderstorms on the approach and in the target area caused many aircraft to turn back, while the Pathfinders could not mark the target, with the result that such bombing as there was on Hamburg itself was widely scattered. Thirty bombers failed to return: Lent scrambled but landed again after twenty-seven minutes without scoring.

During the afternoon of the following day *Major* Helmut Lent and Kubisch flew in G9+AF from Leeuwarden to Stade: the next time Lent flew it was in Bf 110 D5+AA, the personal aircraft of the *Kommodore* of NJG 3. He had been appointed to that high office with effect from the 1st of August. His command of IV./NJG 1 was taken over by *Hauptmann* Hans-Joachim Jabs.

As Kommandeur IV./NJG 1 Helmut Lent had 'his own' machine, Bf 110 G9+AF. It is possible to fit an exact date to this photograph, which was taken at Deelen. The markings on the starboard fin show 73 victories (23 icons plus a 'fifty' emblem in the centre of the top row). Lent scored his 73rd victory on 30 July 43, and his logbook show him at Deelen in 'AF' on 2 August. He took over command of NJG3 on 4 August.

CHAPTER NINE

August to December 1943
Kommandeur NJG 3, the first months

The effective date of Lent's appointment as *Kommodore* of NJG 3 was the first day of August 1943, but it was the 4th of the month before he occupied his office at Stade, west of Hamburg, where the *Geschwader* Headquarters were located. He had overlapped his appointment by flying with IV./NJG 1, his former *Gruppe*, against Bomber Command's final raid in the Battle of Hamburg the previous night.

Oberst Hans Schalk with his successor as *Kommodore* NJG 3, *Major* Hemut Lent, fifteen years his junior in age

There had been individual *Gruppen* bearing the designations I./NJG 3, II./NJG 3, III./NJG 3 and IV./NJG 3 at various times since as early as October 1940, and a *Geschwader* Staff between March and August 1941, but since then the *Gruppen* had been operationally subordinate to NJG 1. Now this confusing arrangement was to be rationalised, and Lent was the officer selected to bring the four *Gruppen* together under one command identity, NJG 3. He was referred to in official documents as '*m.W.d.G.d.Kdore. des N.J.G.3 beauftragt*' – 'tasked with attending to the duties of *Kommodore* of NJG 3'[111], bureaucratic jargon that meant that the appointment was an acting one and subject to confirmation. The officer from whom Lent took over as *Kommodore* NJG 3 was the Austrian-born *Oberst* Hans Schalk, a Battle of Britain *Zerstörer* ace.

Officers of NJG 3 saying farewell to their former *Kommodore*, *Oberst* Schalk, on his hand-over to *Major* Lent

The command of a *Geschwader*, acting or otherwise, was a challenging appointment for a young officer who had celebrated his twenty-fifth birthday a scant seven weeks previously and who, as recently as October 1940, had been a junior officer in charge of a *Staffel* of twelve aircraft. With its four *Gruppen*, each of three *Staffeln*, plus staff flights at *Geschwader* and *Gruppe* level, the *Geschwader* was responsible for the night-time defence of the area around the German Bight and the major ports located there: it had an establishment of approaching 150 operational aircraft dispersed on airfields in northern Germany and Denmark. Units

---

[111] In full: '*Mit der Wahrnehmung der Geschäfte des Kommodores des Nachtjagdgeschwaders 3 beauftragt*'.

of I./NJG 3 were located at Vechta, Wittmundhafen and Kastrup (Denmark); II./NJG 3 units at Schleswig and Westerland; III./NJG 3 units at Lüneburg and Stade; and IV./NJG 3 units at Grove and Aalborg in Denmark. The *Geschwader* was subordinate to the 2nd Fighter Division under *Generalleutnant* Schwabedissen, whose headquarters were also at Stade, as was the *Geschwader* Staff Flight.

Lent brought with him a formidable reputation as an operational pilot with a personal total of 73 confirmed victories, and he was a holder of the Knight's Cross with Oak Leaves. The day after his arrival at his new post he received a telegram. It read:

Major Lent, the newly appointed *Kommodore* of NJG 3, is seen here wearing the *Schwerter*, awarded to him on 4 August 1943.

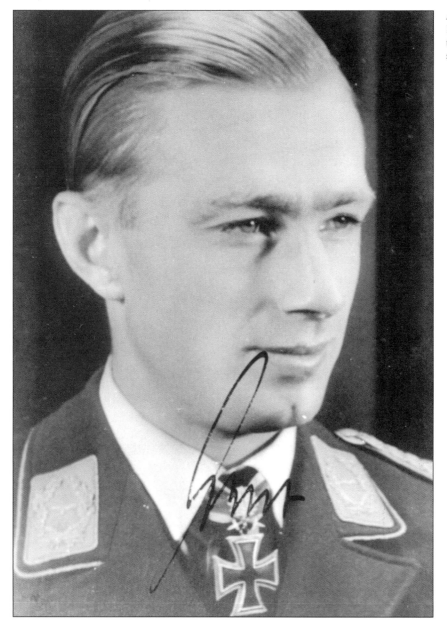

Another portrait of Helmut Lent wearing the *Schwerter*. Lent has signed this photograph.

Führer's Headquarters, 4 August 1943. In recognition of your unswerving heroism I award to you, as the thirty-second soldier of the German Armed Forces, the Oak Leaves and Swords to the Knight's Cross of the Iron Cross. (Signed) Adolf Hitler.

He had also proved himself, in his previous posts as Captain of a *Staffel* and Commander of a *Gruppe*, to be an efficient, dedicated and well-liked officer whom his subordinates, from lowly airman to battle-proven fighter ace, respected and obeyed willingly and unquestioningly. Lent is remembered by Helmut Conradi, mentioned earlier, who writes:

I was posted as an aircraft mechanic in 1941 to the Staff Flight of II./NJG 2 at Leeuwarden, where Helmut Lent was *Gruppenkommandeur*. Together with three other mechanics we looked after Lent's aircraft and those of the Adjutant and the Technical Officer, three Me 110s, and in addition a Dornier 215 that Lent used in bad weather. This machine could stay in the air an hour longer than the Me 110, but it was somewhat slower. Lent already had a number of kills to his name. His attitude towards us was very pleasing, and he treated us very well. With his blue eyes and his fair hair he was an idol and an example at one and the same time.

Entitled '*Rückblick*' ('Looking Back'), a paper survives that sums up Lent's twenty-one months of service as *Gruppenkommandeur* of II./NJG 2 and IV./NJG 1 successively. It was probably written after his death, but by whom is not known:

Afterwards Helmut would often say, 'My happiest time was when I was a *Gruppenkommandeur*. That's when one is in direct touch with the troops.' This was the time of the keen competition between him and Gildner: when Helmut joined the *Staffel*, Gildner was in the lead with more kills. Afterwards either of them always had one more kill than the other.

It would have been very easy for Helmut, as *Staffelkapitän* and later as *Gruppenkommandeur*, just to have picked out the best *Räume* and headed there himself. But comradeship wouldn't let him do so. Despite the healthy ambition that all soldiers have and the desire for medals that every officer certainly feels in wartime, it was not a matter of importance for him to shoot down as many enemies as possible himself, but what was top priority for him was simply that enemy aircraft should be destroyed so that as many tons of bombs as possible should not reach the *Heimat*. And it was a source of much pleasure to him when his work with new crews yielded success and young pilots came back from operational flights with their first kills, because for Helmut, as *Staffelkapitän*, *Gruppenkommandeur* and later as *Kommodore*, one of his most satisfying tasks was to imbue new generations of fliers with the same zeal for attack, destruction and victory that motivated him himself.

His concern for his men led him to visit the kitchens, to sample their food, to inspect their accommodation and the operational readiness rooms where the fighter crews used to spend many hours of the night waiting to be scrambled (He used to say, 'I'm just going to have a sniff about.'), and he was always looking after his men's welfare. He was strict, but not unfeeling, and he waged a constant battle against idleness.

Helmut knew that action was the best example. He was a born leader, an exemplary figure whose presence compelled loyalty, so that he was entrusted with the leadership of a *Gruppe* at twenty-three and of a *Geschwader* at twenty-five. And he justified the trust that was placed in him. One of his sayings was, 'A man grows as his responsibilities grow.' It would be a mistake to assume that his qualities of leadership were confined to his flying abilities alone and were only apparent in the number of enemy aircraft he shot down. It goes without saying that the unique successes that he had achieved since joining the *Nachtjagd* testified not only to his own great eagerness for combat but that they also reflected that combination of a sixth sense that any true hunter must possess plus a certain amount of luck which, however, as Moltke said, only favours the expert. But for a night fighter it is extremely important to fly in the *Räume* that are frequently penetrated by the enemy, because what is the use of the best flying abilities and the boldest readiness for combat if one doesn't come into contact with the enemy? Helmut not only had personal good fortune, but also the good luck to be located in a good area where, it goes without saying, his successes were successes for the leadership, successes for the ground organisation and successes for the ground personnel.

At the *Führer*'s Headquarters at Rastenburg, 10/11 August 1943. *Luftwaffe* officers newly decorated by Hitler. Left to right: Werner Schröer; Heinrich Ehrler; Egmond *Prinz* zur Lippe-Weissenfeld; Helmut Lent; Manfred Meurer; Joachim Kirschner; Theodor Weissenberger.

On the 9th of August Lent left Stade in D5+AA, heading for the *Führerhauptquartier* at Rastenburg, where Hitler was to decorate him with the *Schwerter*. He arrived there the following day after an overnight stop at Jürgenfelde and remained until the 12th, when he returned via Berlin-Staaken, landing back at Stade that evening. He was now free to dedicate himself to the responsibilities that went with the command of a night-fighter *Geschwader*, not least of which, on the operational side, would arise from the fundamental changes of thinking and tactics forced upon the *Nachtjagd* by the RAF's introduction of *Window*. Such changes

did not, of course, take place immediately: but they may be summed up at this point to give an idea of the nature of the tasks that faced Lent in his first months in command.

One thing was irrefutable: the days of *Himmelbett* close control as the standard defence against Bomber Command were over, and it followed that some alternative method of bringing the night fighters into contact with the bombers had to be found. Herrmann's *Wild Boar* Messerschmitts and Focke-Wulfs had demonstrated their capabilities and their potential over Hamburg, and already the twin-engined night fighters were beginning to follow their example, but that was unstructured and no more than a minor step in the right direction.

There were already indications that the initial setback caused by *Window* would be a temporary one, as indeed Harris had expected it would be. Since the first use of *Window* on 24/25 July the percentage of bombers lost had increased steadily raid by raid. This was partly due to the efforts of the single-seater *Wild Boars* of Herrmann's JG 300, but some of the radar operators in the twin-engined machines were beginning to be able to differentiate, partly instinctively, between the comparatively few 'solid' *Lichtenstein* returns from bombers and the very, very many flickering and ephemeral echoes from strips of *Window* and,

Oberst Viktor von Lossberg, seen here as an *Oberstleutnant*, who conceived the highly successful 'Tame Boar' (*Zahme Sau*) method of interception control.

free from the constraints of *Himmelbett*, were hunting independently both
in the stream and over the target.

Among those *Luftwaffe* officers who had foreseen the inherent
weakness of *Himmelbett* was *Oberst* Viktor von Lossberg, an adviser on
night-fighting matters to *Generalfeldmarschall* Erhard Milch, Director-
General of Equipment (Air), and he had already, before the opening of
the Battle of Hamburg, suggested an alternative form of control and
interception. His basic concept was that the fighters would find their way
into the bomber stream as early as possible and fly along with it, instead
of lying in wait in static close-control areas. Von Lossberg's original idea
was that ground controllers would infiltrate fighters into the stream with
the aid of a VHF radio navigation system known as '*Ypsilon*' or 'Y', but at
the same time plain-language 'running commentaries' on the bombers'
position, course, height, likely target and so on would be broadcast from
the control centres, so that the fighters could listen in and navigate
individually and independently into the stream and hunt for prey. Von
Lossberg's system complemented *Wild Boar*, and it was named *Tame Boar*

Major Lent with his
Adjutant, *Hauptmann*
Petersen. In the
background is *General*
Schwabediessen.

('*Zahme Sau*'). The fighters' *Lichtenstein* intercept radars remained jammed for the time being, of course, but the radar operators rapidly developed the knack of keeping in the stream by directing the pilot to fly where the jamming was thickest, and such was the concentration in time and space achieved by Harris's men that it was then much easier for the fighter crews, once in the stream, to pick up bombers with the naked eye. *Window* was already becoming less of an asset to Bomber Command, and more of a liability.

Several variations on the basic German AI radar were already under development, and it was a matter of little difficulty to select one that could not be jammed by the *Window* that Bomber Command was using. The one chosen was *Lichtenstein SN-2*, which operated on a longer wavelength than the *Lichtenstein B/C* with which the night fighters were equipped, and the process of producing it in quantity and replacing the existing *Lichtenstein* sets began at once, but it proved to be quite a lengthy job, so that it was not until late 1943 that the '*Window*-proof' radar was in use in any appreciable numbers. As its wavelength was longer, it needed longer

A crashed Junkers Ju 88 night fighter with SN2 radar aerial. The twin *Schräge Musik* cannon can be seen protruding from the top of the fuselage aft of the cockpit.

aerials, and longer aerials meant a slight decrease in airspeed. At the same time, however, the *Luftwaffe* began to introduce an extremely potent and unsuspected weapon system into their night fighters. Ironically, this device itself also slowed the fighters down a little, but its efficiency greatly offset the disadvantage of the slight loss of overtaking speed. The new weapon suited the *Zahme Sau* system so well that it might have been specifically designed for it, although such was not, in fact, the case. It was

517 One version of the *Schräge Musik* installation. The two MG/FF cannon, with a calibre of 20 mm., protruded from the upper surface of the fuselage. The pilot manoeuvred his machine to a position beneath the bomber and fired the *Schräge Musik* guns upward into his target.

called *Schräge Musik*[112] and comprised two 20 mm. MG FF cannon mounted in the upper surface of the aircraft's fuselage behind the pilot and pointing upward and slightly forward of the vertical at an angle of about seventy degrees. The pilot aimed the guns by means of a reflector

---

[112] *Schräge Musik*, literally 'slanting music' or something similar, was the vernacular expression for jazz music. The name seems to have been given to the new weapons system because of the slanting position of the upward-pointing cannon. There were various versions, both experimental and operational, but the one mentioned here was the equipment most generally used.

sight mounted in the top of his transparent cockpit-cover. He would approach his target slowly from below and astern, possibly slightly off to one side, where the bomber crew could not easily see him against the dark ground beneath, and when he was in position under the bomber he would match his speed to its and stealthily climb to his preferred attack distance – his guns would have been synchronised to that range – aim and open fire. He usually shot between the fuselage and the inner engine on one wing or between the two outer engines, where fuel tanks were located. Individual pilots had their own preference, but the general result was the same – the tanks caught fire, and the bomber was doomed. As soon as he saw flames – which was often after very few shells had been fired, sometimes as few as five – the pilot would dive away to one side or the other and start looking for further prey. As he was usually still moving in the same general direction as the bomber stream and at about the same speed, it was frequently not too difficult to find another victim. Literally, the crews of bombers that met their end in this way never knew what hit them – no warning, a few bangs, flames, and then a blazing dive to oblivion. A bomber that came under an accurate *Schräge Musik* attack had little chance of survival. A lucky few men, but very, very rarely a complete crew, escaped by parachute, and even then they did not suspect the manner in which their aircraft had met its doom. The upward-firing cannon did not use tracer ammunition, and it would not be until much later in the war that Air Ministry Intelligence came to suspect that a new weapon was being used: even then, bomber crews were not warned of the existence of *Schräge Musik*.

Some night-fighter pilots found *Schräge Musik* difficult to use because the aiming was rather awkward: one had to lean back in the pilot's seat and bend one's head back to look through the reflector sight, and that position had to be maintained as one climbed into position below the bomber. Some former *Zerstörer* pilots, steeped in the instinctive reactions required in the cut and thrust of aerial combat by daylight, never came to terms with the clinical way in which the upward-pointing guns had to be used, and some, notably Achim Jabs, would not have the installation in their aircraft, preferring to exchange it for the slight increase in speed that its removal permitted. On the other hand, many pilots, particularly young ones who had never flown in aerial combat by day, became so dedicated to *Schräge Musik* that they relied on it to the exclusion of their forward-firing armament. The most successful night-fighters were those, like Heinz Schnaufer, Martin Becker, Paul Zorner, Georg Greiner and so on, who were equally at home with both weapon systems, the conventional and the innovative. Unfortunately we do not know with certainty what Helmut Lent's attitude was, but it is likely that whatever his personal inclinations he would have understood the potential of *Schräge Musik* and made use of it himself, if only as an example to his subordinates.

It is of interest in passing to note that the officer generally credited with the concept, design and introduction into operational service of *Schräge Musik* was Rudolf Schoenert, who had served under Lent in II./NJG 2 and on whose technical aptitude Lent had commented in a

Major Rudolf Schoenert, who is credited with the introduction of the *Schräge Musik* weapons system. Schoenert, who had been a subordinate of Helmut Lent in 1941/42, ended the war as *Kommodore* NJG 5.

confidential report in October 1942[113]. An NCO armourer, Oberfeldwebel Paul Mahle[114], who had once been a member of Lent's *Zerstörer Staffel* 1./ZG 76, is credited with having worked closely with Schoenert on the project.

Much of Bomber Command's effort during the month of August 1943 was directed, at small cost, against targets in Italy with a view to 'encouraging' the Italians to withdraw from the war: they did so on the 8th September following Allied landings in the south of the country that had begun the previous week. Heavy attacks were made by the RAF

---

[113] See Page 165.

against Mannheim and Nuremberg on the $9^{th}/10^{th}$ and $10^{th}/11^{th}$ of August respectively. Losses, at just over two per cent, were low: possibly *Window* was still having some affect. Then, on the $17^{th}/18^{th}$, Harris's men attacked Peenemünde and lost 6.7 per cent of their force.

Peenemünde, on the island of Usedom on the Baltic coast, was the site of highly secret research and development works at which the assembly and testing of V-weapons[115] – the V1 flying bomb and the V2 ballistic rocket – were carried out. The RAF raid was aimed at the V2 installations and was planned as a precision attack, in contrast to the area attacks that were Bomber Command's stock-in-trade. Very considerable damage was caused to the several individual targets, and the eventual start of the V2 offensive against London delayed, although by how long remains a matter of controversy. The German night-fighter force, including NJG 3, was up in force. A feint attack on Berlin by Mosquitos initially deceived the Germans as to the intended target, and the first night fighters scrambled were sent to the German capital and so arrived late on the scene of the main attack, but nevertheless they achieved considerable success. They claimed 44 kills, which was, in fact, four more than Bomber Command actually lost. NJG 3 alone claimed ten kills. Lent himself took off from Stade at 2312 hours, but not against the bombers. Had he done so, the entry in his logbook would have read *'Nachtjagd'* ('Night Fighting'), whereas it reads *'Einsatz'* ('Operation'). We can perhaps deduce the likely nature of his trip by considering what happened that same night at his previous base, Leeuwarden.

The night-fighters were urgently experimenting with *Zahme Sau* and *Ypsilon* control. Lent's logbook shows that on 14th August he had flown to Castrup near Copenhagen and back on an *Ypsilon* practice flight, followed by two flights (one on the 14th, one on the 15th) entered as 'Practice operation'. It seems likely that when he scrambled on the evening of the Peenemünde raid he was conducting a live 'Y' experiment: strength is given to this hypothesis by the fact that *Hauptmann* Heinz Schnaufer, *Staffelkapitän* of 12./NJG 1, had taken off from Leeuwarden on just such a mission about fifteen minutes earlier, accompanied by three other aircraft flown by *Oberfeldwebel* Karl-Heinz Scherfling, *Feldwebel* Heinz Vinke and *Unteroffizier* Georg Kraft. The Leeuwarden experiment was not a success: both Schnaufer himself and Scherfling had to return to base with engine trouble, while Vinke and Kraft were shot down by an intruder Beaufighter of No. 141 Squadron, RAF, piloted by the British night-fighter ace Wing Commander J. R. D. (Bob) Braham, DSO, DFC.

The Peenemünde raid saw the first official operational use of *Schräge Musik*[116], described earlier. Two Bf 110s of 5./NJG 5 fitted with the device destroyed six bombers in all. On the British side, too, there were

---

[115] *'Vergeltungs-Waffen'* – retaliation weapons.
[116] There had been a number of unofficial 'do-it-yourself' experiments with upward-firing guns by operational pilots such as Prinz Heinrich zu Sayn Wittgenstein, who had had a number of successes on the eastern front with such a system.

significant new initiatives. Bob Braham's Beaufighter was carrying an experimental electronic device, *Serrate*, designed to home on to the radar transmissions from German night fighters. *Serrate* would eventually become a thorn in the flesh of the *Nachtjagd*, particularly when installed in the remarkable Mosquito intruder/night fighter. It was the Peenemünde raid, too, that saw the use for the first time on a German target of a 'Master Bomber'[117], a senior Pathfinder officer who remained over the target throughout the attack and broadcast plain-language instructions to the main-force pilots in order to direct and concentrate the bombing, a concept based on the successful R/T control of his Lancasters by Wing Commander Guy Gibson in the famed 'Dams' raid the previous May. The Master Bomber chosen for the Peenemünde mission was Group Captain J. H. Searby, the commanding officer of No. 83 Squadron, PFF. He had carried out a 'rehearsal' for the task in a raid on Turin on the night of 6/7 August – although he was totally unaware at that time that a special raid was planned and that he was cast to play a leading role in it.

On 22 August, in expectation of a Bomber Command raid that night, Lent, flying G9+AA, deployed tactically from Stade to Lübeck/ Blankensee, ninety kilometres or so to the northeast, possibly because bad weather was expected at Stade, or possibly because *Luftwaffe* Intelligence forecast an attack in North Germany. Whatever the reason for the move, the bombers went to the Ruhr town of Leverkusen and Lent did not take off but stayed on at Lübeck. He scrambled from there at 2331 hours the following night, the 23rd, on his first operational mission as *Kommodore* NJG 3, and the target that Harris had chosen was Berlin.

If Harris calculated that there would still be some significant advantage to be gained from *Window*, he seems to have been mistaken: he sent 710 four-engined bombers to the 'Big City' and lost 56 of them, the majority to night fighters. This, the highest number of bombers destroyed in a single night thus far in the war, represented a loss-rate of 7.9 per cent. Once again *H2S*, which was now gradually finding its way into main-force aircraft as well as those of the Pathfinders, gave very unsatisfactory results over Berlin and bombing was widely scattered, but even so great damage was done to property and the death-rate, at 854, was high. The RAF bombers came in over Holland, aiming almost directly for a turning-point south of Berlin and then turning north to begin their bombing run. Night fighters were sent to radio beacons to await further orders until the pattern of the raid emerged and it became clear where the target would be, and then some found their way into the bomber stream to fly *Tame Boar* while some went to Berlin and flew *Wild Boar* over the target. Among the latter was Lent himself: he headed south from Lübeck and made his first kill over Berlin at 0056 hours, logging it as a Short Stirling, and he destroyed a Halifax twenty minutes later. In the official list of bombers destroyed he is also credited with a Lancaster,

[117] At first – but only for a very short time – called 'Master of Ceremonies'

although there is no mention of it in his logbook[118]. At 0130 he landed away from home at Rechlin/Lärz. His *Geschwader*, NJG 3, claimed 17 kills, while the total number listed by the Germans as being shot down by night fighters was 62, or six more than the number that Bomber Command officially recorded as lost. Quite certainly, although statistics are not available, the *Flak* will also have claimed a number of successes, bringing the German figures to well above the British ones. Something similar it will have been noted, had happened in the Peenemünde raid. It was very unusual for official German figures of enemy aircraft destroyed to be greatly inaccurate, although errors did occur: pilots' claims were closely scrutinised before they were confirmed. With *Himmelbett* it had been fairly easy to match claims to kills, because the fighter was usually under radar control when the bomber was destroyed, but when the fighter was freelancing, particularly in the target-area among many enemy bombers and friendly fighters, not to mention heavy flak, duplicate claims were bound to occur.

Two more attacks on Berlin followed in quick succession. On 31 August/1 September Harris sent 622 aircraft and lost 47 (7.6 per cent), of which Lent claimed two, and on 3/4 September he despatched 316, losing just under 7.0 per cent. Lent scrambled, but did not score.

It is possible that this short series of raids was intended by Arthur Harris to be the opening of the Battle of Berlin, which he conceived as a series of devastating attacks with which he could, if given sufficient bombers, bring the war to a victorious conclusion without the necessity of an invasion by ground troops. The Command's losses, however, were daunting. The three raids had cost 125 bombers and their crews, and Harris, it seems, drew back from risking further losses of this magnitude. Another possible consideration in his mind was whether he should use the Halifaxes and Stirling in the all-out assault on Berlin. Losses of Stirlings and Halifaxes on the first two raids had been disproportionately heavy, with percentage losses of 14 and 10 respectively, so Harris had only sent Lancasters on the final one. Neither of the two heavies, particularly the Stirling, could climb as high as the Lancaster, and the night fighters, now free to choose their own targets, found it easier, and possibly less dangerous, to go for the bombers that were at the lowest level. At this stage, despite the Hamburg reverse, the night fighters had the advantage in the battle.

On 6 September 1943 Lent was awarded the *Frontflugspange für Nachtjäger in Gold mit Anhänger* (Operational Clasp for Night Fighters in Gold with bar), a decoration that was awarded on the basis of the number of operational

---

[118] Errors occur occasionally in Lent's logbook. Lent himself did not make the entries in the book, delegating that task mainly to his *Funker*, Walter Kubisch, but sometimes also to other subordinates. There are indications that the logbook was not kept up to date day by day but was filled in at fairly long intervals, presumably from notes made at the time. Further, it took some long time for claims of 'kills' to be confirmed, and only when that had happened could they go into the pilot's logbook. It is not surprising that errors arose: some of Lent's known victories are not to be found in his logbook.

flights made, 110 being necessary to qualify for the golden award.

As a *Kommodore*, Lent flew operationally only marginally less frequently than he had done when he was the *Kommandeur* of a *Gruppe*, despite the extra responsibilities and heavy workload that went with the new job. He flew against the bombers whenever he could, and he continued to score steadily. He had taken his total tally to 78 when he shot down his two Halifaxes over Berlin during the second of Harris's three attacks, and later in September he claimed a Stirling when Bomber Command attacked Hanover. It was a successful night for his *Geschwader*. Harris's force of 711 bombers lost 26 aircraft, all but four to night fighters, and NJG 3 claimed 11 of them.

In addition to an average of one or two operational flights a week, Lent's logbook shows frequent local flying, air tests, practice interceptions and so on, as well as short visits to airfields on which the *Gruppen*, *Staffeln* and *Kommandos* of NJG 3 were stationed. One interesting trip was to Hanover/Langenhagen on 2 October 1943, where he test-flew a Focke-Wulf Ta 154[119], an experimental high-performance night fighter which, like the de Havilland Mosquito, had a plywood

Rastenburg, 2 August 1943. *Reichsmarschall* Hermann Göring with (from left to right) *Hauptmann* Egmond *Prinz* zur Lippe-Weissenfeld; *Major* Helmut Lent; *Major* Hajo Herrmann; and *Hauptmann* Manfred Meurer, all of whom had been decorated by the Führer.

---

[119] Designated 'Ta' after its designer, Kurt Tank. Only very few of these machines were made. The Germans were unable to find a suitable adhesive for the plywood construction of the fuselage.

This photograph was taken just after *Major* Lent was wounded in action on 3 October 1943. In addition to a relatively serious wound to his hand he suffered superficial injuries to his face, as can be seen from this photograph.

fuselage and which – imitation being the best form of flattery – bore the same name, but with German spelling, '*Moskito*'. That same night Lent flew against bombers attacking Munich without adding to his score, and the next night against a force that bombed Kassel. While carrying out an attack on a Stirling, Lent's Bf 110 D5+AA came under fire from the bomber's guns and he sustained injuries that were later described in his *Wehrpass* as, 'Bullet wound through the left index finger and first joint and the first joint of the thumb, with splinter wounds to the first joint of the thumb and the second and third joints of the index finger.' Despite his wounds he pressed home his attack and destroyed the Stirling and then managed to fly his machine back to Stade, where he landed safely. He did not fly again until the 9th of November.

During this Kassel raid, Lent lost a close friend, his *Kommandeur* II./NJG 3, *Hauptmann* Rudolf Sigmund, formerly his Adjutant with IV./NJG 1, who had received the Knight's Cross from the hands of the *Führer* two months previously and who had 37 kills to his credit when he

Major Heinrich *Prinz* zu Sayn-Wittgenstein wearing the *Eichenlaub* awarded to him on 31 August 1943.

died in action. As casualties within the *Nachtjagd* mounted old, familiar faces were no longer seen, well-known voices no longer heard, old names fading in the urgency of the present moment; and new names achieving fame on the home front, among them Heinz Schnaufer, who had taken over IV./NJG from Lent and now had 28 kills, and Heinrich *Prinz zu* Sayn-Wittgenstein, newly back from great successes on the Eastern Front and now serving under Lent as *Kommandeur* II./NJG 3, who had scored

Hauptmann Paul Zorner wearing the Knight's Cross.

over 50.

It seems that when Lent returned to flying in November he was possibly still not fully fit, because from the 9th to the end of the month he flew far less frequently than he usually did, and only once operationally, on the 26th, when Berlin was the target, but then he landed back at Stade after only 48 minutes in the air without scoring. That, given Helmut Lent's well-earned reputation for leading from the front, was untypical, because in the meanwhile Arthur Harris had returned to Berlin in such strength that it was apparent that the campaign against the Reich capital had now been resumed in earnest. In December 1943 Lent scrambled five times and shot down in all two Lancasters and a Stirling. In the course of an attack on Berlin on the night of the 2nd/3rd December one of the Lancasters and the Stirling became his 81st and 82nd kills, and he claimed the other Lancaster on the 16th/17th, when Berlin was once more the target.

Christmas came and went without a let-up in the battle. Lent flew on the night of 20/21 December, when Leipzig was the target, and on 23/24 December, when Berlin again suffered from Bomber Command's

Autumn 1943. Lent pursues one of his favourite pastimes, hunting. His left arm is in a sling following his being wounded in aerial combat on 3 October 1943.

attentions. On neither occasion did he score, but one officer who did taste success was *Leutnant* Paul Zorner, *Staffelkapitän* of 8./NJG 3, stationed at Lüneburg. Zorner shot down a Halifax in the evening of the 20th and three Lancasters in the early morning of the 24th, bringing his score to nineteen. Zorner recalls a meeting with Lent at that time:

When I joined NJG 3 *Oberst* Schalk was still *Kommodore*. He was an Austrian, but a somewhat strict and unbending officer and certainly a convinced Nazi. When Helmut Lent became *Kommodore* of NJG 3 in August 1943 I had just become *Kapitän* 8./NJG 3. We were stationed at Lüneburg, the only unit there. With the change of *Geschwader-Kommodore* the atmosphere changed for the

Oberfeldwebel Walter Kubisch, Lent's regular *Funker*, wearing the Knight;s Cross awarded to him on New Year's Eve 1943.

better. For Lent, politics played a secondary role, National Socialist indoctrination became unimportant: the only important subjects became night-fighting tactics for the aircrew, the solution of technical problems for the technical staff and, for all of us, a friendly, almost communalist, relationship in our dealings with each other, despite the fact that Lent was a Prussian.

When there was a change of *Geschwaderkommodore* it was not the usual custom for unit commanders to report to the new *Kommodore* immediately. Those who were on the airfield where he was stationed – in his case Stade – came into contact with him immediately, of course, but others only went to Stade if there was a specific reason. I had met Lent previously at Leeuwarden, when he was *Kommandeur*, but I can't recall when I first met him at Stade. Naturally, he visited his subordinate units at their airfields now and then, and that happened with me at Lüneburg between Christmas 1943 and New Year's Day. I remember the visit very well – it was typical of Lent.

Lüneburg was a peacetime airbase, and equipped accordingly, and my *Staffel* was the only unit stationed there. For my officers I had three officers' accommodation blocks with over forty two-room apartments. I had got married in October 1943, and the temptation for me to invite my wife to Lüneburg and for her to live with me on the airfield over Christmas and look after me was understandably very strong. For a wife to live locally was not encouraged, and for her to live on the base was completely forbidden. My wife arrived at Lüneburg on the 19th of December. It seems possible that Lent had got wind of her presence on the base, because shortly after Christmas he arrived there unexpectedly together with his adjutant, *Hauptmann* Petersen, whom he had taken with him from Leeuwarden. I realised that there was no way in which I could conceal my wife's presence, but I thought that I was in a fairly strong position, because I had shot a bomber down on the night of 20/21 December and three on the night of the 23rd/24th. After Lent and Petersen had visited *Staffel* Headquarters, therefore, I invited them both, 'in the name of my wife', to have coffee with us in my apartment. As I had expected, Lent was not surprised by the invitation, and we spent a very pleasant hour over coffee. Lent was very well mannered, Petersen less so. My wife had brought with her a tin of homemade butter cakes – quite a precious item in 1943. Naturally, she offered them to our guests with the coffee. Lent helped himself very modestly, but Petersen scoffed the whole tinful.

As the two were taking their leave, Lent said to me, 'Strictly, your wife shouldn't be here. But you shoot bombers down, so I have no objection.'

On the 22nd December 1943 *Major* Helmut Lent was decorated by *General* Schwabedissen, Commander of the Second Fighter Division, with the *Silberne Verwundetenabzeichen*, the Silver Wound Badge, in recognition of the two wounds he had suffered in action, the first on 10 July 1941, when he was hit in the course of shooting down a Wellington during an RAF raid on Osnabrück, and the second on 3 October 1943. Lent's *Funker*, the then *Unteroffizier* Walter Kubisch, it will be recalled, had been very much more seriously wounded than Lent in July 1941, and he wore the Wound Badge in black. On New Year's Eve 1943 news of a considerably more prestigious decoration reached him. Helmut Lent had a telephone call from the Commanding General of the Night

Another photograph of Walter Kubisch wearing the *Ritterkreuz*. He was only the second night-fighter *Funker* to be so honoured.

Fighters, Joseph ('Beppo') Schmid, who had succeeded Joseph Kammhuber in that position in the course of a major reorganisation of the *Nachtjagd* in September 1943. He informed Lent that Kubisch, by now an *Oberfeldwebel*, had been awarded the Knight's Cross. Kubisch was only the second *Funker* to be distinguished in this way, the first having been *Oberfeldwebel* Gerhard Scheibe, *Bordfunker* to *Hauptmann* Manfred Meurer, *Gruppenkommandeur* of 1./NJG 1. Scheibe's Knight's Cross had been awarded only three weeks previously, and he was destined only to wear it a scant few weeks. Together with Meurer, who had 65 victories to his credit, he would die in action on 21 January 1944.

In earning his Knight's Cross Kubisch, who already held the German Cross in Gold, which had been awarded to him on 19 May 1943, had made a total of 240 operational flights, including 134 by night, and had participated in 9 kills by day and 55 during the hours of darkness. At a party in celebration of Kubisch's honour Lent made a short congratulatory speech and then took off his own Knight's Cross and 'decorated' Kubisch with it, insisting that his *Funker* should wear it until the end of the party, which was also the end of the year.

As 1943 came to its close and the fateful year of 1944 dawned Lent, with 75 night kills, was still the *Nachtjagd's* leading scorer, followed by Heinrich Prinz zu Sayn-Wittgenstein (68), Werner Streib (63) and Manfred Meurer (62).

CHAPTER TEN

January to March 1944
Kommandore NJG 3.
High rank. Nuremberg

AN ALL-LANCASTER force, 421 aircraft strong, hit Berlin on the first night of 1944, and 28 of them failed to return to England. *Major* Helmut Lent claimed one as his 76th night victory and his 84th overall, but such satisfaction as he felt at his achievement was overshadowed by his sadness at the loss of a valued subordinate and friend, *Ritterkreuzträger Hauptmann* Paul Szameitat, *Kommandeur* of I./NJG 3, who had shot down 29 RAF bombers.

January 1944. Walter Kubisch wearing the Knight's Cross awarded to him on the last day of 1943.

The total number of kills recorded by the *Nachtjagd* on the night of 1/2 January 1944 was 23, shared by only thirteen pilots. *Hauptmann* Ludwig Meister of I./NJG 4 shot down four, but the outstanding performance of the night was that of *Prinz* zu Sayn-Wittgenstein, with six victories. It was the second time that Wittgenstein had achieved this impressive feat, but the first time he had done so had been on the Eastern front in July 1943, just before he returned to the west, when the comparatively low-flying Ilyushin Il 4 medium bombers of the Red Air Force represented much easier targets than the heavy bombers of the Royal Air Force. This time his destruction of six Lancasters marked his promotion to *Major* and appointment that very day to the post of *Kommodore* NJG 2. A gifted pilot, Wittgenstein saw it as his obligation as a member of the aristocracy to excel at everything he did, including night fighting, and he was burningly ambitious to score as many kills as he possibly could. By the end of the night his tally had reached 74, so that he was ten short of Helmut Lent's total score but only two behind his night-fighting tally.

Wittgenstein, a former bomber pilot, flew a Ju 88G. According to Walter Kümmritz, who was his *Funker* until late November 1943, the Prince had had all the items that slowed the aircraft down, such as the radio operator's rear gun and any aerials that he thought were unnecessary, including those for blind flying, removed. He kept his favourite aircraft, C9+AE, highly polished, and it was about 40 kph faster than the standard Ju 88G. He retained the two *Schräge Musik* cannon, however, much preferring them to the forward-facing guns.

With the advent of *Tame Boar* night fighting, the incidence of multiple kills in a night by individual crews had begun to escalate. Until Hamburg and the demise of *Himmelbett*, for example, the number of pilots claiming five or more victories in one night in the west[120] had amounted to seven over a period of nine months. Now, from August to December 1943, a further four had achieved the feat: one pilot, *Hauptmann* Wilhelm Herget, *Kommandeur* of I./NJG 4, had shot down eight heavy bombers during the night of 20/21 December when Bomber Command attacked Frankfurt. There are several points that attract attention in this context. Firstly, it was during this period, the final five months of 1943, that a number of factors that increased the efficiency of the *Nachtjagd* were coming into play: SN-2 radar; *Schräge Musik*, the Ju 88 in increasing numbers; and the fact that by progressively decreasing the length of the bomber stream[121] Harris was bringing the bombers closer together, thus to some extent playing into the fighters' hands and making it easier for them to move on to one bomber after another. Looking ahead, it is

---

[120] Records of those claiming two, three or four kills in a night are not readily available.

[121] In planning his raids, Harris introduced a number of tactical measures aimed at minimising casualties. He mounted decoy raids, he 'split' the bomber stream to confuse the defences as to the primary target, he sent two forces to the same target with a time-gap between in the hope of catching the fighter force refuelling and rearming on the ground, and so on. He also progressively reduced the length of time that the main force were over the target, thus effectively reducing the length of the stream.

worthy of note that in the twelve months of 1944 'five or more in a night' was accomplished no fewer than nineteen times. Yet it is a matter of some surprise and speculation that Lent, until his death the most successful of night fighters, never shot down more than three bombers in one night, and that he only did that on four occasions, the first time in August 1943.

Berlin was again the target of a major raid on the night of 2/3 January, and although Lent scrambled and was airborne for over two hours he did not score. He took off again on the night of 4/5 January, presumably in response to a raid on Berlin by 13 Mosquitos, and also the following night, when the primary target was Stettin. Still his night victories did not exceed 76. Wittgenstein, determined to become the leading scorer in the *Nachtjagd*, remained two kills behind. But Wittgenstein was in reality only competing against his own ambitions, because it is improbable in the extreme that Lent saw him as a threat to his reputation, or even that he considered himself to be in competition with the Prince.

Lent's flying logbook shows that on 10 January he flew in a Bf 110 from the Staff Flight, D5+BA, from Stade to Jürgenfelde and that he returned to Stade from Berlin/Staaken in the same machine on the 12th. Jürgenfelde was the feeder airfield for Hitler's Operational Headquarters in East Prussia, the *Wolfsschanze* at Rastenburg, and Lent had been summoned there to attend a ceremonial gathering of élite *Luftwaffe* officers who were to receive the certificates for their decorations from the hands of the *Führer* himself. Hitler presented Lent with those for the *Ritterkreuz*, the *Eichenlaub* and the *Schwerter*. In the company of a number of other officers who had also been honoured at

Taken early in 1944, this photograph shows Lent with members of the local hunt at Stade. To his left is the local MFH (*Kreisjägermeister*).

Führerhauptquartier Lent then travelled to Berlin by rail, and from Berlin he went to Göring's lavish estate, Karinhall, which lay in the *Schorf Heide*, a wide expanse of wooded heath land to the north-east, as a guest at a celebration of Göring's 51st birthday on the 12th of January. Presumably another pilot ferried D5+BA from Jürgenfelde to Staaken, because at 2025 hours on the 12th BA, with Lent at the controls and Kubisch in the radio-operator's position, took off from that airfield on the return journey to Stade.

A raid on Brunswick on the 14th/15th January 1944 provided both Lent and Wittgenstein with an opportunity to increase their score, when the *Nachtjagd* crews severely punished the 500 RAF bombers taking part. The historian Martin Middlebrook comments as follows on the raid[122]: 'The German running commentary was heard following the progress of the bomber force from a position only 40 miles from the English coast and many German fighters entered the bomber stream soon after the German frontier was crossed near Bremen. The German fighters scored steadily until the Dutch coast was crossed on the return flight. Eleven of the lost aircraft were Pathfinders.' Multiple scores were again apparent in the analysis of the night fighters' successes. From a total of 31 claims (Bomber Command lost 38 Lancasters) *Leutnant* Wandelin Breukel of II./NJG 2 scored six; *Hauptmann* Peters (III./NJG 3) four; and *Major* Helmut Lent, three. Heinrich zu Sayn Wittgenstein, only shot down one. The 'league table' situation at the end of the night was Lent – 79, Wittgenstein – 75.

As was the case with many of Harris's operations, the cost-effectiveness of the Brunswick raid was questionable. Along with the thirty-eight missing Lancasters the Royal Air Force had also lost approximately 270 trained aircrew, of whom only about 40 survived as prisoners of war while one evaded, eventually finding his way back to England. Yet according again to Middlebrook, 'This raid was not a success. The city report describes this as only a "light" raid, with bombs in the south of the city, which had only 10 houses destroyed and 14 people killed. Most of the attack fell either in the countryside or in Wolfenbüttel and other small towns and villages well south of Brunswick'.

Lent did not fly when 769 bombers attacked Berlin on 20/21 January, but Wittgenstein did, and he added three Lancasters to his score. In despatching the third, he went in so close to his victim that one of the Lancaster's airscrews sheered approximately two metres from one the wings of his JU 88. The aircraft went down out of control. After falling from about 8,000 metres to less than 1,000, Wittgenstein managed to bring it under some sort of control, and after a hair-raising flight to belly-land it at Erfurt. As luck would have it an aircraft from Deelen landed at the same airfield, so Wittgenstein commandeered it and flew it back there, while the other crew returned by train. Lent 79, Wittgenstein 78.

---

[122] 'Bomber Command War Diaries', by Martin Middlebrook and Chris Everitt, first published by Viking in 1985.

Magdeburg was Harris's chosen target the following night, 21/22 January, and within 50 minutes *Prinz* Wittgenstein had shot down four Lancasters and a Halifax. Helmut Lent claimed only two bombers that night. Wittgenstein (*Kommodore* NJG 2) 83, Lent (*Kommodore* NJG 3) 81. It was the first time since early 1942 that Lent had not been at the top of the unofficial 'league table' of kills. At last Wittgenstein had achieved his ambition to be the best night fighter, but a cruel Fate decreed that he would never know that he had done so. He manoeuvred into position beneath a sixth bomber. '*Major* Wittgenstein was just about to open fire, when suddenly there was a cracking and flashing in our aircraft. The port wing began to burn, and the aircraft went into a dive. I saw the cabin roof above our heads fly off, and I heard a shout on the intercom – *Raus!* I pulled my oxygen mask and my helmet off, and I was flung out of the machine. After a short time I pulled the ripcord...' Thus wrote Fritz Ostheimer, Wittgenstein's *Funker*, subsequently. He and Kurt Matzuleit, the Third Man in the crew, survived, but Wittgenstein died, the victim, in all likelihood, of a Mosquito intruder[123]. Another leading ace was also killed in action that night, *Hauptmann* Manfred Meurer, *Kommandeur* of I./NJG 1, who had shot down 65 Bomber Command machines and was a holder of the Oak Leaves to the Iron Cross.

Following his two successes on the night of Wittgenstein's death, Lent did not score again in January, although he took off operationally a further twice when Berlin was attacked on the 27th and the 29th of the month. February was a month without kills: Lent was away from his unit for the first three weeks or so on 'rest and rehabilitation' leave in the Austrian ski-resort of Kitzbühel, and he only flew operationally once in what remained of the month, when Harris attacked Schweinfurt on the 24th/25th. From a career point of view, however, February was significant. On the second of the month *Major* Lent headed a short list of officers recommended for accelerated promotion, in his case to *Oberstleutnant*. Without such a recommendation he would not in theory have been eligible for elevation to that rank until July 1948 – had the war not finished before then. As it was, he was promoted with effect from 1 March, and at the same time his appointment as *Geschwaderkommodore* NJG 3, which so far had been on an acting basis, was confirmed.

Another officer who featured on the same list of accelerated promotion recommendations as Helmut Lent was *Oberleutnant* Paul Zorner: as described earlier, Lent had made the acquaintance of Zorner's bride at Lüneburg in December 1943. Zorner recalls:

> At the end of February 1944 my *Staffel*, 8./NJG 3, was moved from Lüneburg to Nordholz, near Minden. In the first days of March the weather was bad, and we didn't expect there would be any raids. Nevertheless, we remained on stand-by. At about eight o'clock in the evening of the 1st or 2nd of March Area Headquarters reported a single enemy aircraft approaching and said that the

---

[123] It is probable, but not certain, that the Mosquito pilot who shot down Wittgenstein was Flight Sergeant D. Snape of No. 141 Squadron.

Gruppenkommandeur had ordered that in view of the bad weather situation I myself was to scramble to intercept it. I was to head north and await further instructions. After I had been in the air for about fifteen minutes the controller informed me that the enemy aircraft had turned away and that I was to land. I was not to go back to Nordholz, however, but to Stade. I landed there as instructed, and I went to the operations room, where I was told to report to the *Kommodore, Oberstleutnant* Lent, immediately. I asked myself what could be up, but my conscience was clear. In the headquarters building I met *Oberleutnant* Raht[124], the *Kapitän* of a *Staffel* stationed at Schleswig, who told me that he too had been ordered to report to the *Kommodore*. And still the penny didn't drop. We were taken in to see Lent, who greeted us with a friendly grin and told us that we had been given early promotion to *Hauptmann*. The whole story of a single enemy bomber, the order to fly to the north and so on had been set up by Lent in order to get us to Stade without suspecting anything so that he could tell us personally about our promotion. In the normal course of events I would not have been promoted for another thirteen months. And it goes without saying that the stars for our epaulettes were there, waiting to be put on straight away. Then Lent brought out a bottle of champagne. When I got back to Nordholz the following day they already knew the whole story, so we had another celebration. Once more, this whole affair was typical of Lent. I never met him again, but he wrote me a personal letter of congratulation when I got the *Ritterkreuz*.

The battle against the bombers continued to take a steady toll on the night fighters, with probably as many crews dying as a result of inexperience and bad weather as from enemy action. But even experience was no guarantee of safety. The number of night-fighters' gravestones that bear the inscription, '*Unbesiegt vom Feind*' ('Unconquered by the Foe') is legion. In mid-March 1944 Lent wrote a letter home that included the following:

> On the way back I had a chance meeting with the good Prince Lippe. We had a very pleasant chat before I took off again. Sadly it was the last time I would see him. A week later he crashed in the Ardennes in bad weather and lost his life. It is not a nice feeling to lose old comrades, with whom one has shared many a fine war experience, one after the other. But who can tell why God has done this? We human beings are far too small, and also far too powerless, to understand his actions.

Major Prinz Egmont zur Lippe-Weissenfeld, victor in 51 night-time encounters with Bomber Command, was *Kommodore* NJG 5 when he met his death on 12 March 1944, but he had only held that post for three weeks. Previously, until 20 February, he had been *Kommandeur* III./NJG 1, and his new appointment had taken him to Döberitz, west of Berlin. On the 12th of March he set out from Döberitz to fly to Saint Dizier in France to take formal leave of his previous unit, but over Belgium he met bad weather and crashed into high ground in the Ardennes near Saint Hubert. He and the other two on board were killed. Lippe-Weissenfeld

---

[124] Gerhard Raht, (58 kills).

Helmut Lent, *Kommodore* NJG 3, in conversation with one of his *Staffelführer,* *Oberleutnant* Hans Raum. Raum survived the war with 17 victories to his credit.

had served with Lent at Leeuwarden with 4./NJG 1 and II./NJG 2, when the two had become close comrades and friends.

The Battle of Berlin was nearing its conclusion. It had reached its peak of intensity in January 1944, when Harris mounted six maximum-effort raids on the capital of the *Reich* and three major attacks against other long-range German targets. January had been the month that saw Bomber Command suffer its highest losses and the *Nachtjagd* achieve its

Oberstleutnant Helmut Lent was promoted to that rank on 1 March 1944 and awarded the *Brillanten* on 31 July the same year. This photograph of him with Walter Kubisch must have been taken during that period.

greatest number of kills. In February there had only been one attack on
Berlin, plus three major raids on German cities (Leipzig, Stuttgart and
Schweinfurt); and there was also just one Berlin raid during March, plus
five against other German cities (Stuttgart twice, Frankfurt, Essen and
Nuremberg). The centre of gravity of Bomber Command's effort was
beginning to shift away from Germany and towards targets in France,
with flying-bomb launching sites, which were appearing at a disturbing
rate, and targets associated with the forthcoming Allied invasion taking
increasing priority. Lent's apparently reduced level of personal
involvement in the battle was no doubt a direct result of changes such as
these. On 22/23 March, however, he resumed his run of successes.
Frankfurt was the target, and Lent shot down two Lancasters of the 26
that, together with seven Halifaxes, did not return to England. It was a
good night for the *Nachtjagd*, which claimed 30 successes, of which Lent's
Geschwader accounted for 13. *Oberleutnant* Heinz Rökker of I./NJG 2

Illesheim, April 1944.
Oberleutnant Martin
('Tino') Becker receives
his *Ritterkreuz* from
Major Heinz Reschke.
Reschke was killed in
action later that same
month.

Lent and Kubisch in front of Ju 88 D5+MT. Lent's logbook only shows him as flying in this particular machine on one occasion, on 24 March 1944, when he claimed two four-engined bombers during a raid on Berlin.

made three kills, *Hauptmann* Gerhard Raht of II./NJG 3 – whom Paul Zorner had met at Stade – made four, but the outstanding achievement of the night belonged to Martin ('Tino') Becker of I./NJG 6, who destroyed three Lancasters and three Halifaxes in the space of an hour.

Two nights later, on the night of the 24/25 March 1944, the German capital city suffered its final Bomber Command attack of the Battle of Berlin, and indeed of the war. It was a costly anti-climax to a huge undertaking that had not lived up to Harris's expectations nor to his forecasts. 811 bombers set out, and 72 failed to return. Unexpectedly high winds scattered the RAF force, and many of the returning bombers strayed into the anti-aircraft defences of the Ruhr Valley, where the Flak took a heavy toll. Of the night fighters, Rökker shot down a further three, *Oberleutnant* Martin Drewes three, *Oberleutnant* Heinz Schnaufer three, and in all the night fighter force claimed 31. Helmut Lent's contribution was two heavy bombers, which brought his personal total of kills to 93.

That night Helmut Lent and Walter Kubisch had a third man with them in the Bf 110 that they were flying, D5+MT. *Leutnant* Werner Kark, in peace time the editor of a leading Hamburg newspaper, was the official war correspondent of NJG 3. He had been attached to a series of front-line *Luftwaffe* units since 1940, flying many operations as a full member of crew over England, Greece, Africa and Russia before being posted to NJG 3, where he trained and flew as *Bordmechaniker*. Kark made it his practice only to report from personal experience. The following article appeared in the *Oberdonau Zeitung* of 31 March 1944:

With the *Luftwaffe*, March 1944:

The air defences of Germany look back upon hard weeks and months. By day and by night the worst possible weather conditions have continuously made operational flying difficult in the extreme. Recent *Wehrmacht* communiqués have frequently reported that successes have been achieved 'despite the most difficult defensive conditions' against an enemy who skilfully uses the protection of thick sheets of cloud to his own advantage, and hidden behind this statement are not only bitter aerial combats but above all nerve-racking struggles on the part of all the crews against the terrors of icing, ground fog and cloud and drizzle over take-off and landing grounds. In certain conditions today pilots take off and land completely blind. The great unknown factor in our operational flying is not the enemy's guns and his escort fighters, but above all adverse weather conditions. In the winter months there is an undeniable relationship between the bad-weather areas and the number of enemy aircraft destroyed.

Straight into Action!

When our search radars picked up a strong force of British bomber units assembling in the early evening of 24 March there were good conditions for take-off and landing at all the night-fighter fields in the *Reichsgebiet* for the first time in a long period. There was no moonlight, but there was a splendid starlit sky and a bright streak in the northern heaven. 'It's going to be a fruitful night,' said *Oberstleutnant* Lent as we climbed over the wing into the cabin of the Messerschmitt 110. During the last raid he had brought himself back to the top of the list of successful night fighters again with his 82nd and 83rd victories.

Scramble! The enemy is approaching on an easterly heading over the West Friesian islands, not making a feint but heading directly for Berlin. At this very moment our fighters are racing along the runways at their bases, gathering at their operational altitude and being controlled directly into the bomber stream. 'Bomber's Death' will again reap a terrible harvest among the enemy squadrons tonight!

The first kill!

What wonderful visibility there is in this first shining early-spring night! The broad sea, dark islands, knife-sharp coastline, the canopy of searchlights spreading protectively above the towns, the venomous muzzle-fire of the Flak, the bursting shells, the coloured recognition signals of our fighters like will-o'-the-wisps in the sky – the eerily beautiful picture of the nocturnal air battle in all its breathtaking splendour spreads out before us as we enter the arena. The first enemy aircraft, the Pathfinders, have reached the mainland. After them follows the main force, a never-ending stream of bombers on its way to Berlin.

In our cabin there is completely silence. The flak fire on the outskirts of the town grows stronger. The beams of the searchlights form a network of light in the darkness. Quite calm and precise, we suddenly hear on our intercom: 'There's one ahead of us, *Herr Oberstleutnant!*' *Oberfeldwebel* Kubisch, the *Kommodore*'s *Bordfunker*, currently the only one of his trade in the *Nachtjagd* to hold the Knight's Cross, sits there motionless. Lent goes in at full speed. 'Now he's on our left,' says Kubisch. Suddenly something hits the fuselage of the Messerschmitt like the crack of a whip. We have run into the slipstream of the enemy bomber flying ahead of us. 'I've got him – I can see him,' comes from the front seat. Slowly we creep up on the enemy.

The *Kommodore* opens fire. Dull thuds vibrate through the fighter's fuselage. There are dazzling flashes in the cockpit. All our guns are sending a long burst into the heavy four-engined bomber aircraft ahead of us. 'He's burning,' says *Oberstleutnant* Lent, 'he's really burning!' It comes from his mouth as casually as if he were sitting at his office desk. At the same time we catch sight of the burning enemy. Its wide wings are swathed in flame. In a steep dive it races towards the earth like a torch. Searchlights pick it up and follow it down over the silent landscape until it hits the ground. A blazing pyre, black smoke, then fiery embers. The first kill this memorable night, and certainly a Pathfinder.

Blood is the Price of Terror!

A quarter of an hour, half an hour later. Fires are burning strongly all around us. The agitated probing of the searchlights in the sky, the thin lines of tracer from other night fighters, burning enemy bombers and coloured flares show that the bomber stream is still advancing through our airspace. We continue searching, constantly changing our heading. 'Ahead and to the right!' says Kubisch. 'Still further to the right!' A new contact. Once again the enemy machine takes skilful evasive action. We follow him, turning, climbing, diving all the time, copying his every manoeuvre. Behind this enemy aircraft is one

Lent, *Kommodore* NJG 3, is seen here with *Major* Husemann, his most successful *Gruppenkommandeur.*

of Germany's best night fighters!

Suddenly, ghost-like, the Tommy looms up ahead of us. Massive shape, wide wings, twin fins, four powerful engines. The *Kommodore* presses on the firing buttons. For us these are moments of high tension. Will his aim be true?

A sinister night-time picture. We have experienced its like many times when hunting above the *Reichsgebiet*. Then suddenly the faint silhouette of the heavily damaged enemy bomber appears above us. A broad sheet of flame from the centre of the fuselage tells us that he is badly hit. Behind him he is trailing thick banners of smoke. Once, twice, three times a small shadow sweeps past the tail unit of the bomber. The British are bailing out! But the pilot must still be at the controls. The bomber is still capable of flying, and he is trying to escape.

A second attack! Our cannon and machine guns hammer out again. It is the *coup de grâce*. The bomber loses height more and more swiftly, descending towards the wide countryside in a steep dive. Like a shadow, careful and alert in case despite everything the enemy still recovers, we follow him until finally, some distance from us, a huge ball of fire on the ground marks his end. This is another cargo of bombs that will not reach Berlin.

We leave the battle area. The stream is still heading to the east. We know that comrades from other *Geschwader* will infiltrate the bomber stream from all directions and claim fresh victims. On the broad bombers' road to Berlin tonight more fires from shot-down bombers than ever before will show the British airmen that once again a very heavy price must be paid in blood for terror attacks on the capital of the *Reich*.

This was Bomber Command's final major raid on the German capital, not only of the so-called Battle of Berlin but also of the entire war. Historically, however, the Battle is considered to have lasted until the end of the month of March, and Harris sent two more major raids to Germany during that period, one against Essen on 26/27 March and the other one against Nuremberg on 30/31 March. Poised to expect yet another long-range penetration, the German defences were taken by surprise by the strike at Essen and the RAF lost only nine machines from a force of 705. Lent did not fly that night. Then came the Nuremberg raid, and the outcome could scarcely have been in starker contrast.

Nuremberg, an industrial and cultural city in Bavaria with very strong associations with the National Socialist Party – Adolf Hitler described it as 'the most German of cities' and before the war chose it as the venue for major Party rallies and congresses – was intrinsically a difficult target, because its location dictated that any bomber force heading for it had to fly almost all the way there and back over Germany and occupied territory, unlike, for example, Berlin, where the bombers could take advantage of long sea crossings before braving the land-based fighter and flak defences. The route chosen for the night of 30/31 March was planned to avoid major flak concentrations such as the Ruhr and Frankfurt areas, and the meteorologists forecast favourable cloud cover that would provide some defence against enemy night fighters, even though the long, straight track into the target area was ideally suited to

Tame Boar interception. Unusually, the raid was mounted during the full-moon period, although it must have been obvious that if the cloud cover failed to materialise the bomber stream would be highly vulnerable. Much reliance was placed on the jamming of *Nachtjagd* control frequencies, deception broadcasts, diversion raids and Mosquito intruder operations.

The weather forecast, on which so much depended, was totally inaccurate. There was little cloud cover, unexpected winds blew the bombers off track and took a large number of them over the heaviest flak defences of the Reich, those of the Ruhr, and many of the bombers produced contrails – unforeseen by the weather forecasters – that showed the night fighters not only the bombers' route, thus enabling more fighters to be called up, but also the position of individual aircraft. The *Nachtjagd* enjoyed a field day – an appropriate metaphor given that 'Nachtjagd' translates as 'Night Hunt' – and the *Flak*, too, had considerable success.

By any standards the Nuremberg raid was a disaster for the British. Of the total of 950 aircraft that Harris sent out that night, 795 were heavy bombers allocated to the main target, while the remainder were to fly various types of support operations. When the surviving Lancasters and Halifaxes returned to England and were counted, 95 of their number were found to be missing, while a further ten or so crashed in England. Only minimal damage was caused in Nuremberg, where just 69 civilians died – about one for every 12 bombers despatched – while deaths of RAF aircrew amounted to 545, with a further 152 men becoming prisoners of war. The best available estimate for the number of German night-fighter crewmen who died is eleven.

Helmut Lent's personal contribution to the total of kills made by the *Nachtjagd* that night was limited to a single Lancaster, much to his frustration. As a whole, however, his *Geschwader* enjoyed considerable success: I./NJG 3 (Vechta) claimed five kills; II./NJG 3 (also Vechta), fifteen kills; III./NJG 3 (Stade), seven kills. Lent took off from Stade at 2340 hours. Allowing for a ground speed of 215 mph, and assuming that Lent flew more or less in a straight line to the target area, he might have been expected to pick up the bomber stream near to the point to the north of the target at which they were turning in on the 75 mile approach leg to the aiming point, and this, indeed, seems to have been what happened. He scored his single success at 0121 hours between twenty and forty kilometres (twelve and twenty-four miles) north of Nuremberg, by which time the attack was nearing its end: the main bombardment had been scheduled to begin at 1010 hours and to last seventeen minutes. Why Lent was scrambled so late in the proceedings is not known. The successful pilots of III./NJG 3, also flying from Stade, all scored their victories about an hour earlier than Lent did, and so must have been in the air well before the *Kommodore*.

War correspondent Werner Kark again flew as Third Man with Lent and Kubisch on the night of the Nuremberg raid, and on the following day this article by him appeared in the German press:

This memorable night had already had an unusual prelude. We were ordered up to cockpit readiness. 'A red herring, a feint attack,' said the veterans among us: when was the last time that the British had come in bright moonlight and clear visibility? Nobody could remember a similar occasion. For months now we had accepted take-off on instruments, cloud layers up to an altitude of several thousand metres and thick darkness in the battle zone as the natural accompaniment to our difficult job.

Still unconvinced, and in grave doubt about the whole sense of our orders, we taxied out to take-off in 'Cäsar-Anton'[125]. The wings glittered in the bright light of the half-moon. Silver light shimmered on the runways, the hangar-roofs and the barrack blocks as *Oberstleutnant* Lent swept over the airfield at full throttle. If the British bomber formations should really dare to attack tonight there is no doubt in our minds that once again they would be on the receiving end of a bitter lesson of air-historical significance. But who among us could imagine the breathtaking events that would take place in this battle in the moonlight above the cities of Southern Germany, events that lay ahead of us, the like of which none of us, even the oldest and most experienced, had ever known? And we had flown many times by night along the aerial routes over Germany!

Now we know that bomber streams are approaching German territory from the northwest. We are kept continuously informed on the R/T of the location of the leading machines. As their squadrons are approaching the target on a broad front strong forces of German night fighters from operational airfields storm into their flanks, and then a continuous air battle spreads out over hundreds of kilometres.

Ahead of us are dazzling lights: cones of searchlights shine out in the darkness, flak fire suddenly erupts above the towns. Flares are floating down.

We are approaching the target area, and in front of us bombers galore are going down. 'Man, man, man, it's all happening here!' the *Kommodore* shouts suddenly over the intercom. 'Kubisch – keep a good lookout!' he adds. The *Funker* peers intently at his instruments.

We are flying into the very field of battle. Hitherto on such occasions our eyes have always taken in the painful drama of the towns under attack; until tonight fires, explosions, target-indicators and areas of incendiary bombs have been the visible evidence of the nocturnal air battle, but tonight a look around shows us that this time it is the enemy alone who is being subjected to one of his hardest tests of this war.

The fires that we saw were the fires of fatally stricken British bombers crashing. In place of his Pathfinders' markers there are the torches of aircraft going down in flames, and the flickering flashes in the sky mark the bitter aerial combats between our fighters and their enemies. At this moment it is hard to concentrate on one's job in the aircraft and pay attention to one's own safety. This breathtaking drama is unfolding before us even before we reach the combat area. While we are burning inwardly to bring our own victims down from the sky, our comrades are doing great work. We used to think that

---

[125] *Cäsar-Anton* – phonetic alphabet for the Bf 100's identification letters (D5+CA).

20, 30 or even 40 kills over Frankfurt, Hanover or Kassel marked the acme of our personal experience in these nights of fire, but in these moments all our previous experiences and expectations are exceeded. The facts tell us the truth. At the very moment that the *Funker* calls out to the pilot, 'There's one up there,' the aerial battle reaches a renewed climax. Below us the fires from the crashed bombers illuminate a thin covering of cloud. The flames of burning machines below it light it up blood-red. Around us it is as bright as day. Two, three, four combats have flared up very close to us. A fighter is just diving steeply down on its prey.

To our starboard streams of tracer flash past our wings, and above us we can make out the sharp outline of a Halifax swathed in flame from tail unit to cockpit. On our port side a bomber explodes in whirling fragments.

Now we have picked up a prey of our own. Our foe seems to be overcome with fear. He is twisting and turning for his life in this inferno. But the *Oberstleutnant* doesn't let his victim off the hook. We follow him into a dive, pull up with him, go over on to the left wing, then the right one, so that everything in the cabin that is not fastened down floats up, ghost-like. Our target comes into our sights for a fraction of a second. Our pilot fires a long burst. Blood-red flashes streak from the barrels of our cannon. The shells hit his starboard wing, tear it off. For a instant wreckage fills the air, and then the bomber goes down vertically and hits the ground. There is a ball of fire on the earth, a thick black cloud of smoke from the explosion, the 87th night kill of *Oberstleutnant* Lent[126].

When we get back to base the *Kommodore* is dissatisfied with himself and with the world. 'Our comrades shot too many down!' he says – and then laughingly adds that nevertheless tonight has been one of his great experiences with the *Nachtjagd*.

We will never forget this night. Even less so will the British terror fliers.

At 0121 hours, when Lent made his kill, the bombing of the city was at its height, and he was still some distance to the north of the aiming point. His kill is recorded as having taken place 'between 20 and 40 kilometres north of Nuremberg'.

Lent's disappointment at only shooting down a single bomber when he could see the havoc that the *Nachtjagd*, including other members of his own *Geschwader*, was wreaking on Bomber Command is readily understandable. There must still have been a few targets to be attacked after he had made his kill, but he did not succeed in adding to his score. Even with pilots as experienced and as talented as Lent, luck still played a part in their success. The *Kommandeur* of IV./NJG 1, Heinz Schnaufer, who had become the second-highest scorer when Wittgenstein died and now had 51 kills, was also in action on the night of the Nuremberg raid, and he was even less successful than Lent, gaining not a single victory.

Lent was, and had been since the early days of the war, a national hero, and he and his achievements featured regularly in the state-controlled media. Another war correspondent, Wilhelm Glöde, also had an article about Lent published on 1 April 1944, but he approached his subject

---

[126] There appears to be some confusion here. The generally accepted list of victories records this as Lent's 86th night-time kill.

About April 1944. *Oberstleutnant* Helmut Lent in conversation with *Hauptmann* Heinz Schnaufer, *Kommandeur* IV./NJG 1. Schnaufer, with a final score of 121, was the only night-fighter pilot to score more victories during the war than Lent did.

from a different angle:

The 'front runner' among our successful night fighters, *Major* Helmut Lent, was promoted to *Oberstleutnant* on 1 March 1944, so becoming at the age of 25 the youngest *Oberstleutnant* in the *Wehrmacht*. To date he has logged 87 victories by night and 8 by day.

A grey late-winter's day lies over the broad marshland meadows. The windows of the express train are steamed up and the crush in the corridor is so oppressive that it would be presumptuous to speak of one's impressions of the landscape. But on the drive back from Landsberg – the small diversion gains me an hour – I am much better able to form a picture of the stretch that for years was the road to school of the man who is the reason for this journey to the Warthe Marsh – *Oberstleutnant* Helmut Lent, the holder of the *Ritterkreuz mit Eichenlaub und Schwertern*, whose parental home is the vicarage in Pyrehne. The thickly wooded slopes of the Messin Forest with the beautiful Lake Dolgen stand out against the marshland. The home village of our leading night fighter lies on the small dunes before them.

The one-horse carriage rattles along the hard-frozen road that winds along from Döllensradung past humble fields, a clump of pine-trees and a lonely camp. We drive directly towards the church spire of Pyrehne. At once the broad village green reveals the colonist village, burnt down on more than one occasion but now rebuilt. Afterwards, in the Pastor's office, I learn that Pyrehne was once a fishing village on the edge of the marsh, but that it is not one of the marshland villages in the narrower sense.

Over afternoon coffee with the parents the conversation soon comes round to the main subject – the early life of the holder of the *Schwerter* in his father's house in the small, cosy village between heath-land and marsh. Coming after his two brothers, now village priests in Hochzeit and Spiegelberg, Helmut, as the youngest, was their father's favourite. Full of pride he speaks about the deeds of his son, emphasising that he has remained true to his youthful character. When he stays a few days on leave in the parental house he is rarely to be seen in uniform. Among his boyhood friends he prefers to be known as *'Pastors Helmut'* rather than to be gaped at and bowed to as *'Herr Oberstleutnant'*

Major Heinz Wolfgang Schnaufer, seen here wearing his Knight's Cross with Oakleaves, Swords and Diamonds.

with medals and decorations. One of his closest friends from his very early days is the verger. At one time to help him with ringing the church bells seemed to the small Helmut to be a dream of supreme bliss. The two of them, the old verger and 'Pastor's Helmut' don't write long letters to each other. Only once, after Helmut was promoted to *Major*, did it seem to the old man that the comradely *'Du'* was no longer appropriate. But with complete sincerity the *Eichenlaubträger* insisted on the traditional form.

With silent pride the father calmly says that in his view the ambition to reach the heights must already have arisen in Helmut when, as a ten-year-old, the church roof was being renewed. During one mid-day break he climbed on the scaffolding, to the horror of the roofer, and began swinging in the foreman's chair as if from a rope tied to the thickest branch of the apple tree. He also told of the way in which Helmut used to join his contemporaries in happy games and, as 'Artillery Commander', soon became their self-elected leader: all his memories become alive, make the proud father's heart glow, because they provide the background to the rapid climb of the young hero: to be, at 25 years of age, the holder of high honours and a *Geschwader-Kommodore* is begrudged him by very, very few: he is simply the hardest and best among the most dedicated.

In the Lent home they seem to have their own method of counting the days. A particular event is not referred to by day and year, but the father thinks a moment and then says, 'That was just after the *Eichenlaub*, approximately at the time of the 37th kill.' The visits to the *Führerhauptquartier*, to Karinhall, the promotions and the times he was wounded represent somewhat irregular, but nevertheless frequent, rungs on the ladder of time. There is a lot to tell about the young girl from Hamburg who became his wife, of the baby girl who is the joy of his off-duty hours, of his faithful Kubisch, the first *Funker* in the German Air Force to win the *Ritterkreuz*. Pictures and newspaper cuttings soon cover the table.

Twilight interrupts us. The carriage is waiting outside the door again, telling me it is time to go home. Now the ice-cold east wind is blowing from directly in front of us. An overcoat and blankets keep me warm. Long transport convoys roll towards the front line along the big metalled road to the East. The small home village of the great night fighter seems to draw back into the edge of the forest, as if it is looking for protection from the night, his time for hunting.

CHAPTER ELEVEN

March to October 1944
Kommodore NJG 3. The final months

Lent, now an *Oberstleutnant*, with his wife Lena and their daughter Christina. The photograph was taken on about Christina's second birthday.

T HE END of the Battle of Berlin with the disastrous attack on Nuremberg on the night of 30/31 March 1944 marked, for the time being at least, the end of Harris's degree of freedom in the selection of targets for his bomber force. The planning for '*Overlord*', the Allied invasion of the Continent, was well advanced, and the great enterprise could not long be postponed. Bomber Command would be needed to make an important contribution to both to the preparatory operations and eventually to the landings themselves. With effect from 15 April the two Allied strategic air forces, the US 8th Army Air Force and Bomber Command, came under the control of the Supreme Commander, General Dwight D. Eisenhower. Unhappy though Harris was with this arrangement, still believing that the best contribution that his Command could make to ultimate victory lay in the destruction of the German

infrastructure, he had no option but to fall into line, and once he had done so he led his Command in the invasion-related operations with great skill and dedication. Bomber Command attacks on military, transport and communications targets in France and Belgium increased while those against targets within Germany decreased. The result was that the night-fighter units stationed in Holland, Belgium, France and the west of Germany saw more action and scored more victories than did those units that lay further back from the invasion front, among which were those belonging to Lent's NJG 3.

Lent's flying logbook gives little indication of his command activities. April 1944 seems to have been a very quiet period as far as flying was concerned. Over and above a moderate amount of local flying from Stade he paid only eight visits to other airfields during the month, for a total flying time of less that ten hours. Only one of these trips is recognisable as probably having been to visit one of his units, that on 14 April to Westerland/Sylt, where IV./NJG 3 was stationed. His logbook does not show him making a single operational flight during the month, although he is credited in the 'Nonnenmacher List' with the destruction of a Lancaster on the night of 22/23 April, when Düsseldorf, Brunswick and railway yards at Laon were attacked by Bomber Command for the loss of 42 bombers[127]. Beginning on the 24th of April he flew an eight-day tour that took him successively from Stade to Kitzingen, Echterdingen, and Ingolstadt, all in southern Germany, and to Parndorf

Lent visits Saint Trond in Spring 1944. From left to right: Lent, *Kommodore* NJG 3; Unknown; Schnaufer, *Kommandeur* IV./NJG 1; Jabs, *Kommodore* NJG 1.

---

[127] As recorded elsewhere omissions from Lent's logbook were not unusual.

Coffee at Saint Trond, Spring 1944. Lent, Schnaufer and Jabs.

in Austria. Ingolstadt was the home base of 1./NJG 101 and Parndorf that of II./NJG 101, while Kitzingen was the base of 1./NJG 102 and Echterdingen that of II./NJG 102. NJG 101 and NJG 102 were not mainstream night-fighter *Geschwader* but smaller units whose primary function was the operational training of night-fighter crews. Until approximately the autumn of 1943 new crews had been trained at *Nachtjagdschule 1* at Schleissheim or at *Nachtjagdschule 2* at Stuttgart/Echterdingen[128]. Interestingly, the training at these early night-fighter schools seems mainly to have been aimed at teaching the crews to fly during the dark hours, and live night-fighter interception and combat techniques were not practised there: the training aircraft did not even carry radar, and newly-trained crews were expected to learn the practical aspects of their trade 'on the job' when they reached their operational units. Unlike the original night-fighter schools, however, NJG 101 and NJG 102 had an operational function and were integrated into the air defence system, with the instructors, in addition to their teaching function, carrying out live interceptions in exactly the same way as did pilots of the main front-line *Geschwader*. Senior, experienced and decorated officers frequently visited training units to talk to the trainees, to stimulate their morale and to advise on changing and developing operational techniques, and it is probable that Lent's visits in April 1944 came into this general category.

During May NJG 3 saw rather more action, although it was not until

---

[128] *Nachtjagdschule* – Night Fighter School.

the eleventh of the month that Lent entered '*Nachtjagd*' in his logbook, when six separate targets in France were attacked by Harris's crews. Lent took off from Stade in D5+CA at twenty minutes to midnight on the 11th and landed just over two hours later, but he had been unable to add to his score. The following night, the 12th, saw him airborne again, but again he did not destroy a single enemy bomber. For Lent, however, there was nevertheless something special about this particular sortie. One imagines that it must have been with a feeling of sadness that he switched off the engines of his Bf 110 after taxiing the machine to its dispersal point. The Bf 110, in its *Zerstörer* and night-fighter versions, had been his regular mount since June 1939, and it was the type of aircraft in which he had scored all but a few of his 95 kills to date. Now he was converting to the standard aircraft flown by NJG 3, the Ju 88, and according to his logbook he never flew the Bf 110 operationally again, although he did make one last trip in it, to Kastrup and back, the following day. From now on his regular aircraft would be the Junkers 88G-6 D5+AA, the 'D5' signifying NJG 3 and the 'AA' signifying *Kommodore*.

The first operational sortie that Lent made in D5+AA was on the night of 21/22 May, a night when Bomber Command attacked Duisburg and lost 29 Lancasters, but Lent landed back at Stade after only sixteen minutes in the air, again without having shared in the spoils. Two nights later, however, his luck changed when the German defences claimed 18 Lancasters from a force of 361 attacking Dortmund, of which Lent shot down two. His total score was now 97. Despite scrambling a further three times before the end of May, he was unable to increase his tally until mid-June. While there is no evidence that he was consciously aiming at the magic number of 100, he would not have been human had it not been in his thoughts. During May, as in April, he made frequent visits to other airfields, some of which housed *Gruppen* of NJG 3. Other trips, such as, for instance, one he made to Deelen, Headquarters of NJG 2, on 5 May were no doubt liaison visits.

On 6 June 1944 the long-expected invasion of Europe began. From then on most of Bomber Command's efforts were directed with great effect against tactical targets in France in support of the Allied advances into Europe – road and rail communications, concentrations of troops and armour, fuel storage facilities, airfields and so on – and there were also front-line bombing operations in direct support of the advancing Allied troops. V1 flying-bomb sites and storage installations came under attack by an increasing number of bombers, and in their turn V2 rocket launching sites and support facilities, more and more of which were appearing in France and Holland, were targeted. For some time Bomber Command did not area-bomb German cities and towns at all, but a new target of increasing significance did take the Lancasters and Halifaxes more and more over the *Reich* and so within easier reach of the *Nachtjagd* again – oil. The Americans had long held the view that one of the most effective ways in which long-range heavy bombers could be used was to disrupt supplies of the oil that fuelled the German war machine, particularly their air forces: typically, Harris had been less enthusiastic, categorising oil as a 'panacea target'. Now, however, that Bomber Command was under the overall command of the Supreme Allied Commander, Harris accepted the categorisation of oil as a priority target and obeyed Eisenhower's orders to attack oil installations, mostly in the Ruhr area, and he achieved unexpectedly good results. His bombers, aiming at markers dropped by *Oboe* Mosquitos, frequently attained a higher degree of accuracy by night than the American B-17s and B-24s did in daylight. The Joint Oil Offensive played an enormous part in ultimate victory. As Harris himself would write in 'Bomber Offensive' after the war, 'The triumph of the offensive against oil was complete and indisputable.'

In belated response to the invasion the *Luftwaffe* began a hectic tactical repositioning of both day and night fighter units, including the redeployment of the flying units of Lent's NJG 3 to Butzweilerhof, near Cologne, and to Le Culot in France. Lent's first recorded flight following the opening of the invasion was on the evening of the 14th of June, the day after his 26th birthday, when he flew from Stade to Butzweilerhof, landing there at 2014 hours. Walter Kubisch was not with him in the Ju 88, but his seat was occupied by a *Funker* by the name of Lütringhaus. Also in D5+AA were Werner Kark and probably a fourth man, a *Zweiter Funker* (Second Wireless Operator). Just after midnight they took off again to intercept a force of Lancasters and Halifaxes that were attacking German troop positions and railway targets. Only four four-engined bombers were lost that night, and Lent did not score. Then, the following day, he flew in D5+AA to Le Culot, and in the early hours of Friday the 16th took off to intercept a moderate force of 224 incoming Mosquitos, Lancasters and Stirlings heading for the railway yards at Lens and Valenciennes. In conditions of good visibility the RAF bombers struck accurately at their targets, but they lost eleven of the Lancasters, all to night fighters, with Lent claiming three of them.

This night's events marked a high point in Lent's operational career. Two relevant documents survive, one the text of an interview that he gave to a radio reporter shortly afterwards:

> First of all we were called up to cockpit readiness, but we were soon stood down again. At about half-past eleven things got serious – we were ordered off! I was one of the first into the air, and I headed west. Quite soon after we were airborne I could make out the target, because the enemy were using a new type of target marker. I thought I was going to arrive too late again, but then everything worked out OK. Unfortunately my excellent wireless operator, *Oberfeldwebel* Kubisch, was not with me on this operation, but his stand-in did extremely well, so that I was able to get into the stream in good time. The whole combat with the three bombers didn't last long: from the first kill to the last it only took seven minutes. All three burned better than I have seen for a long time, and they caught fire so quickly that one member of my crew, who hadn't previously taken part in a kill, said to me, 'Break off! Break off!' and I had to remind him that I knew myself when I needed to break off. They were

three four-engined bombers. I think they were Lancasters, but everything happened so quickly that I couldn't identify them one hundred per cent.

In the second surviving text, published in the press on 20 June, Werner Kark describes the same operation:

Bombers are flying from the darkness of space towards their target. But our night fighters intercept their path. The tense silence on board is suddenly broken. The *Funker* speaks clearly and precisely: 'I've got a bomber on the starboard. I bit more starboard. Down a bit, down a bit more.' It is silent again as our pilot curves, climbs, dives, sometimes at full throttle, sometimes slowly. Then at last come the words from the front that we have been waiting for – 'Thank you. I have him!'

From the semi-darkness of the sky the silhouette of a four-engined bomber grows bigger and bigger. Calmly our pilot manoeuvres into an attacking position. Then his cannon flash, and flames shoot from the bomber's two starboard engines. Like a flaming projectile with a huge tail of fire he sweeps past us in a steep dive into the depths. Even before he hits the ground with what looks like a series of explosions we have picked up another doomed four-engined machine approaching the target. It was the flight mechanic[129] who saw him first. The enemy is weaving wildly. 'Just calm down, young man,' says our pilot in measured tones. An instant later the Lancaster flies through a full burst of shells from his cannon. Luck is with us tonight!

As this enemy machine goes down to the earth at a steep angle, enveloped in flames from rear turret to cockpit, we pick up a third target. This machine meets its fate with the same breathtaking speed as the first two.

'Gentlemen, that was my 100th victory!' For an instant we see the hellish fire on the ground as the third bomber crashes, and then we turn to our pilot with smiles. It is *Oberstleutnant* Helmut Lent, the *Kommodore* of a night-fighter *Geschwader*. In the excitement of the night we had almost forgotten the event that Lent, with complete justification, had been looking forward to.

Lent's achievement in shooting down 100 enemy aircraft earned him another citation in the *Wehrmachtsbericht*, his fifth in all. Modest though he might be, he unquestionably had good reason to feel a degree of satisfaction with his own performance. Although a number of day-fighter pilots had amassed more than 100 victories – indeed some had scored well over 200, mostly on the Russian front – he was the first night-fighter man to do so. His nearest rival, Heinz Schnaufer, although gaining fast, had still only scored 78.

Lent's personal success, however, does not appear to have been matched by that of his *Geschwader* as a whole. On 22 June he sent an extraordinarily prolix 1800-word letter to each of his four *Gruppenkommandeure* criticising them for their apparent under-achievement and suggesting ways in which they might improve their

---

[129] In the latter part of the war it was customary for night fighters to carry an extra man to assist in operating the radar and/or to keep a watch for British bombers or intruder fighters. He was often loosely referred to as '*Bordmechaniker*' (flight mechanic).

At Le Culot after his 100th kill. To Lent's left is War Correspondent Werner Kark, who also acted as Third Man in Lent's aircraft.

Also at Le Culot after Lent's 100th victory, 16 July 1944. To his right is reserve *Funker* Lüttringhaus.

operational performance. Whether he conceived and drafted the missive personally, or whether it was issued on instructions from higher authority, will presumably never be known, but its contents are puzzling, reading as they do more like a verbose rewrite of a training manual entitled 'Officer Qualities' than a letter from a leader of fighting men exhorting his subordinates to greater efforts. The letter ends:

We have reached the most crucial phase of this war. As a result of the introduction of new weapons the trust in our leaders, and above all in final victory, on the part of the German people in the homeland and of the German

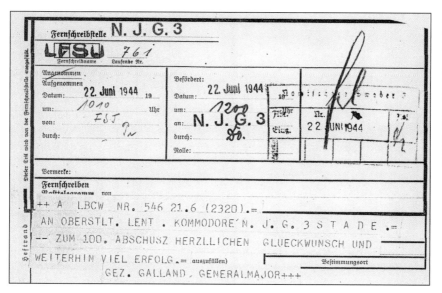

Among the telegrams of
congratulation to
Helmut Lent on his
100th victory was this
one from Adolf Galland.
It reads, 'To
Oberstleutnant Lent,
Kommodore NJG 3.
Sincere congratulations
on your 100th victory.
Much success in the
future.'

soldier at the front has grown tremendously. The final spurt is just beginning.
I am convinced that final victory is not far off, if the lowly night fighter, from
whatever *Gruppe* he might be, faces the enemy with increased operational
dedication, with greater determination, and above all with more kills. The
Kommandeure have in their hands the means to make a decisive contribution to
this aim.

Generalmajor Joseph
'Beppo' Schmid (his
name is misspelt) was
rather more fulsome in
his praise than Galland:
'On the occasion of your
100th victory I send
you, in grateful
appreciation of the
valuable contributions
that you have made in
energetic and most
valuable operations to
the effective conduct of
night fighting, and
thereby to the
protection of the
German *Heimat*, my
appreciation and most
sincere congratulations.
On to new success with
Hals- und Beinbruch.

It is interesting to speculate what led Lent to write this extraordinary document which, one would think, was more likely to discourage those to whom it was addressed than to motivate them to greater effort. Could all his *Gruppenkommandeure* be so lacking in basic leadership qualities that it was necessary for him to catalogue their corporate inadequacies in such detail? And if the criticism was aimed at perhaps one, two or three of his four *Kommandeure*, the document was inherently divisive because those not meriting criticism would certainly know at once who the inadequate leaders were. A senior officer who is dissatisfied with the performance of a junior officer interviews the subordinate in private – 'on the carpet' – and spells out his inadequacies to him in detail; if he judges it appropriate he encourages the junior by advising him on ways in which he might improve his performance, or possibly he makes it clear to him that if he does not improve there will be disciplinary consequences. Ironically, given the many criticisms in Lent's letter, it included this comment by him: 'On four occasions I observed that the officers, from *Kommandeur* down, were strongly given to criticism. Healthy criticism has always been the starting-point for better performance. But criticism by itself without learning the appropriate lessons is the best sign of poor *ésprit de corps*.'

On the 23rd June Lent was scrambled from Le Culot just after midnight without success. Then, either later that same night or on the 25th/26th – the record is unclear – he shot down two Lancasters from forces of bombers attacking flying-bomb sites: the V1 attack on England had begun a week after the invasion and heavy casualties were already being caused in London and the South East of England. Then, on 27/28 June, against another similar force, he shot down a further Lancaster, bringing his total score to 103, his night-time score to 95.

Lent left Le Culot and returned to Germany on 30 June. During the following two weeks he flew widely to various airfields, mostly in North Germany, but there is no clue to the reason for these excursions. Back at Le Culot on the 16th of July he flew operationally on the 18th/19th and the 20th/21st, claiming two bombers each night, although only one each night appears in the Nonnenmacher List: presumably the other two did not receive official confirmation. When Lent left Le Culot on 22 July for Stade his score stood at 105.

Lent's logbook shows him resuming the earlier pattern of frequent visits to other airfields following on from his return to Stade, but the visits were interspersed with night scrambles, the first in the early hours of the 25th July. With the immediate demands of the invasion less pressing, Harris was able to mount a three-raid offensive against Stuttgart, sending out 614 heavies and losing 21 in the first attack – the *Nachtjagd* claimed 24 victories. Helmut Lent, flying from Stade, shot down a Lancaster. The second attack was on the following night, but although Lent went into action he did not score. On the final night of the Stuttgart 'trio', however, the 28th/29th July, Bomber Command also sent 106 Lancasters and 187 Halifaxes to Hamburg. Lent, *Kommodore* of NJG 3, shot down two bombers, both of them Halifaxes, of the 10 bombers –

Pages from Lent's *Wehrpass* (Service Record Book) showing his honours and awards: Iron Cross Grades 2 and 1; Narvik Shield; Operational Clasp in Gold; Individual mentions in *Wehrmachtsbericht*; Oak Leaves; Swords; Bar to Operational Casp in Gold; *Brillanten*; Wound Badge in Silver.

9 of which were Halifaxes – claimed by his *Geschwader*. As no Halifaxes took part in the Stuttgart raid, so it is clear that all NJG 3's successes were against the force attacking Hamburg. Lent's overall score went up to 108 and his night score to exactly 100.

On 31 July 1944 this official communiqué was issued:

> The *Führer* has awarded the Oak Leaves with Swords and Diamonds to the Knight's Cross of the Iron Cross to *Oberstleutnant* Helmut Lent, *Kommodore* of a night-fighter *Geschwader*, as the 15th soldier of the *Wehrmacht*.

The *Brillanten*, as the award was colloquially known, was for practical purposes the highest decoration that a member of the German armed forces could earn[130]. That only fifteen had been awarded in almost five years of war, during which its closest British equivalent, the Victoria Cross, was awarded approximately 120 times, testifies to its rarity. Lent was the first night-fighter pilot to have earned the honour[131]. Congratulatory telegrams flowed in, among them one from Hermann Göring:

> My dear Lent,
> Full of pride and gratitude I congratulate on the highest German decoration for gallantry, which you, the first and the most successful German

---

[130] A higher grade of the Order of the Iron Cross was introduced in December 1944, the Golden Oak Leaves with Swords and Diamonds, but it was only awarded once, to *Major* Hans-Ulrich Rudel, the outstanding *Stuka* pilot who destroyed 333 Soviet tanks on the Eastern Front.

[131] Only ten *Luftwaffe* officers received the *Brillanten*, and only two of them were night-fighter pilots. *Major* Heinz Schnaufer's decoration was promulgated on 16 October 1944, just a week after Lent's death, when Schnaufer shot down his 100th bomber. He went on to finish the war with 121 kills to his name.

Foreign Minister Ribbentrop's telegram of congratulations on the award of the *Brillanten* reads: 'On the award of the highest German decoration for bravery I send to you my most sincere congratulations. Heil Hitler!'

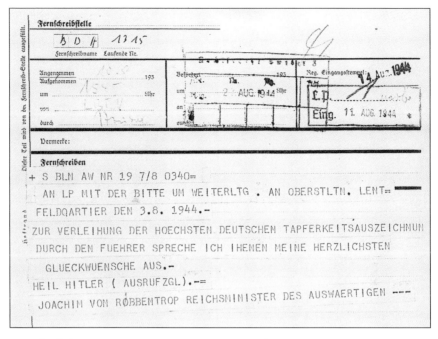

night fighter, now wear. No one is more able than I am to measure what unforgettable services you have performed in the battle for the destiny of the German people.

With unbridled readiness for action and death-defying bravery you have fought night after night to defend the *Heimat* against the enemy's terror bombers, destroying opponent after opponent. It is your example that invariably motivates the men of your *Geschwader* to gallant feats of arms in the most bitter conflicts. In you, therefore, the entire German nation joins me in our admiration of one of our bravest soldiers. I combine my acknowledgement

General Milch's congratulations are rather more formal: 'Most sincere congratultions on the award of the Oak Leaves with Swords and Diamonds. Heil Hitler.

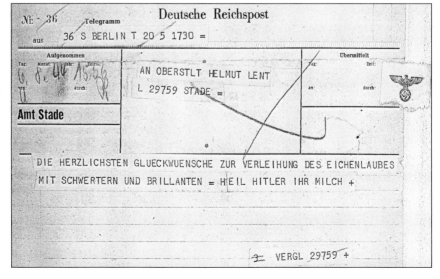

of your glorious achievements both as a single combatant and as a commanding officer with my best wishes for your future and further proud victories.

Yours, Göring, *Reichsmarschall* of the Greater German *Reich* and Commander-in-Chief of the *Luftwaffe*.

During the night of 16/17 August, according to the Nonnenmacher List, Lent claimed his 109th victim, although there is no entry in his logbook even to show him flying operationally that night. There is, however, a '*Nachtjagd*' entry for the following night, the 17th/18th, showing him scrambling operationally from Stade at 2301 hours on the 17th and

landing just after two hours later, but there is no mention of a kill. One of Bomber Command's main targets that night was Kiel, and the Nonnenmacher list shows that I./NJG 3, III./NJG 3 and IV./NJG 3, by this time back from France and stationed at Schleswig, Düsseldorf and Wittmundhafen respectively, shot down all but one of the ten claims made by the night fighters that night, with Lent contributing one kill. The probability is that Lent, or whoever was maintaining his logbook, had made a date error.

25 August 1944. *Oberstleutnant* Helmut Lent receives the *Brillanten* from the hands of Adolf Hitler at Rastenburg.

By this time Lent's pattern of flying was as before – frequent liaison trips to other operational airfields, including, but not confined to, those occupied by his own *Gruppen*. On 24 August he flew to Rastenburg to receive his *Brillanten* from Adolf Hitler, arriving back at Stade on the 26th having called in at Jüterbog, Ingolstadt, Darmstadt and Reinsehlen on

Lent wearing the
Brillanten, probably
taken at Rastenburg on
25 August 1944.

the way. On 11 September, when the RAF attacked Darmstadt, he shot
down a single Lancaster, so bringing his score to 110. It is generally
accepted that this was the final tally that Helmut Lent reached during
the war. The Nonnenmacher list, however, records one more kill by
Lent, his 111th, a Lancaster on the night of 16/17 September 1944, but
no details such as time and location are given, and we are left with
something of a mystery.

Bomber Command lost three Lancasters on the night in question,
two of them from a force attacking targets in Holland and Germany in
preparation for Operation 'Market Garden', the Arnhem landings,
which began the following day. Both the Lancasters that were lost were
attacking flak positions a Moerdijk, near Dordrecht in Holland, and it
is believed that they collided with each other over the target. In any

event, neither could have been a victim of Lent, who had taken off from Stade during the afternoon of the 16th and flown to Grove in Denmark, his flight being logged as '*Einsatzverlegung*' (Operational Deployment). Lent, according to his logbook, scrambled operationally from Grove at 2341 hours on the 16th and landed at the same airfield at 0145 hours on the 17th: there is no mention of his having shot down a bomber[132]. Coincidentally, however, a Lancaster was lost that night in northern latitudes.

Lent's *Brillanten* are now in the Museum of Defence History at Rastatt, Germany, but not on public display. They are seen here in front and rear view.

On 11/12 September 1944 a force of Lancasters from Nos. 9 and 617 Squadrons, some of them carrying 12,000 pound 'Tallboy' bombs, had flown from England to the Russian airfield of Yagodnik, near Archangel. On the 15th of the month they had attacked the mighty German battleship '*Tirpitz*', which was moored in Altenfjord in Norway. The bombers returned to Yagodnik after the attack[133] and flew back to Britain during the night of 16/17 September. One of them, PB416 KC-V of No. 617 Squadron, crashed in Norway.

It is fascinating to speculate that Lent – and possibly other night fighters – might have been sent to Grove with a view to intercepting the Lancasters on their way home, and that Lent had made a successful interception. Such evidence as there is[134], however, argues against the

---

[132] This is not necessarily of significance. At this later stage in Lent's career there are a number of similar omissions. Possibly it was the practice not to enter victories in one's logbook until official confirmation of the claim was received.

[133] This was, as it transpired, the raid that in practical terms ended the career of *Tirpitz*. She was hit by a Tallboy and had to be towed to Tromsö, where RAF Lancasters finally sank her on 12 November 1944.

[134] Lent was airborne from 2341 on the 16th until 0125 on the 17th: Presumably these times were in GST (German Summer Time), which was two hours ahead of Greenwich Mean Time, so he was in the air from 2141 until 2325 GMT on the 16th. RAF records, however, contain the statement that the Lancaster, 'Acknowledged QDT from Dyce at 0121 GMT. Nothing else heard'. A 'QDT' was a radio fix.

likelihood: but it would be interesting to know who his victim really was.

There were scattered RAF raids, none of them major, over Germany on 28/29 September 1944. Lent took off on what was destined to be his last operational mission at 0309 hours on the 19th, but he did not make contact with the enemy, and he landed again after 36 minutes. At about this time – possibly a day or two after this abortive flight – Lent paid a short visit to his home village of Pyrehne. There was a very happy reason for his trip, to collect baby clothes that had originally been used by his daughter Christina, now just over two years old.. Helmut's wife Lena was expecting their second child at the beginning of October, and Lent was convinced that it would be a son.

Someone who remembers Lent from this period is Walter Briegleb, a night-fighter pilot who was posted to IV./NJG 3 in September 1943, just after Lent had become *Kommodore*. Stressing that his personal contacts with Lent were few, as was to be expected when he was a junior officer and Lent an *Oberstleutnant* and *Kommodore* whose headquarters were at a different airfield, Briegleb comments as follows:

> You ask me for my personal opinion of Helmut Lent. Although he was still a young man – *Oberstleutnant* and *Kommodore* of a *Geschwader* and still only 25 – his personality, his understanding and his trustworthiness shone out. His professional competence, his successes and his unassuming presence combined to give him both human appeal and total authority. Operationally, there can be no doubt, he was a hard fighter, but he never attempted to drive his pilots into reckless 'adventures'. He expected us to fight bravely but prudently, avoiding unnecessary risks. Anyone shooting down two or three in a night was under instructions to act independently and return to base, and not to take off again if he did not feel able to undergo the nervous strain of flying another mission. When I shot down two bombers on the night of 5/6 January 1945 I thought of this advice on the part of Lent and landed at the nearest airfield.

Walter Briegleb recalls two incidents that were typical of Lent. In June 1944 Lent paid a visit to Briegleb's airfield, Varel, and Briegleb, by now a *Staffelkapitän* with seven victories, reported to him. Lent awarded the young officer the Iron Cross First Class, but did not have a medal with him and so he took off his own EK1 and pinned it on Briegleb's chest. The second incident was in early October 1944, when Briegleb came into contact with a Wellington, probably a minelayer, over the sea. The Wellington was 'stubborn' and put many bullet-holes in Briegleb's 'faithful *Berta*', D5+BV, before succumbing to Briegleb's cannon fire. Briegleb was still over the sea when his starboard engine cut. He reported his situation to base and was ordered by Lent himself to fly to Wittmundhafen and make a wheels-up landing there. Briegleb headed for Wittmundhafen, but not wanting to lose his favourite aircraft he concentrated all his 'know-how' and landed there on one engine. Everything went smoothly, but he had disobeyed a direct order from his *Kommodore* and expected to be reprimanded. It was with some trepidation that he reported to Lent by telephone, but Lent congratulated him on his smooth landing and on his 16th kill. Briegleb describes Lent as 'a comrade and an example'.

Walter Briegleb draws attention to Lent's instruction that pilots shooting two or three bombers down in a night were to return to base and not scramble again if they did not think they could stand the nervous strain. Lent himself never shot down more than three in a night, and he only did that on four occasions, so that of his total of 103 night victories only twelve were scored in batches of three. This argues a high degree of caution and selectivity on Lent's part, which is highlighted by a statistical comparison with the record of Heinz Schnaufer, whose final score was to exceed that of Lent. Of Schnaufer's total of 122 confirmed victories, 62 – almost exactly half – were scored in batches of three or more. He scored three in a night on ten occasions, four in a night five times, five in a night once and seven in a night once.

A few short days after the incident that Briegleb describes Lent's God, it seems, withdrew His protection from His favoured son.

CHAPTER TWELVE

5th to 7th October 1944
The death of Helmut Lent and his crew

AT 1246 HOURS on Thursday the 5th of October 1944 Helmut Lent took off from Stade in his Ju 88, D5+AA, We*rknummer*[135] 751081, to make the 140-mile journey to Paderborn. It was a perfect day for flying, with good visibility, a little scattered cloud and a slight wind from the east. On board the aircraft in addition to Lent were *Oberfeldwebel* Walter Kubisch, his *Funker*; *Leutnant* Werner Kark, the war correspondent, flying as gunner; and *Oberleutnant* Hermann Klöss as Second *Funker*.

The final family photograph. Helmut Lent visited his home village of Pyrehene in September 1944, the month before that in which he died. This photograph was taken during that, his final leave. Left to right: Brother Werner; Sister Ulla; Mother; Father; Brother Joachim; Sister Käthe; Helmut. Werner is in uniform, having been conscripted as a military chaplain.

---

[135] *Werknummer* – factory number, manufacturer's number.

Lfd. Nr. des Fluges	Führer	Begleiter	Muster	Zulassungs-Nr.	Zweck des Fluges	Abflug Ort	Flug Landung Tag	Tageszeit	Ort	Tag	Tageszeit	Flug-dauer	Kilometer	Bemerkungen
1527	Lent	Kubisch	Ju 88	D5+AA	Einsatzverlegung	Stade	3.10.	1446	Marx	3.10.	1507	21		
28	"	"	"	"	"	Marx	"	1649	Stade	"	1710	21		
29	"	Kubisch, Klöss, Kark	"	D5+AA	"	Stade	5.10.	12.46	—	—	—	—		*Am 5.10.44 13.20 Uhr 500 westl. Flugplatz Paderborn abgestürzt.* *Die Richtigkeit der Flüge von Lfd. Nr. 854 – 1529 wird bescheinigt.* *i. A. den 6.11.44* *Petersen*

Lent, the *Kommodore* of NJG 3, had arranged to visit his friend and colleague, *Oberstleutnant* Hans-Joachim Jabs, *Kommodore* of NJG 1, to discuss operational matters of mutual concern.

Shortly before Lent's arrival at his destination at 1320 hours American heavy bombers had bombed the airfield at Paderborn/Nordborchen, leaving craters on the concrete runway. Enemy aircraft, however, were no longer in the vicinity. An emergency grass runway had been cleared and marked out for Lent, and it seems that there was an overhead electric cable in the vicinity of the approach lane. In default of more precise information, we must assume that this cable had not been considered a hazard when the emergency grass runway was marked out.

There were several witnesses to what happened then; typical of their reports is that of *Unteroffizier* Walter Kotecki:

> I was at the anti-aircraft gun site at the *Ilse* works on the west of the airfield. I saw the aircraft on the approach, coming in to land with its engines throttled back. It suddenly went into a left turn. I noticed that the port engine was stopped. The rear of the fuselage stalled and the aircraft flew a short distance further in a stalling condition. Then it seemed to me that the pilot saw the overhead high-tension wire and pulled the aircraft round to the left. The port wing came into contact with the ground and the starboard wing cut through the high-tension wire. There was a bright blue tongue of flame. Then the aircraft hit the ground and caught fire immediately. I did not see whether the undercarriage was retracted.

Obergefreiter Herbert Illing, a member of the Airfield Salvage Team at Paderborn, also witnessed the crash. His report agreed with that of Kotecki but added a little detail:

> I was at the western boundary of the airfield working on a crashed Bf 110. I saw the Ju 88 make a circuit of the airfield and then come in to land with its undercarriage retracted. The runway controller fired two red lights and the aircraft went into a turn to port. The port engine was stopped with its airscrew feathered. The rear fuselage sagged and the aircraft flew a further 20 – 25 metres in a stalled condition. I then saw the aircraft make a tight turn to port and go into a sideslip. Then all I saw was a bright flash and the fire when it hit the ground.

The final pages of Helmut Lent's logbook showing the details of his 1529th flight as a night fighter. The columns show Lent as the pilot with Kubisch, Klöss and Kark as his crew flying in Ju 88 D5 I AA. They took off from Stade at 1246 hrs. on the 5th October 1944. The comments in the *'Bemerkungen'* column read, 'Crashed 500 (metres) west of the airfield at Paderborn at 1320 hrs., 5.10.40. Below is written in a different hand, 'The correctness of the flights serial numbers 524-1529 is certified.' It is signed by Heiner Petersen, Lent's adjutant.

Unteroffizier Alfred Günther saw the Ju 88 coming in low overhead: its port engine was stopped and the aircraft was banked steeply to the left. He saw the left wingtip touch the ground and the right wing strike the overhead electric cable and tear it down. He and two other soldiers ran to the point of impact:

> The crew had been thrown out and were lying approximately ten to fifteen metres from the burning machine. Together with an anti-aircraft gunner who came running up I dragged *Oberstleutnant* Lent away from the wreckage and then carried him to the edge of the road. I took the injured *Oberstleutnant* in a vehicle from the fire-fighting section to the local hospital in Paderborn. By the time I got back to the accident site in an ambulance from the hospital the other members of the crew had been taken away.

All four members of the crew, Lent, Kubisch, Klöss and Kark, were dreadfully injured and unconscious. They were taken to hospital in Paderborn, where Kubisch, who had suffered severe burns, internal injuries and extensive fractures, died in the course of an emergency operation. A few hours later Klöss died from head injuries, and the following morning Kark too died from similar causes.

Achim Jabs was Lent's close friend; both *Kommodore* were accommodated in married quarters in the former Court House in Reinfeld, between Lübeck and Hamburg, and their wives were good friends. Jabs immediately went to Lent's bedside. This is his account[136] of what followed:

> Of all four members of the crew, Lent was the least seriously injured. He was suffering from severe shock and concussion, and both lower legs were fractured. The same day he regained consciousness for a few minutes, and he recognised me. He was unable to tell me what had caused the crash.
>
> The chief doctor at the hospital recommended the amputation of one of Lent's lower legs, which had been torn open to the bone, because he feared that gangrene might set in. This suggestion was, however, overruled by a senior *Luftwaffe* surgeon, Professor Häberle, whom Hermann Göring had charged with the treatment of the Lent crew. Häberle ruled that it would be unwise to amputate because of the severe shock that Lent had suffered in the crash. An operation to repair the fractures was carried out, and, according to the medical experts, a very good pinning of both lower legs as accomplished.
>
> Lent recovered consciousness again for a few moments after this operation. I was able to tell him of the birth of his second daughter Helma, who had been born a short time after the crash. Lent was deeply disappointed that the baby was not the son that he had been looking forward to. This second daughter looked a lot like Lent.
>
> On 7 October, when I had to leave Lent to attend the funeral of the *Kommandeur* of I./NJG 1, Hauptmann Förster, who had died in a crash in a Heinkel 217 at Münster/Handorf, he came to himself again, and when I took

---

[136] From an article by Jabs in '*Jägerblatt*' in 1969.

my leave he said, 'You'd better hurry,' and then lapsed into unconsciousness once more, and he never woke up again. During my absence from Paderborn it was discovered that Lent was indeed infected with gangrene. Professor Häberle was summoned and the leg was amputated, but Lent died on the operating table.

Later Jabs enlarged slightly on this account: 'The Head Doctor of the Paderborn hospital in which Lent was being treated told me that he had to amputate immediately, because in his opinion Lent was already infected with gangrene. I was ordered by Göring to inform the doctor that the Chief Medical Officer of the 2nd *Fliegerkorps*, a famous surgeon, would come to take over the further treatment himself. This delay of several hours sealed Lent's fate. When eventually the surgeon from the 2nd *Fliegerkorps* arrived he attempted to remove the leg on the operation table, but the gangrene was already in Lent's body, so that he died during the night.'

Copies exist of witness statements and an official Accident Report form, duly filled in, but do little to explain exactly what caused so experienced a pilot as Helmut Lent to crash his aircraft. The nearest that the completed form come to definitive findings is in the section headed '*Vermutliche Ursache der Störung*' (Presumed Cause of the Accident)[137], in which the option '*Führungs- oder Bedienungsfehler*' (Pilot or crew error) is

Headed 'NJG 1 comment on the crash of *Oberstleutnant* Lent,' this statement was issued on 26 January 1945.

Nachtjagdgeschwader 1   Gefechtsstand, den 26.Januar 1945
————————————————————

Betr.: Stellungnahme NJG 1 zum Absturz des Oberstleutnant L e n t .

    Beide anliegenden Augenzeugenberichte stellen ein Ausbrechen
    der Maschine nach links fest. Weitere Zeugen haben gehört, dass
    der linke Motor vor der Landung aussetzte. Oberstleutnant Lent
    selbst bestätigte dieses. Durch Ausfall des linken Motors schob
    die Maschine nach links weg, war im Gleitflug nicht mehr zu
    halten und stürzte ab. Das Warnungssignal vom Platz (Rotschiessen)
    hatte auf den Absturz keinerlei Einfluss.

---

[137] A more exact translation would be 'Presumed Cause of the Fault', but the form is apparently a general-purpose document that was used to record and comment on technical trouble of any sort.

underlined. The summary of the findings, dated 26 January 1945, is laconic in the extreme: 'Both attached eyewitness reports state that the aircraft broke away to the left. Other witnesses heard the port engine cut before the landing. *Oberstleutnant* Lent himself confirmed this. When the port engine stopped the machine swerved to the left, could not be held in a glide and crashed. The warning signal from the airfield (red signal lights) had no influence on the crash.'

In default of a more detailed analysis of the possible causes of the tragedy – and it may be, of course, that a more thorough investigation was carried out but that the relevant records have been lost over the years – we must look to the report on the technical examination of the crashed aircraft for enlightenment. As part of the investigation the port engine was dismantled in the workshops at Paderborn and a broken component discovered, which apparently accounted for the failure of the engine. It was established positively that the airscrew of the failed engine was fully feathered, that the undercarriage was retracted and that the

General der Flieger Wollf, Commanding General of the 11th *Luftgau* (Air District), sent this telegram to Helmut Lent on the evening of the day of his crash at Paderborn. Lent died two days later. The telegram reads, 'Dear Lent, With heartfelt concern the thoughts of all in *Luftgau* 11 go out to their best and bravest night-fighter *Geschwaderkommodore*. We all salute you in comradeship and admiration. My wife and daughter join me in sending greetings to your dear wife, who was at one time together with my wife at Hermannswerder. We wish you a good recovery and convalescence. Heil Hitler! Your faithful *General der Flieger* Wollf.

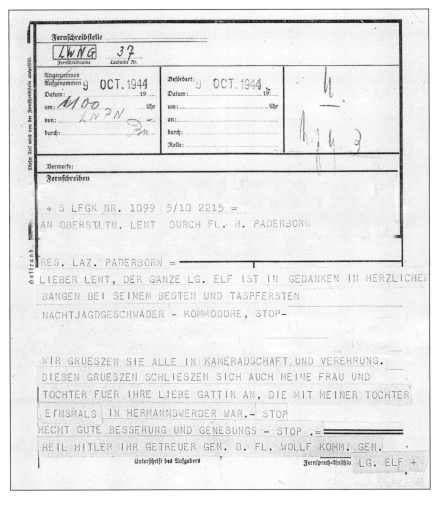

Deutsche Reichspost

Telegramm

64 S AUS DEM FELDE 31 10/10 2215 =

Aufgenommen | NACHGESANDT AUS HAMBURG | Übermittelt

FUHLSBUETTEL 11/10 1000 = .

Amt S POST | FUER FRAU LENA LENT IN STADE =

ZU DEM SCHWEREN VERLUST DER SIE DURCH DEN FLIEGERTOD IHRES

GATTEN BETROFFEN HAT SPRECHE ICH IHNEN MEIN AUFRICHTIGES UND

TIEFEMPFUNDENES BEILEID AUS = ADOLF HITLER +

Für dienstliche Rückfragen

T/0127 — 8.44   X C 187 DIN A 5 (Kl. 2)

flaps and elevator trim tabs were set for normal flight.

The statements by witnesses give no indication at all as to just when during the approach and landing procedure the port engine stopped, but the feathering of an aircsrew was a matter of seconds only and to land a Ju 88, or even to overshoot, on one engine was neither difficult nor dangerous for a competent pilot. The fact that the undercarriage was not lowered could mean that Lent intended to make a belly landing or that he did not intend to land but proposed to overshoot and go round again. One possibility that has been suggested is that he wanted to overfly the grass landing strip to check for possible bomb damage before committing himself to a landing, but the low level at which he approached, as indicated in witness statements, would seem to argue against that likelihood.

On 10 October 1944 Hitler sent his condolences to Lena, Helmut's widow, in this telegram: 'I send to you my most sincere and deeply-felt sympathy on the heavy loss that you have suffered in the flier's death of your husband. Adolf Hitler.'

Fliegertod des Oberstleutnants Lent

Aus dem Führerhauptquartier, 11. Okt.

Ergänzend zum Wehrmachtbericht wird gemeldet:

Geschwaderkommodore Oberstleutnant Helmut L e n t , Inhber der höchsten deutschen Tapferkeitsauszeichnung, fand den Fliegertod. Mit ihm verliert die Luftwaffe ihren erfolgreichsten Nachtjäger, der im Kampf gegen die nächtlichen Terrorangriffe der englischen Luftwaffe 102 Luftsiege errungen hat.

Mit 75 Tagesabschüssen gegen einen zahlenmäßig überlegenen Gegner errang die III. Gruppe eines an der Eismeerfront eingesetzten Jagdgeschwaders unter Führung von Ritterkreuzträger Hauptmann Doerr am 9. Oktober ihren 3000. Luftsieg.

Bei den Kämpfen im Banat hat sich die Grenadierbrigade (mot.) 92 unter Führung von Oberst Hillebrand durch vorbildliche Härte und Standhaftigkeit besonders ausgezeichnet.

Oberstleutnant L e n t
PK.-Aufn.: Kriegsberichter Doelfs (PBZ

Only the first two paragraphs of this newspaper report deal with the death of Helmut Lent.: From the *Führer's* Headquarters, 11 October. *'Geschwaderkommodore Oberstleutnant* Helmut Lent, holder of the highest decoration for gallantry, has died a flier's death. With him the *Luftwaffe* loses its most successful night fighter, who scored 102 aerial victories in the battle against the nightly terror attacks by the British Air Force.'

The most puzzling aspect of the problem is that the aircraft's landing flaps were found to be set for normal flight; that is, they were fully retracted into the wing, not lowered at all. For a landing, either normal or single-engined, they should have been fully lowered, and the lowering of flaps is so integral and automatic a part of the landing procedure, a procedure that Lent had followed many thousands of times, that for him to have overlooked doing so would seem so unlikely as to verge on the impossible. And so the position of the flaps suggests strongly that Lent intended to go round again.

A hypothesis that seems best to fit such evidence as is available is that Lent approached the emergency runway intending to land and with his port engine feathered and presumably with his flaps down. At a late stage in the approach he decided, for some reason that we shall never know, but possibly on seeing the red signals fired from the ground, or maybe on catching sight of overhead cables, to overshoot. He raised his flaps and opened up the throttle of his starboard engine, but in doing so gave too much power, causing the aircraft to cartwheel over its dead engine and so to hit the ground.

There are, of course, other possible explanations for the accident, but none would seem to point to any conclusion other than that reached by the investigators at Paderborn, pilot error. There was a saying among aircrew of the *Luftwaffe*, half humorous, half serious – '*Jede Landung ist eine heilige Handlung*', which translates loosely, and in the case of Helmut Lent perhaps rather appropriately, as 'Every landing is a deal with God.'

CHAPTER THIRTEEN

Official Act of Remembrance & interment;
Family Memorial Service

The Lent family's announcement of his death.

A STATE ACT of Remembrance was held for Helmut Lent in the *Reich* Chancellery in Berlin on Wednesday the 11th of October 1944, beginning at ten o'clock in the morning. *Reichsmarschall* Hermann Göring took the salute as Lent's coffin, draped in the national flag of the Third Reich, was borne into the great Mosaic Hall. Ahead of the coffin, carrying Lent's honours and decorations on a velvet cushion, *Oberstleutnant* Werner Streib, the Inspector of Night Fighters, marched in slow time. Six steel-helmeted officers, all holders of the Knight's Cross,

Mein über alles geliebter Mann und guter, treuer, sonniger Lebenskamerad, Christinchens treusorgender Vater

Helmut Lent

Oberstleutnant und Geschwaderkommodore in einem Nachtjagdgeschwader, Träger des Eichenlaubs mit Schwertern und Brillanten zum Ritterkreuz des Eisernen Kreuzes und anderer hoher Kriegsauszeichnungen

geboren am 13. Juni 1918, starb am 7. Oktober 1944, vom Feinde unbesiegt, den Fliegertod.

Als sein letztes Vermächtnis wurde uns am 6. Oktober 1944 unser zweites Kind, Helma-Elisabeth, geboren.

Im Namen aller Angehörigen

In unsagbarem Schmerz

Lena Lent, geb. Senokosnikow.

Stade, Harburgerstr. 185
Hamburg und Pyrehne, Kreis Landsberg/Warthe

escorted the coffin and stood as guard of honour during the ceremony: *Oberstleutnant* Günter Radusch; *Oberstleutnant* Hans-Joachim Jabs; *Major* Rudolf Schoenert; *Hauptmann* Heinz Strüning; *Hauptmann* Karl Hadeball and *Hauptmann* Paul Zorner[138]. Göring's speech included the following passage:

Act of Remembrance, Berlin, 11 October 1944. *Reichsmarschall* Hermann Göring takes the salute as the coffin of *Oberstleutnant* Helmut Lent is borne past to lie in state.

Berlin, October 1944. Senior officers in the capital of the Reich in order to be present at the *Staatsakt* for Helmut Lent. Left to right: Wolfgang Timmich, *Kommodore* NJG 4; Hans-Joachim Jabs, *Kommodore* NJG 1; Werner Streib, *Inspekteur der Nachtjagd*; *General* von Döring, 3. *Jagddivision*; Günter Radusch, *Kommodore* NJG 2. Radusch took over command of *Kommodore* NJG 3 after Lent's death.

---

[138] By the end of the war these seven officers had shot down the impressive total of 392 enemy aircraft.

The Guard of Honour at Lent's coffin. Left to right: Jabs; Schoenert; Hadeball; Radusch; Strüning.

A man who achieves so many things, such a warrior, such an example and such a teacher, will forever live with us and among us. Just as he was the model for the new force, so too will his spirit mark the *Nachtjagd* in the future. As we take our leave from him at this hour, and as we remember his life, we cannot but be aware that his sacrifice imposes a duty on us all, the duty to be worthy of that sacrifice. A hero's life such as this cannot be snuffed out, and at this very moment, when the battle to the end will be most difficult, we too feel the strength to fight it.

At this hour of farewell, my dear Lent, the *Führer* expresses to you his thanks and his recognition, and to these thanks from the *Führer* I add those of the *Luftwaffe*, the

Göring delivers his address at the *Staatsakt*.

gratitude of the German people and my own thanks. Today, when dark clouds surround Germany, the deeds of men such as you were shine so brightly that we need not fear the darkness. You were ready to fight and to die: and now, my good, gallant Lent, join the ranks of the heroes.

Göring salutes Lent's coffin.

The following day Lent and his crew were interred in a common grave in the military cemetery at Stade. *Generalleutnant* Schmid, Commanding the First Fighter Corps, laid wreaths from the Führer and from *Reichsmarschall* Göring, the first of many tributes laid by high-ranking officers and civilian dignitaries. *Generalmajor* Ibel, Commander of the Second Fighter Division, made a graveside speech to the memory of Helmut Lent, Walter Kubisch, Werner Kark and Hermann Klöss, while State Secretary Ahrens, Governor of Hamburg, spoke on behalf of the civilian population.

Hertha, the wife of Helmut's brother Joachim, was among the mourners, and later she wrote a letter to the many members of the Lent family, describing the ceremonies in both Berlin and Stade. Her letter provides a moving record of the occasions. It begins, 'Dearest All, sincerest thanks to all of you for your loving letters on the passing of our beloved Helmut. We have had so many letters that it is impossible for us to answer them all and thank everyone individually. I am sending you this typewritten letter, which I hope will answer all your questions at one time.' Hertha described the crash of Lent's aircraft and then continued:

Dignitaries at the interment of the Lent crew. Front row, left to right without topcoat: *Generalleutnant* Max Ibel. Then, wearing leather coats, *Generalleutnant* Joseph Schmid; Secretary of State *Obergruppenführer* Ahrens; *General der Flieger* Wolff.

We got the news of Helmut's accident from his in-laws early on the Sunday morning, and on Sunday afternoon we learned that he had died. On Thursday we travelled to Pyrehne, where we met up with his other brothers and sisters, and we travelled overnight to Berlin in order to be at the Air Ministry by eight-thirty in the morning. From there we were taken by car to the State funeral service in the Reich Chancellery at ten o'clock. The service in the Mosaic Room was very splendid. There is a great deal that one could say

Helmut Lent's coffin is borne to the common grave. The bearers seen here are, from left to tight, Schoenert and Hadeball in the front row, Zorner and Strüning in the second row.

about it, but you have heard about it on the wireless and in the newspapers, and now on the newsreel at the cinema as well. Then we were driven to Stade, near Hamburg, for the interment. In fact it was our wish that Helmut should be buried in Pyrehne, his home village, but his wife so much wanted him to be buried in Stade. And indeed it is very fine to know that he is resting side by side with his flying comrades in a single grave.

Oberstleutnant Hans-Joachim Jabs, friend and comrade of Helmut Lent and carrier of his Order Cushion, stands back as the coffin is carried past him to the grave. (Left of photograph).

The coffin of *Oberfeldwebel* Walter Kubisch is carried to the grave. Kubisch was promoted posthumously to the rank of *Leutnant*.

Generalmajor Max Ibel delivers his memorial address.

At half-past one at night, when we were in the Stade Hotel, we were got out of bed by an air-raid alarm. The following morning we breakfasted together with the other guests, and we introduced ourselves. Kark and Dr. Klöss were both married with no children, and Kubisch was planning to marry at Christmas. His fiancée, who like him comes from Saxony, is a dear, fine person. In civilian life Kark was the Editor of the *Hamburger Tageblatt*. Dr. Klöss comes from Ulm and was married in Berlin.

During the morning there was a long alarm, and we could hear bombs dropping nearby. We could hear the rattle of a low-flying aeroplane's machine-guns over the town, and we prayed that there wouldn't be an air-raid warning during the ceremony. An officer picked us up from the hotel at half-past two.

The coffin of War Reporter and 'Third Man' in Lent's crew, *Leutnant* Kark, is carried to the common grave.

We entered the cemetery by a side path, and Helmut and his comrades came towards us from the other side. The funeral music began just as we met and the guard of honour moved off to the place of burial, where the other funeral guests, the military and guard detachments were already assembled, in the following order: the band, the guard of honour and ourselves. After only a few bars of music had been played a major came hurrying up and stopped everything. The music came to a stop, the guard of honour halted, the coffins were lowered to the ground and we were quietly conducted past and shown to our seats. We sat there waiting for things that were supposed to happen, but which didn't. We thought there was going to be an air-raid alarm. The priest had been told in advance that out of consideration for Helmut's wife, who quite remarkably was at the ceremony only six days after her confinement, he should only give a short sermon.

At half-past three, thirty minutes late, the service resumed. What had caused the delay? A general had announced that he would be present, and he still hadn't turned up!

While we were waiting we had time to take a good look round. We mourners were all seated about fifteen metres from the common grave, which was beautifully decorated all over with evergreen foliage. The military details and representatives of the Party were drawn up in a square around us and the grave. To our left there were about a hundred airmen carrying wreaths. In all there were thousands of people.

The funeral music began at a quarter to four and the coffins were brought up and placed in front of the grave. Each place was marked out with small pine

Two of the coffins prior to the burial ceremony. The coffin-bearers, all holders of the *Ritterkreuz*, who can be seen in this picture are Zorner (to the right of the white wreath); Strüning (immediately to the right of the left-hand coffin); Jabs (in the background); and Hadeball.

Troops drawn up prior to the burial ceremony.

trees. For Helmut and Kubisch, *Eichenlaubträger* formed the guard of honour – Helmut was an *Eichenlaubträger* himself – with *Ritterkreuzträger* for the others. Helmut's friend *Kommodore* Jabs carried the decorations cushion. Then the band played, 'Who knows how soon my end will come?' The *Superintendent*[139] of Stade, who is also the Divisional Padre, gave the sermon. Even without the late start Helmut probably turned in his grave! It was a shocking sermon about the countryside, forests and meadows based on the text, 'But they that wait upon the Lord shall renew their strength: they shall mount up with wings as eagles,' which was identified with the gallant life of airmen, and so on. We were deeply shocked that no tribute was paid to Helmut in his coffin for his services to God and his Redeemer. We were all very relieved when this nonsense, which was a disgrace to the Evangelical Church, came to an end. Joachim and Werner had been to see the *Superintendent* in advance and told him of Helmut's very clear view of Christ. The *Superintendent* had told them that he had to be fair to everyone and take into consideration that Dr. Klöss belonged to the official church of the Party. There were no prayers, no 'Our Father', no blessing. Then *General* Ibel, Helmut's boss, spoke. He painted a good soldierly picture of each of them and acknowledged their acts of heroism. If you come to see us you can read his speech.

The coffins were carried to the grave by parachute troops. There were steps down. Air Force tradition dictates that the pilot is the last man to leave his machine, so Helmut was the last one to be carried down. The band played

---

[139] *Superintendent* : a senior clergyman in the Evangelical Church.

(*Top*) The coffin of Walter Kubisch is carried to its final resting place.

(*Bottom*) Lent's coffin is lowered into the grave. To the left are Jabs (carrying medal cushion), Hadeball (barely visible); Schoenert, Zorner.

Generalleutnant Joseph ('Beppo') Schmid at the side of the common grave before the coffins are covered.

'*Ich hatt' einen Kameraden*'[140] softly, and the wreaths were carried down – one from the *Führer*, one from the *Reichsmarschall*, and then wreath after wreath. The Master of the local Hunt, a farmer with whom Helmut was close friends, a fine, sincere Christian, sounded '*Jagd aus*'[141] on a French horn. That was very fine. There were words of tribute from various representatives, and then we were able to pay our final respects. My sister-in-law, Lena, was wonderfully brave. Helmut's father, his two brothers, Uncle Paul and Pastor Braune from Lobetal, each read a short passage from the Bible so that the word of Christ should be spoken at Helmut's grave.

Lena was taken back to the hospital by one of the doctors there, where we had coffee with the others, and then we went by car to the officers' quarters, to Helmut's house, where he had lived with his family for almost one and a half years. We wanted to see his home and say hello to little Christina. The following day, Friday, the christening of little Helma Elisabeth took place in the Wilhardi Church in Stade. Father-in-law christened her. My sister-in-law also attended the ceremony, and then she chatted with us in her home for about an hour. The following morning we went back home.

★　　　★　　　★

---

[140] 'I had a Comrade', a traditional military song.
[141] '*Jagd Aus*': literally, 'Hunt over', the traditional call to mark the end of the hunt. The English equivalent is, 'Going Home.'

On 31 October 1944, Reformation Day, following the ceremonial pomp in Berlin and the deep sadness of the interment in Stade that marked the German nation's loss of its best known and lionised night-fighter commander, the Lent family and the villagers of Pyrehne mourned the passing of 'Pastor's Helmut' at a solemn family service of commemoration in the village church. Helmut's elder brother, Pastor Joachim Lent, gave a memorial address in which he spoke movingly of Helmut's love of, and loyalty to, his fatherland and of his sense of duty as an officer, but also of his modesty and humility despite the high rank and honours that he had achieved. He also alluded obliquely to the support that his brother Helmut had given him in his difficulties with the National Socialist authorities that arose from his religious views:

Obergruppenführer Ahrens salutes Lent's coffin in the common grave. *Generalleutenant* 'Beppo' Schmid is on the left of the photograph.

> We all have a great deal to thank him for, above all I myself. As both a brother and a Christian, and particularly as the latter, he demonstrated his help to me in many difficulties of religion. For me to describe it all in detail is unfortunately impossible, but those who are privy to the facts will know what I mean. When help of that kind ended in success he would express his pleasure in moving words that at the same time demonstrated his humility. On one occasion he wrote, 'I am enormously pleased that our *Unternehmen Michael*[142] has ended in success. What is quite clear is that all thanks are due to God our Father and that I was, so to speak, only his tool. That in itself is a great

---

[142] 'Operation Michael' or 'Action Michael'.

thing. After all it was, and still is, my duty to help as much as was in my power. I did so willingly.'

Above all Joachim stressed Helmut's Christian faith: 'He went into battle as a Christian, and as a Christian in battle he felt that he was in God's hands. He accepted his victories as a Christian. Time and time again he unambiguously testified his belief in Christ. He went into battle as a Christian. Before each night mission he read his New Testament and then said a prayer. And thus before each battle he came before God's countenance, knowing that he would be in God's hand.' It was with a quotation from the last letter that Helmut had written to him that Joachim finished his address:

Lena Lent, Helmut's widow, sent this card as a token of thanks for condolences received. It reads: 'For the many proof of sincere sympathy for the hero's death of my beloved husband, *Oberstleutnant* Helmut Lent, *Kommodore* of a night-fighter *Geschwader*, I send my heartfelt thanks. In the name of all members of the family.'

'Though cities descend in ashes, if God builds His church on their ruins this has been a fruitful time.'

Seen against the background of religious intolerance and persecution in the Third Reich, this was a courageous address. Joachim made no mention of Party or Führer, speaking only of his brother's honour as a soldier and his loyalty to his fatherland and *Heimat*, and above all of his belief in and allegiance to Jesus Christ. Joachim's words when alluding to *Unternehmen Michael* suggest that Joachim, as a member of the *Bekenntniskirche*, had in fact clashed with the Party authorities, and been

Für die vielen Beweise aufrichtiger Teilnahme beim Heldentode meines geliebten Mannes, des

Oberstleutnant

Helmut Lent

Kommodore in einem Nachtjagdgeschwader, sage ich meinen herzlichsten Dank.

Im Namen aller Angehörigen

Lena Lent

Stade, Harburgerstr. 185.

helped by Helmut[143], on more than the one occasion described earlier in this book, and indeed that likelihood is supported by much hearsay reporting for which there is no available documentary confirmation.

Hertha, Joachim's wife, also described the family memorial service in Pyrehne in the circular letter that she wrote to the family:

The gravestones of the Lent crew photographed in 1999. Lent's grave is on the left.

> Last Tuesday, Reformation Day, was our commemoration service for Helmut in Pyrehne. This was, at last, the proper celebration for our beloved Helmut. The church was beautifully decorated with firs, autumn leaves and winter asters. In a true Reformation Day holy service brother-in-law Werner preached the sermon on the text, 'Blessed are they that mourn, for they shall be comforted'. Four hymns by the choir enhanced the ceremony. Joachim gave a commemorative address, a copy of which I am enclosing with this letter. Please pass it on, so that Helmut will be known as a believer in Christ. We were all very grateful for this ceremony. There was a great deal of sorrow that kept many people away, but the church was full. The headmaster and a delegation of teachers came from the Landsberg School. In his address Joachim mentioned the shocking experience that we had had with the local newspaper, the *General Anzeiger*. We wanted to put this memorial notice in the paper,

---

[143] It is likely that Helmut Lent gave similar support to his other brother, Werner, who also experienced difficulties with the authorities, including the *Gestapo*. See Page 149.

Oberst Lent's gravestones. He was promoted posthumously.

'Believing in his Saviour Jesus Christ, my beloved husband, my ever-cheerful life's companion, the good father of little Christina, our dear son and brother, *Oberstleutnant* Helmut Lent, ended his young life in the service of his beloved Fatherland. We take comfort in the word of God, Jeremiah 3,13: "Yea, I have loved thee with an everlasting love: therefore with a loving kindness have I taken thee unto me," followed by our signatures. The newspaper refused to print this announcement. They wanted to print a different one in the military style that is so common these days. The manager said to my sister-in-law, 'Do you want me to have my newspaper closed down because of your announcement?' As they couldn't come to an agreement my sister-in-law said emphatically that no announcement at all should be printed, not even the one that the newspaper wanted. The outcome was that, to everyone's displeasure, the newspaper's version appeared in the paper. This passage is not in your copy of the commemorative address, but otherwise it is word-correct.

It was very fine that we were able to be together in Pyrehne in so large a family circle. One is very grateful for such things these days. My sister-in-law Lena was unable to come because of her maternal duties, but her sister represented her.

Now we are all back home again. The world hasn't changed. Everything goes on as it was before. Only our heartache remains, particularly that of my poor bereaved sister-in-law. One thing, however, makes us happy and thankful - the unshakeable certainty that the Word of God gives to us. From that Word we give you this one true comfort, which we are going to have inscribed to our Helmut on the memorial cross in the Pyrehne graveyard: 'I know that my Redeemer liveth.'

CHAPTER FOURTEEN

Postscripts

A S HERTHA LENT had revealed in her letter to the family, the editor of the local newspaper, the *General Anzeiger*, had refused to print an obituary notice to Helmut drafted by the family on the grounds that the wording breached the rules laid down by the National Socialist authorities, which required that an obituary to any soldier killed in action should included the words '*Gefallen für Führer, Volk und Vaterland*,' ('Died for *Führer*, People and Fatherland'). Instead, and contrary to the wishes of the family, the paper had printed an obituary notice that conformed to the National Socialist norm. The editor of a national newspaper, the *Deutsche Allgemeine Zeitung*, was more accommodating, and on 24 November this obituary notice appeared:

> In the certain belief in Jesus Christ, the *Brillantenträger Oberstleutnant* Helmut Lent gave his young life in action for his Fatherland. Jeremiah 31.3.
>
> Lena Lent, née Senokosnikov,
> Johannes Lent, Pastor,
> Marie Lent, née Braune.
> Stade / Pyrehne.
>
> As a last bequest from my dear husband, God in His goodness gave me a healthy daughter, Helma Elisabeth.

This obituary notice did not escape the attention of the security police, and in January 1945 the *Deutsche Allgemeine Zeitung* contained this report:

> *Lent's last will saves his family from Concentration Camp.*
> *Obituary omits Belief in the Führer.*
>
> The last will and testament of *Oberstleutnant* Helmut Lent, a holder of the Diamonds to the Iron Cross, has saved his wife and father from a concentration camp.
>
> The *Gestapo* began proceedings against his widow Lena Lent, Pastor Johannes Lent and the responsible editor of the DAZ for the 24 November 1944 on the grounds of the anti-State text of the obituary notice for *Oberstleutnant* Lent.
>
> The obituary contained no single mention of belief in the people and the Führer on the hero's death of the *Brillantenträger*, but only of the Christian faith.

t neue Wendung

Lents letzter Wille rettet seine Familie vor dem KZ

Nachruf ohne Führerglaube

Der letzte Wille des Brillantenträgers Oberstleutnant Helmuth Lent hat seine Frau und seinen Vater vorm KZ gerettet.

Die Gestapo hatte eine Untersuchung eingeleitet gegen die Witwe Lena Lent, den Pfarrer Johannes Lent und den verantwortlichen Redakteur der DAZ vom 24. November 1944 wegen staatsfeindlicher Fassung der Todesanzeige für Oberstleutnant Lent.

In der Anzeige war mit keiner Silbe der Volks- und Führerglaube, sondern nur der christliche Glaube im Heldentod des Brillantenträgers erwähnt, weiter nichts.

Der Wunsch des Toten

Die Beschuldigten konnten aber nachweisen, dass Oberst-Leutnant Lent in Vorahnung seines Todes seine Todesanzeige selber abgefasst und ausdrücklich jede Bezugnahme auf den oder die nationalsozialitsische Idee untersagt hatte.

Das Verfahren musste daher eingestellt werden.

Oberstleutnant Lent, geb. am 13.8.1918 in Pyrehne, Kreis Landsberg, erhielt nach 100 Nachtjagdsiegen am 2.8.44 die Brillanten.

Frau Lena Lent ist die Tochter eines Hamburger Fabrikbesitzers und hat ein Kind aus der Ehe mit Helmuth Lent.

Im festen Glauben an Jesus Christus hat d. Brillantenträger

Oberstleutnant Helmut Lent

sein junges Leben im Einsatz für sein Vaterland vollendet. Jer 31, 3

Lena Lent, geb. Senokosnikow
Johannes Lent, Pfarrer. Marie Lent, geb. Braune

Stade/Pyrehne

Gottes Güte schenkte mir als letztes Vermächtnis meines lieben Mannes ein gesundes Töchterchen Helma Elisabeth

OBEN: *Helma Elisabeth Lent betrachtet ein Bild ihres gefallenen Vaters.*

UNTEN: *Die Todesanzeige in der DAZ.*

The article in the *Deutsche Allgemeine Zeitung* in January 1945. It is translated in the main text.

The dead man's wish

The accused were able to prove that in anticipation of his death *Oberstleutnant* Lent had himself drafted the obituary notice and had specifically forbidden any mention of the National Socialist ideology.

The proceedings had therefore to be terminated.

Oberstleutnant Lent, born 13.8.1918 in Pyrehne *Kreis* Landsberg, was awarded the *Brillanten* on 2.8.44 after shooting down 100 enemy aircraft by night.

Frau Lena Lent is the daughter of a Hamburg factory-owner. She has one child from her marriage to Helmut Lent[144].

Helmut Lent was promoted posthumously to the rank of *Oberst*, presumably from the date of his death, but there seems to be no record of just when the promotion was promulgated.

On January the 12th 1944 the Red Army began its massive winter offensive against Germany, sweeping forward irresistibly through Poland and East Prussia with an overwhelming superiority of men and material, its massed tanks, heavy artillery and vast numbers of aircraft, brushing aside German opposition and clearing the way ahead. The spearhead of the mighty offensive pointed to Berlin. By the end of January the Red Army had reached the Oder at Frankfurt and were only a hundred miles or so from the German capital. Pyrehne, on the Russians' direct route to Berlin, was occupied by enemy troops. Thousands upon thousands of Soviet fighting men from many diverse ethnic origins were being brought forward for the final assault, united in a fierce determination to crush the hated enemy and inflicting remorseless depredation upon anything or anybody German, military or civilian, man or woman, in a largely uncontrollable orgy of destruction, looting and rape. One of the countless victims of the mayhem was Helmut Lent's father. Many years later Lent's sister Ursula wrote:

> On the subject of the death of my father I should, as the last eyewitness, like to give an authentic account of it. There are so many versions in circulation, including distorted versions in print, that I feel impelled to set the record straight once and for all. These are the facts. Early on 16 February 1945 there was an announcement, 'All women to the age of 50 and all men to the age of 65 assemble in the village square.' Father told me that he was convinced that this meant deportation to Siberia. In fact we had to chop down trees in the Kleinheider woods, where the Russians wanted to make an airfield. The church was blown up for the same purpose. When I got home from work after dark there was a loud banging of a rifle butt on the back door. As usual Father went to answer, while I put on an old headscarf and went out through the front door to my hiding place in an old cottage behind our neighbour Dümmke's farm. Our mother, incidentally, had never hidden herself. I had

---

[144] This is, of course, incorrect. Lent's second daughter, Helma Elisabeth, was born on the day of his fatal crash. The photograph accompanying the article in the newspaper is captioned, 'Helma Elisabeth Lent looking at a picture of her dead father.' The girl shown is in fact Christina, Lent's first daughter.

CATALOGUE

OF

COINS

COMPRISING

ENGLISH AND FOREIGN GOLD AND SILVER COINS
INCLUDING A SMALL SERIES OF CROWN PIECES
SPECIMEN SETS

MEDALS

COMPRISING

A GROUP AWARDED TO OBERSTLEUTNANT LENT, LUFTWAFFE,
WITH OAK LEAVES, SWORDS AND DIAMONDS TO THE KNIGHTS CROSS OF
THE IRON CROSS
A GEORGE MEDAL AND BAR GROUP OF THREE
A GEORGE MEDAL GROUP OF SIX
A CONSPICUOUS GALLANTRY MEDAL (FLYING)
AND
OTHER ORDERS, DECORATIONS AND MEDALS
INCLUDING
The Property of THE REV. J. H. G-W. GREEN
The Property of DR. L. A. PARGETER
AND
OTHER OWNERS

WHICH WILL BE SOLD BY AUCTION

BY MESSRS.

SOTHEBY & Co.

P. C. WILSON	A. R. A. HOBSON	A. J. B. KIDDELL	T. H. CLARKE	C. GRONAU
R. J. RICKETT	P. M. H. POLLEN	G. D. LLEWELLYN	R. P. CAME	M. J. WEBB
LORD JOHN KERR	EARL OF WESTMORLAND		J. MARION (U.S.A.)	H. M. ROBINOW
P. POUNCEY	J. M. LINELL	R. A. B. DAY	C. B. CHATWIN	H. J. RICKETTS
		M. J. STRAUSS		

Associates :

JOHN CARTER, C.B.E.   N. MacLAREN   H. A. FEISENBERGER   J. F. HAYWARD

AFFILIATED COMPANY: PARKE-BERNET GALLERIES INC. NEW YORK
New York Representative : SOTHEBY'S OF LONDON LTD.   *President :* P. M. H. POLLEN

AT THEIR LARGE GALLERIES, 34 & 35, NEW BOND STREET, W.1

By courtesy of Morton and Eden Ltd. Of 45 Maddox Street, London, an extract from the catalogue for the sale at Sotheby and Co. on 18 July 1966 at which memorabilia of Helmut Lent were auctioned.

hardly arrived there when Mother came rushing in through the door: 'Come quick! Father has just been shot!' He had collapsed in the doorway, where everything had happened. Mother told me that Father had been very worked up about everything that had happened that day – the idea that we were going to be deported, having to hand in his only remaining suit and so on – and he shouted at the drunken Russian, 'What else do you want from us! You've taken everything already! Why don't you just shoot us! I want to go to Lord Jesus!' The news that the old priest was lying dying in the vicarage must have spread like wildfire, among the Russians as well, because that night, when there had always been terrible things happening as far as the women were concerned, thousands of Russians poured into the village, yet we did not see a single Russian with bad intentions. After some time three officers arrived, apparently on orders from higher up, to look after Father. I saw one, after he had seen the bullet wound, make a dismissive gesture with his hand, as if to say, 'Hopeless.' He then put a headscarf on my head and said something to me, and the only word that I could understand, which he said several times, was '*Doktore.*' That was a ray of hope for me, and I went with him without fear to

Correspondence between Frau Christina Delavre and Phillips, the Auctioneers, on the subject of the award certificates stolen by a British officer after the war. She failed to recover the documents.

Phillips

Fine Art Auctioneers & Valuers since 1796

Blenstock House, 7 Blenheim Street, New Bond Street, London, W1Y OAS   Telephone 01-629 6602   Telex No: 298855 Blen G.

Also at Edinburgh, Glasgow, Leeds, Knowle, Oxford, Norwich, Merseyside, Bath, Exeter, Chester, Colwyn Bay, Dublin, Geneva, The Hague, Toronto, Montreal, Ottawa, Boston & New York.

Mrs. Christina Delavre,   19th December, 1984
Anton-Burger-Weg 145,
D-6000 Frankfurt/M. 70,   AGH/CB
WEST GERMANY.

Dear Mrs. Delavre,

Thank you for your letter of the 11th of December concerning the Helmut Lent Citations.

We have enquired with our solicitors as to the legal position and they will be reporting to us in the New Year. It is felt, however, that you are unlikely to have any claim in law on the title of these items and that the person who sold them had every right to do so. We will instruct you of our solicitors' findings.

Yours sincerely,

Andrew G. Hilton
Director

Directors: C.J. WESTON F.I.A.(Scot)   C.R. HAWKINGS F.I.A.(Scot)   N.HAWKE   P.J. HAMPTON F.S.V.A.   D.BOYD   P.S.L.VINEY   A.G. HILTON   D.R.BAKER
Departmental Directors: P.P. Beaumont   B.L. Koetser   J.C. Matthews   E.J.G. Smith   M.R. Cowley A.S.V.A.   Secretary: F.T. Griffin F.A.I.A.   E.A.P.A.   M.B.I.M.
PHILLIPS SON & NEALE   Regd. office as above   REGD. IN ENGLAND NO. 647900   VAT REGD. NO. 239.5023.66
Regional Directors: D.Y. Borthwick F.I.A.(Scot)   J.B. Haycraft F.R.I.C.S.   R.H. Hollest F.R.I.C.S.

Registered/Special Delivery   Christina Delavre
                                                            nee Lent

Messrs. Phillips
attn. Mr. Paul Penn-Simkins
Blenstock House
7 Blenheim Street
New Bond Street
London W1Y OAS
England   11 December, 1984

Dear Mr. Penn-Simkins,

Referring to our telephone conversation of to-day, I herewith submit a written claim concerning the three documents relating to my father, the late Col. Helmut Lent. The three certificates (bestowal of orders) are the property of Col. Lent's rightful heirs, i.e. his widow, Mrs. Helene Lent, his only children: my sister, Mrs. Helma Lehnert (nee Lent) and myself. Col. Lent died in 1944, and the three documents were taken away from my mother by a British officer during the occupation of Germany.

As we want to retrieve the a. m. certificates we would be most obliged if you could let us know what further steps we have to take.

With our thanks in advance,

                                        Yours sincerely,

see the Russian *Kommandant*. Of course, I would never have gone by myself. I had to remain outside and was immediately surrounded by soldiers who tried to talk to me. When the officer came out there was another flood of words, but again the only one that I could make out was '*Doktore*.' In a flash of inspiration it occurred to me that there was a man in that part of the village who could speak Polish. The officer wanted to take me back home, but I led him in the opposite direction, which made him rather mistrustful. But he came with me and waited outside the farm while I brought the 'interpreter' out. The Russian told me that they were very upset about what had happened, but they could not always control the hordes of troops following up. A doctor would be there the next morning. This was obviously only said to comfort me, because he knew that Father would not see another morning. But nevertheless they did show some concern for the dying priest, and that in the middle of the most bitter of wars. Then, after a few hours of awesome self-control, our father went to his eternal home, the only concern that he expressed being for his wife and child. The following day we tried to talk the church elders into doing something about a burial, but they were all afraid. When we returned from the village after this unsuccessful visit we saw from the garden two senior officers in long greatcoats ringing at the door. We approached the house very slowly and mistrustfully, until they went away. Then our neighbour Frau Dümmke came up to us excitedly, 'Where were you? They wanted to talk to you, probably about the funeral.' But it was already too late. More and more soldiers came streaming into the village, clearing and occupying the houses, and there was no way in which we could stay, and we left our home. I later heard from a trustworthy source that the Russians buried our Father, presumably in the garden of our neighbour Born. For me why they showed such sympathy in the death of our father is hard to explain... One thing however is quite clear. The death of my father had nothing to do with his son in the Air Force.

★   ★   ★

The Lent family scattered, one of millions uprooted in the final throes of the Second World War. Lena, with her and Helmut's two daughters Christina and Helma, had the comparative good fortune to live in an Allied zone of occupation. A letter from Lent's mother written from Bülzig in the German Democratic Republic in January 1946 provides some slight insight into the fate that overtook those displaced when the Russians invaded their land, the *Heimat* that Lent had fought so hard to defend:

The 17th of February was the most momentous day of my life, not to say the hardest one. During the night our beloved father breathed his last, and that very evening we had to leave our home. Ursula and I had laid our dear dead one out properly, but we were not allowed to bury him. I was very glad that I still had my Ursula with me, because by myself everything would have been unbearably difficult. Parting was bitter, even though we could look forward to meeting again in the light on the other side. I was plagued with worries and fears for my child Ursula, but God's guardian angels were clearly with her. 'For He shall give His angels charge over thee: to keep thee in all thy ways.' I sensed that very strongly.

We managed to keep her hidden for weeks in barns, haylofts and cellars, but we were frightened to death, and our hearts were full of woe...

Ursula and I were back in Pyrehne twice during those months, but I wished that I had not seen it again. Our beautiful church blown up, the vicarage almost completely destroyed, because Pyrehne was in the battle zone for a long time and an airfield had been built close to the village. The decorations in the church for the memorial service for our dear Helmut lay under the ruins, and our house devastated and empty. It was a terrible picture of death and horror. My heart almost broke, and it God's mercy and compassion that our dear father did not have to see it. But such an ending, after we had been just forty years in Pyrehne. Yes, the judgement of God has descended upon us and the German nation.

★   ★   ★

In July 1966 the London Auction House Sotherby's offered for a number of Lent's honours, decorations and badges for sale on behalf of an anonymous seller. Included were his Oak Leaves, Swords and Diamonds to the Knight's Cross; his Iron Cross First Class; his German Cross in Gold; his Iron Cross Second Class; his Long Service Medal in Silver; his Sudeten Medal with Clasp; his Pilot's Badge; his Wound Badges in Black and Silver; his Front Line Flying Clasps in Black and Gold; and his Narvik Shield. The items were bought in one lot by an anonymous bidder for the total sum of £500. In transpired that the purchaser was the famous *Luftwaffe* fighter ace *General der Flieger* Adolf Galland, who was acting on behalf of the Federal German Ministry of Defence, who then presented the collection to the Museum of Defence History (*Wehrgeschichtliches Museum*) in Rastatt, Germany.

The items were in fact put up for auction by Helmut Lent's elder daughter Christina after consultation with her mother, Lena, who was in

The *Bundeswehr* Barracks at Rotenburg (Wümme) near Bremen, named after Helmut Lent.

urgent need of cash to pay for an operation.

In 1984 three of Lent's award certificates, which had been stolen by a British officer at the end of the war, came up for auction by another auction house. Christina claimed that the certificates were the property of the Lent family, but was informed by the Auctioneers, who took legal advice, that she had no title in law.

In today's Germany there are very few memorials to members of the fighting forces in the Second World War. Lent is an exception. In

A modern day view of the aproach road to the Lent Kaserne air force base

A recent photograph of the house in Leenwarden, Holland, used by IV./NJG 1 as an officer's mess

Rotenburg *an der* Wümme, between Bremen and Hamburg, there is a *Bundeswehr* barracks that was originally conceived in the mid-nineteen-thirties as a central equipment store for the *Luftwaffe* of the Third *Reich*. Building was completed in December 1936 and the following month, January 1937, the first troops moved in. In 1939 the central stores moved to Silesia, leaving only a *Flak* depot and an aircraft repair facility there until the beginning of 1940, when operational flying units were first based there. Among the miscellaneous units that flew from Rotenburg during the war were KG 500, St.K. 2 and a *Gruppe* of JG 11. Taken over by British occupation troops in April 1945, the barracks remained under British control until handed over to the *Bundeswehr,* the Federal German Armed Forces, in September 1958. On 18 July 1964 the barracks were named the 'Lent *Kaserne*' after the pastor's son from Pyrehne who, in fighting to defend his country and his folk, had shot down 110 enemy aircraft.

Glossary of German Words and Phrases

Abitur University entrance examination.

Abzeichen Badge.

Alarmstart Scramble! Alarm take-off.

Alleinflug Solo flight.

allgemein (adj.) General.

andere (adj.) Other.

Anzeiger Advertiser, gazette.

Band Band, gang.

beauftragt Tasked.

Bedienung Crew, staff etc.

Bedienungsfehler Crew error.

Bekenntniskirche Confessional Church.

Beobachter Observer.

Bericht Report.

Berichter Reporter.

blau (adj.) Blue.

Blitzkrieg Lightning war.

Bordmechaniker. Flight mechanic (aircrew member).

Bordschützer Air gunner.

Braut Bride, fiancée, 'intended' etc.

Brillanten 'Diamonds' The sixth grade of the Iron Cross, the highest decoration for gallantry. Only ten were awarded to officers of the Luftwaffe. (With one exception – see text).

Brillantenträger Holder of the Brillanten (q.v.).

Bucht Bay, bight.

Bund association, league etc.

deutsch (adj) German.

Diktat Diktat, ultimatum, a harsh settlement forced upon someone, usually a defeated enemy.

Donnerkeil Thunderbolt.

Dritte (adj.) Third.

Dritter Mann 'Third Man': an extra man carried as a lookout in Bf 110 night fighters.

Dunaja Abbreviation for 'Dunkle Nachtjagd', q.v.

Dunkle Nachtjagd Literally 'dark night fighting'. Radar-assisted close-control interception.

Düppel German equivalent of British Window. Foil - coated strips of paper dropped from aircraft to interfere with enemy radar.

Ehre Honour.

Eichenlaub Oak Leaves. The third grade of the Iron Cross.

Eichenlaubträger Holder of the Oak Leaves to the Iron Cross.

Einsatz Operation, operational flight.

Einsatzüberführung Operational deployment.

Eisbär Polar bear.

Eisernes Kreuz Iron Cross.

EKI Iron Cross First Class.

EKII Iron Cross Second Class.

Erholung Recuperation.

Erholungsheim Recuperation home, recuperation centre etc.

Erholungsurlaub Recuperation leave.

Erinnerung Memory, remembrance

Erinnerungsmedaille Commemorative medal.

erweitert (adj.) Advanced, as applied, for example, to a qualification.

Experte Expert (noun). In a Luftwaffe context, an ace. A pilot became an ace when he had shot down five enemy aircraft.

Fahnenjunker Officer-cadet.

Fähnlein Small group, troop (military).

Fähnleinführer Troop leader.

Fähnrich Junior officer rank equivalent to Leutnant (q.v.) on probation.

Fallschirm Parachute.

Fallschirmjäger Paratroop(s).

Feindflug Operation. Literally 'enemy flight'.

Feldmarschall Field Marshal.

Feldpostnummer Field Post Office number.

Feldwebel Sergeant.

Fernnachtjagd Literally 'long-range night fighting'. Luftwaffe intruders over Britain.

Fernnachtjäger Intruders.

Flak Anti-aircraft artillery (abb.).

Flakartillerie Anti-aircraft artillery.

Fliegerkorps Air Corps.

Flugzeug Aeroplane, aircraft.

Flugzeugführer Pilot.

Freya The Freya was an early acquisition radar.

Front Front line.

Frontflug Front-line flight sortie, mission etc.

Führer Leader, pilot.

Führerfehler Pilot error.

Führerhauptquartier Führer's Headquarters.

Funker Wireless operator, radio operator, signaller, radar operator etc.

Gebiet Area, region, district etc.

Gebirgsjäger Mountain troops.

Gefallen Fell, died: fallen, dead.

Gefechtsstand Operational control centre.

Gefreiter Rank equivalent to Lance Corporal (army), Leading Aircraftman (RAF).

General General (rank).

Generalleutnant Lieutenant General.

Generalmajor Major General.

Gerät Equipment, piece of equipment etc.

Geschwader Luftwaffe unit comprising, typically, four Gruppen (q.v.).

Gesellschaft Company.

Gestapo State Secret Police.

gross (adj.) Big.

grün Green.

Gruppe Literally, Group. A Luftwaffe unit made up of, typically, three Staffeln (q.v.), each of nine aircraft.

Gruppenkommandeur Commander of a Gruppe.

Gürtel Belt.

Hals-und Beinbruch Flyer's good-luck wish: 'Break your neck, break a leg.'

Hamster Hamster.

Handel Trade.

Handelsgesellschaft Trading company.

Handlung Deal, business, trade etc.

Hauptfeldwebel Senior Warrant Officer, Sergeant Major.

Hauptmann Captain (rank).

Hauptquartier Headquarters.

Heer Army.

Heide Heath, heathland, moorland

heilige (adj.) Holy.

Heimat Home, homeland etc.

hell (adj.) Light, bright.

Helle Nachtjagd Literally 'bright night fighting'. Night fighting in cooperation with searchlights.

Henaja Abbreviation for 'Helle Nachtjagd', q.v.

Hering Herring.

Himmelbett Code word for radar-assisted close-control interception. Literally 'four-poster bed'.

Hitlerjugend Hitler Youth Organisation.

Hochschule High school.

Hochzeit Wedding, marriage,.

Horchdienst Luftwaffe early warning organisation, listening service.

Ingenieur Engineer.

Jagd Hunt (noun).

Jagdflieger Fighter crewman or crewmen; fighter pilot or pilots.

Jagdflug Fighter flight, fighter mission, fighter operation etc.

Jagdführer Fighter Leader.

Jäger Fighter (can refer to either an aircraft or its pilot)

Jägerleitoffizier Fighter controller. Abbreviated 'JLO' (q.v.).

jeder (adj.) Every.

JLO Abbreviation for Jägerleitoffizier. Pronounced 'Eelo'.

Jugend Youth .

jung (adj) Young

Jungvolk Literally 'Young People'. Junior Hitlerjugend.

Jungzugführer Platoon Leader in the Jungvolk (q.v.)

Kamerad Comrade.

Kampfflieger Bomber crewman/ crewmen, bomber man/man.

Kapitän Captain: in the Luftwaffe, a post, not a rank.

KG Abbr. of Kampfgeschwader (Bomber Geschwader).

Kirche Church

KL Klemm in aircraft numbers. E.g. KL 35 = Klemm 35.

Klasse Class.

Kollege Colleague, comrade.

Kommandeur Commander. Officer commanding a Gruppe.

Kommando A small independent unit or command.

Kommodore Commodore: Commanding officer of a Geschwader (q.v.)

Kreis District.

Krieg War.

Kriegsberichter War correspondent, war reporter.

Landung Landing.

Languste Lobster.

Legion Legion, as in Legion Kondor (Kondor Legion).

Legion Kondor The Condor Legion, which fought in Spain during the Civil War.

Leicht (adj.) Light: Can also mean 'easy' or 'simple' when applied to a task.

Leistung Achievement.

Leutnant Lowest commissioned rank. Equivalent to Pilot Officer etc.

Lichtenstein B/C Type of AI radar.

Löwe Lion.

Luft Air.

Luftflotte Air Fleet.

Luftkriegsschule School of Air Warfare.

Luftwaffe Air Force

Mädel Girl(s), maiden(s).

Major Major (rank)

Marienkäfer Ladybird.

Marine Navy.

mein (possessive adjective) My

Musik Music

Nachtjagd Night fighting.

Nachtjagdschule Night-fighter school

Nachtjäger Night fighter, night-fighter pilot.

Narvikschild A shield awarded to participants in the Narvik Campaign in 1940.

Naxos German device to detect and home on RAF H2S navigation radar.

Oberfähnrich Senior Fähnrich (q.v.)

Oberfeldwebel Rank equivalent to Flight Sergeant (RAF).

Obergefreiter Senior private, Private First Class etc.

Oberleutnant Rank equivalent to Lieutenant (Army); Flying Officer (RAF).

Oberst Colonel: rank equivalent to Group Captain.

Oberstleutnant Lieutenant-Colonel. Rank equivalent to Wing Commander.

Pastor Pastor, vicar etc.

Pfadfinder Boy scout (literally, pathfinder).

Pokal Goblet.

Raum (pl.Räume) Area.

Reichsgebiet The territory of the Reich.

Reichsmarschall Marshal of the Reich. A rank held only by Hermann Göring.

Reichssippenamt Reich Office of Genealogy.

Riese Giant

Ritterkreuz Knight's Cross (to the Iron Cross).

Ritterkreuzträger Holder of the Knight's Cross.

rot (adj.) Red.

Rotte A tactical formation of two aircraft, a pair.

Rottenkamerad Wingman.

Rotterdam Gerät 'Rotterdam Set' etc. German name for H2S.

Rückblick Look back (noun); backward look).

Sau Sow: can also be used to refer to boar generally.

Schein Certificate: (can also mean 'shine').

Schild Shield.

schräg Slanting, oblique etc.

Schräge Musik Jazz music (colloquial). Upward-firing cannon installed in the upper surface of a night fighter's fuselage.

Schule School.

Schwarm A tactical fighter formation, usually comprising three or four aircraft.

schwarz (adj) Black.

schwer (adj.) Hard, difficult. Can also mean 'heavy'.

Schwerter Swords. The fifth grade of the Iron Cross.

See Sea (may also mean lake).

Seeburg Tisch 'Seeburg' Table. A horizontal map, illuminated from below, upon which the tracks of bomber and fighter were displayed.

Soldbuch Pay-book.

Sonderstaffel Special duties Staffel.

Spange Clasp, bar (to medal).

Spanner Various meanings: code word for an infra-red device for target interception.

spat Late.

Sperrflug Blockade flight.

staatlich (adj) State.

Stab Staff.

Stabsingenieur Staff Engineer.

Staffel The smallest independent operational unit of a Geschwader. It comprised typically nine aircraft.

Staffelkapitän Officer commanding a Staffel.

Start Take-off.

Stern Star.

Stieglitz Goldfinch.

Storch Stork.

Störung Fault etc.

Stösser Bird of prey.

Superintendent Superintendent. A senior clergyman in the Evangelic Church.

Taifun Typhoon.

Tante Aunt.

Tiger Tiger

Tisch Table.

Überführung Move, transfer, deployment etc.

Unbesiegt vom Feind Unconquered by the foe.

Unternehmen Operation, project, action etc.

Unteroffizier Corporal.

Urlaub Leave.

Ursache Cause.

vermutlich (adj.) Presumed.

Verwundetenabzeichen Wound badge.

Volksschule Elementary school.

von hinten unten From astern and below – night-fighter attack practised in the early stages of the Nachtjagd.

Wehrmacht The German armed forces (Marine, Heer, Luftwaffe)

Wehrmachtbericht Armed Forces Bulletin. To be mentioned by name in this publication was the equivalent of being Mentioned in Dispatches in the British forces.

Wehrpass Service record book.

weiss (adj.) White.

Werknummer Factory number.

wild (adj.) Wild

Wilde Sau 'Wild Boar'. Freelance night fighting over the bombers' target.

Wolf Wolf.

Wolke Cloud.

Würzburg The Würzburg was a radar originally used to control guns and searchlights. It was widely employed in the Himmelbett fighter-control system.

Würzburg Riese Giant Würzburg.

Ypsilon The letter 'Y'. German radio navigation system.

zahm (adj.) Tame.

Zahme Sau 'Tame Boar'. Freelance night fighting within the bomber stream.

Zeitung Newspaper

Zerstörer Destroyer (naval).

In the Luftwaffe, a heavy fighter, for example the Bf 210.

Zug Various meanings: here, platoon.

zweite (adj.) Second.

zweiter Funker Second radio-operator: an extra *Funker* introduced into a night-fighter crew as radio/radar work became more complex.

Helmut Lent's Victories

BELOW is a table drawn up in an attempt to identify as many as possible of Helmut Lent's aerial victories in the course of a career as a fighter pilot lasting from September 1939 to October 1944. Some of the identifications are more positive than others, and I have categorised them A, B or C, with A meaning 'virtually certain', B meaning 'probable' and C meaning 'possible'. Lent became *Kommodore* of NJG 4 in August 1943, and from that point in time his logbook was less meticulously maintained than it had previously been, and accurate times and locations of the crashes of the bombers he shot down are not recorded. Before he took over command of NJG 4, Lent had spent virtually all his time as a night fighter operating from airfields in Holland, principally Leeuwarden, so that the great majority of his victims came down either on Dutch territory or in the surrounding waters, concentrated in a small area in which it was comparatively easy to associate claims and crashes. To do so was much more difficult in the battle against the bomber streams that ranged over Germany: and in addition, of course, the *Nachtjagd* was fighting a desperate, and ultimately retreating, battle against increasing numbers of bombers, and accurate record-keeping was one of the many things that had to be sacrificed in the urgency of raw survival. So it was that whereas up to July 1943 the majority of Lent's victims can be identified, from then until the end of the war virtually none can.

This tables shows 111 kills, but Lent is usually credited with only 110.

Total kills	Night kills	Date	Time	Location	Aircraft type.	Unit	Serial No., Sqdn. Ident	Comment / Target	CAT
1	-	2.9.39	1710	Lodz, Poland.	PZL 24	PAF	-	Invasion of Poland	A
2	-	18.12.39	1440	Near Borkum (G)	Wellington IA	37 Sqdn.	N2888 LF-A	German Bight	A
3	-	18.12.39	1445	Near Borkum (G)	Wellington IA	37 Sqdn.	N2889 LF-P	German Bight	A
4	-	9.4.40	0855	Bratenjordet, Nor.	Gloster Gladiator	NAAS	427	Invasion of Norway	A
5	-	27.5.40	0820	Bodö, Norway	Gloster Gladiator	263 Sqdn.	-	Norwegian Cam.	A
6	-	2.6.40	1425	Norway	Gloster Gladiator	263 Sqdn.	N5893	Norwegian Cam.	A
7	-	15.6.40	1245	Near Trondheim	Bristol Blenheim	254 Sqdn.	L9408	Reconnaissance	A
8	1	12.5.41	0140	Süderstapel (G)	Wellington IC	40 Sqdn.	R1330 BL-H	Hamburg	B
9	2	12.5.41	0249	Nordstrand (G)	Wellington IC	40 Sqdn.	R1461 BL-Z	Hamburg	B
10	3	28.6.41	0158	SW Bremervörde (G)	Whitley	102 Sqdn.	T4297 DY-?	Bremen	A
11	4	30.6.41	0140	S Wesermünde (G)	Stirling I	7 Sqdn	N6001 MG-?	Hamburg	B
12	5	30.6.41	0205	SW Bremervörde (G)	Stirling I	7 Sqdn	N3644 MG-Z	Hamburg	B
13	6	4.7.41	0043	Exloermond (H)	Wellington IC	301 Sqdn	R1492 GR-?	Bremen	A
14	7	6.7.41	0056	W Coevorden (H)	Whitley V	10 Sqdn	Z6793 ZA-?	Münster	A
15	8	8.7.41	0055	SE Assen (H)	Whitley V	77 Sqdn	Z6799 KN-?	Osnabrück	A
16	9	10.7.41	0220	NW Meppen (G)	Wellington IC	40 Sqdn.	B1770 BL-C	Osnabrück	A
17	10	13.7.41	0055	Veendam (H)	Hampden I	50 Sqdn	AE226 VN-?	Bremen	B
18	11	16.7.41	0049	E Groningen (H)	Wellington II	104 Sqdn	W5513 EP-P	Hanover	A
19	12	25.7.41	0354	Boazum (H)	Wellington IC	57 Sqdn	R1369 DX-?	Kiel	C
20	13	15.8.41	0320	N. Ameland (H)	Whitley V	51 Sqdn	Z6819 MH-X	Hanover	A

Total kills	Night kills	Date	Time	Location	Aircraft type.	Unit	Serial No., Sqdn. Ident	Comment / Target	CAT
21	14	29.8.41	0340	S. Ameland (H)	Hampden I	49 Sqdn	AE126 EA-N	Duisburg	A
22	15	7.9.41	0125	E. Leeuwarden (H)	Whitley V	78 Sqdn	Z6681 FY-?	Hüls	A
23	16	8.9.41	0404	Terwipsel (H)	Wellington IC	9 Sqdn	Z8845 WS-?	Berlin	B
24	17	8.9.41	0459	Drachten (H)	Wellington IC	115 Sqdn	R1798 KO-B	Berlin	A
25	18	13.10.41	0006	Westergeest (H)	Wellington IC	40 Sqdn	X9822 BL-J	Bremen	A
26	19	13.10.41	0033	Zuiderzee (H)	Hampden	144 Sqdn	AD965 PL-?	Hüls	A
27	20	8.11.41	0121	N Akkrum (H)	Wellington IC	75 Sqdn	X9976 AA-?	Berlin	A
28	21	17.1.42	2145	Terschelling (H)	Whitley V	51 Sqdn	Z9301 MH-N	Emden	B
29	22	21.1.42	2228	W Terschelling (H)	Whitley V	51 Sqdn	Z9311 MH-J	Emden	A
30	-	6.2.42	1510	W Terschelling (H)	Hampden I	455 Sqdn	AE308 UB-L	Mine laying (Day)	A
31	23	26.3.42	0032	N Alkmaar (H)	Manchester I	61 Sqdn	L7518 QR-O	Essen	A
32	24	27.3.42	2210	N Terschelling (H)	Hampden I	408 Sqdn	-	Mine laying	-
33	25	27.3.42	2242	N Terschelling (H)	Hampden I	408 Sqdn	-	Mine laying	-
34	26	29.3.42	2159	N Terschelling (H)	Manchester	61 Sqdn	L7394 ZN-?	Mine laying	C
35	27	11.4.42	0023	S Den Helder (H)	Wellington IC	311 Sqdn	Z8838 KX-Z	Essen	A
36	28	13.4.42	0032	N Terschelling (H)	Hampden I	420 Sqdn	P1239 PT-Y	Essen	B
37	29	18.4.42	0155	N Terschelling (H)	Wellington IV	300 Sqdn	Z1267 BH-P	Hamburg	B
38	30	15.5.42	2245	N Terschelling (H)	Wellington III	9 Sqdn	X3482 AA-J	Mine laying	C
39	31	3.6.42	0106	E Medemblik (H)	Hampden I	408 Sqdn	AT154 EQ-B	Essen	A
40	32	4.6.42	0055	NNW Alkmaar (H)	Halifax II	76 Sqdn	R9457 MP-A	Bremen	A
41	33	6.6.42	0034	S Hoorn (H)	Wellington IC	156 Sqdn	DV812 GT-?	Essen	A
42	34	6.6.42	0116	Ijsselmeer (H)	Wellington IV	301 Sqdn	Z1331 GR-C	Essen	A
43	35	21.6.42	0048	N Ameland (H)	Hampden I	420 Sqdn	AT185 PT-A	Emden	A
44	36	24.6.42	0112	N Terschelling (H)	Wellington IC	103 Sqdn	T2921 PM-T	Mine laying	A
45	37	24.6.42	0146	NW Vlieland (H)	Wellington IC	103 Sqdn	DV831 PM-R	Mine laying	A
46	38	26.6.42	0237	NW Enkhuizen (H)	Wellington IC	18 OTU	T2612 ??-H	Bremen	B
47	39	26.6.42	0256	Noordwijk (H)	Whitley V	24 OUT	BD266	Bremen	B
48	40	3.7.42	0125	SW Assen (H)	Wellington IV	301 Sqdn	Z1314 GR-M	Bremen	B
49	41	9.7.42	0130	Rottumeroog (H)	Wellington III	75 Sqdn	X3557 AA-?	Wilhelmshaven	A
50	42	27.7.42	0235	NW Vlieland (H)	Halifax	-	-	Hamburg	-
51	43	27.7.42	0239	NW Vlieland (H)	Wellington	-	-	Hamburg	-
52	44	5.9.42	0250	SW Leeuwarden (H)	Lancaster I	61 Sqdn	R5682 QR-R	Bremen	B
53	45	14.9.42	0502	NW Terschelling (H)	Wellington	-	-	Bremen	-
54	46	9.11.42	2038	Ameland (H)	Halifax II	102 Sqdn	W7864 DY-F	Hamburg	B
55	47	17.12.42	2022	N Sloten (H)	Lancaster	44 Sqdn	ED355 KM-D	Nienburg	A
56	48	17.12.42	2038	E Urk (H)	Lancaster I	44 Sqdn	ED333 OF-B	Soltau	B
57	49	8.1.43	2024	W Texel (H)	Lancaster	-	-	Mine laying	-
58	50	21.1.43	2111	N Schiermonnikoog	Wellington	-	-	Mine laying	-
59	51	1.3.43	2139	N Ameland (H)	Halifax II	419 Sqdn	DT641 VR-R	Berlin	B
60	52	5.3.43	2020	W Harlingen (H)	Halifax II	76 Sqdn	BB282 MP-R	Essen	C
61	53	5.3.43	2224	W Wieringen (H)	Lancaster I	83 Sqdn	W4847 OL-V	Essen	B
62	54	29.3.43	2346	NW Lemmer (H)	Wellington III	426 Sqdn	BJ762 OW-O	Bochum	A
63	55	4.4.43	0027	E Texel (H)	Lancaster	-	-	Essen	-
64	56	20.4.43	0339	W Staveren (H)	Mosquito	-	-	-	-
65	57	5.5.43	0008	S Enkhuizen (H)	Stirling III	7 Sqdn	BK773 MG-T	Dortmund	A
66	58	5.5.43	0018	SE Hommerts (H)	Stirling I	149 Sqdn	EF 343 OJ-B	Dortmund	A
67	59	14.5.43	0255	N Harlingen (H)	Halifax II	78 Sqdn	JB924 EY-M	Bochum	A

68	60	24.5.43	0216	SW Workum (H)	Halifax II	10 Sqdn	DT789 ZA-Z	Dortmund	A
69	61	22.6.43	0309	W Vlieland (H)	Lancaster	-	-	Krefeld	-
70	62	23.6.43	0206	W Urk (H)	Halifax	-	-	Mülheim	-
71	63	26.6.43	0111	W Urk (H)	Wellington X	466 Sqdn	HF544 HD-?	Gelsenkirchen	A
72	64	28.7.43	0237	NW Terschelling (H)	Lancaster	-	-	Hamburg	-
73	65	30.7.43	0210	-	Lancaster	-	-	Hamburg	-
74	66	24.8.43	0056	Berlin (G)	Stirling	-	-	Berlin	-
75	67	24.8.43	-	Berlin-Tegel (G)	Lancaster	-	-	Berlin	-
76	68	24.8.43	0116	Berlin-Spandau (G)	Halifax	-	-	Berlin	-
77	69	1.9.43	0054	W Berlin (G)	Halifax	-	-	Berlin	-
78	70	1.9.43	0103	E Berlin (G)	Halifax	-	-	Berlin	-
79	71	22.9.43	2241	-	Stirling	-	-	Hannover	-
80	72	3.10.43	2227	-	Stirling	-	-	Kassel	-
81	73	2.12.43	1958	-	Lancaster	-	-	Berlin	-
82	74	2.12.43	2020	-	Stirling	-	-	Berlin	-
83	75	16.12.43	1907	-	Lancaster	-	-	Berlin	-
84	76	2.1.44	0249	-	Lancaster	-	-	Berlin	-
85	77	14.1.44	1849	-	Lancaster	-	-	Brunswick	-
86	78	14.1.44	1905	-	Lancaster	-	-	Brunswick	-
87	79	14.1.44	1910	-	Four-engined	-	-	Brunswick	-
88	80	21.1.44	-	-	Lancaster	-	-	Stuttgart	-
89	81	21.1.44	-	-	Lancaster	-	-	Stuttgart	-
90	82	22.3.44	2126	-	Lancaster	-	-	Frankfurt	-
91	83	22.3.44	2135	-	Lancaster	-	-	Frankfurt	-
92	84	24.3.44	-	-	Four-engined	-	-	Berlin	-
93	85	24.3.44	-	-	Four-engined	-	-	Berlin	-
94	86	31.3.44	0121	N Nuremberg (G)	Halifax	578 Sqdn	MZ508 LK-N	Nuremberg	C
95	87	23.4.44	-	-	Lancaster	-	-	Düsseldorf	-
96	88	23.5.44	0021	-	Lancaster	-	-	Dortmund	-
97	89	23.5.44	-	-	Lancaster	-	-	Dortmund	-
98	90	16.6.44	0052	-	Lancaster	-	-	Invasion targets	-
99	91	16.6.44	0056	-	Lancaster	-	-	Invasion targets	-
100	92	16.6.44	0100	-	Lancaster	-	-	Invasion targets	-
101	93	25.6.44	-	-	Lancaster	-	-	Invasion targets	-
102	94	25.6.44	-	-	Lancaster	-	-	Invasion targets	-
103	95	28.6.44	-	-	Lancaster	-	-	Invasion targets	-
104	96	19.7.44	0141	-	Lancaster	-	-	Wesseling	-
105	97	21.7.44	0207	-	Lancaster	-	-	Various	-
106	98	25.7.44	0114	-	Lancaster	-	-	Stuttgart	-
107	99	29.7.44	0147	-	Halifax	-	-	Hamburg	-
108	100	29.7.44	0157	-	Halifax	-	-	Hamburg	-
109	101	17.8.44	-	-	Four-engined	-	-	Kiel	-
110	102	12.9.44	-	-	Lancaster	-	-	Darmstadt	-
111	103	17.9.44	-	-	Lancaster	-	-	-	-

APPENDIX C

Award Certificates

There follows a selection of official certificates for awards made to Helmut Lent during his career in the *Luftwaffe* from April 1936 to October 1945.

Top left Pilot's Badge

Top right Iron Cross, 2nd Class

Left Narvik Shield

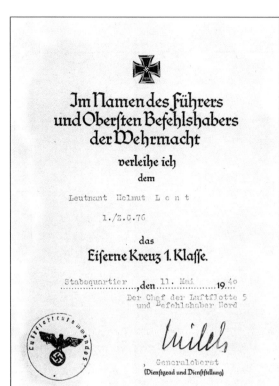

Top left Iron Cross, 1st Class

Top right Honour Goblet

Right Wound Badge in black

Vorläufiges Besitzzeugnis

**Der Führer
und Oberste Befehlshaber
der Wehrmacht**

hat

dem Oberleutnant Helmut Lent

**das Ritterkreuz
des Eisernen Kreuzes**

am 30.August 1941 verliehen.

Berlin, den 1. September 1941
Der Chef des Luftwaffenpersonalamts
I.V.

Generalmajor

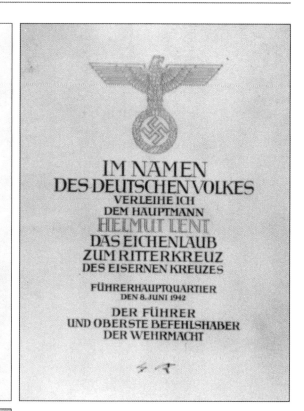

Top left Official notification for
the Knight's Cross

Top right Certificate for the
Oakleaves to the Knight's Cross
signed by Hitler

Left Definitive Certificate for the
Knight's Cross signed by Hitler

VORLÄUFIGES BESITZZEUGNIS

DER FÜHRER
UND OBERSTE BEFEHLSHABER
DER WEHRMACHT
HAT

DEM   Major Helmut L e n t

DAS

EICHENLAUB MIT SCHWERTERN
ZUM RITTERKREUZ
DES EISERNEN KREUZES

AM   2. August 1943   VERLIEHEN.

Hauptquartier d.Ob.d.L.DEN   3. August   1943
Der Chef des Luftwaffenpersonalamts

IM NAMEN
DES DEUTSCHEN VOLKES
VERLEIHE ICH
DEM MAJOR
HELMUT LENT
DAS EICHENLAUB MIT SCHWERTERN
ZUM RITTERKREUZ
DES EISERNEN KREUZES
FÜHRERHAUPTQUARTIER
DEN 2.AUGUST 1943
DER FÜHRER
UND OBERSTE BEFEHLSHABER
DER WEHRMACHT

Top left Official notification for the Award of the Swords to the Knight's Cross.

Top right The Award document for the Swords signed by Hitler

Right Official notification for the Award of the Diamonds to the Knight's Cross.

VORLÄUFIGES BESITZZEUGNIS

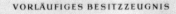

DER FÜHRER
UND OBERSTE BEFEHLSHABER
DER WEHRMACHT
HAT

DEM Oberstleutnant Helmut L e n t

DAS EICHENLAUB
MIT SCHWERTERN UND BRILLANTEN
ZUM RITTERKREUZ
DES EISERNEN KREUZES

AM   31. Juli 1944   VERLIEHEN.

Hauptquartier d.Ob.d.L..DEN 31.August   1944
Der Chef der Personellen Rüstung und
National-Sozialistischen Führung der Luftwaffe

Generaloberst

Alphabetical Index of Names

As a very general rule, ranks etc. are those that apply when a person is first mentioned. 'fnu' means 'first name unknown'.